For Michael H......
the st...
overseas...

so much help and support,

With gratitude

Jan .

Date slip
over page

WORK FROM WASTE
Recycling wastes to create employment

WORK FROM WASTE

RECYCLING WASTES TO CREATE EMPLOYMENT

by

Jon Vogler

Published by Intermediate Technology Publications Ltd. and Oxfam

Acknowledgements

The research for this book was done during visits to eight developing countries financed by the Overseas Development Administration of the British Government, who also met the costs of publication, and I am deeply grateful for this help. However, all views expressed are my own and are not necessarily those of O.D.A.

Thanks are due to Oxfam who funded the typesetting of the book. I should like also to thank the many Oxfam staff and project holders, all over the world, who have assisted repeatedly throughout the project, and other bodies, too numerous to mention, who provided expert advice.

Published by Intermediate Technology Publications Ltd., 9 King Street, London, WC2E 8HN, U.K. and Oxfam.

ISBN 0 903031 79 5

Printed and bound in Great Britain
by Billing and Sons Limited
Guildford, London, Oxford, Worcester

iv

Contents

This book is dedicated to the thousands of poor people who live by collecting and processing waste and especially to those who befriended me and freely gave information for this book.

"Let not ambition mock their useful toil,
Their homely joys, and destiny obscure;
Nor grandeur hear with a disdainful smile,
The short and simple annals of the poor."
Thomas Gray 1716–1771

Preface

Who is the book for?

Although 'Work from Waste' is written primarily for use in developing countries, it may also be of interest in industrialized countries, for communities and groups practising local self-reliance. It covers a wide range of technologies and can be used by people with various levels of skill. It is hoped that two groups of people in developing countries will particularly benefit from it. Firstly, the unemployed who see no reasonable hope of any other kind of job. Secondly, those who are already employed in the collection and recycling of waste but do not make an adequate living from it. There are millions of these people; they form a large minority in every Third World town and city, and include many women, children, the handicapped and ex-prisoners. They generally have little skill and no capital or equipment beyond a few sacks or a small cart. They usually collect material and sell it unprocessed, in tiny quantities, to middlemen and it is these merchants who, because they process and transport it in larger quantities, can sell it at increased value.

The reasons why the small collectors rarely increase the value of what they sell are many: not enough cash to finance stocks, no transport, no equipment or premises and no ability. Yet there are many technologies which are simple and require little or no capital; the purpose of this book is to bring these to the attention of the poorest and least skilled. As only a small proportion of such people can read, it may be necessary for a friend to read and explain the book to them. Therefore, the readers of the book in the first instance will be those who work, either professionally or from goodwill, to help the poor. They will include extension workers, missionaries, field staff of development agencies, teachers and instructors in training colleges and universities, village leaders and overseas volunteers. Not all will be technically trained and, for their sake and that of their listeners, the language and ideas have been kept as simple as possible and a full glossary of technical terms is provided.

This book may, in addition, be useful to those small and medium companies which have been built up by enterprising people, often with limited capital and skill. Through running their own business or factory they have developed confidence in their ability to introduce new activities, use new materials, employ better techniques and make additional products. To them this book should be an encyclopaedia of wastes, their origins, uses and methods of processing, which will stimulate new activities and create employment in this way.

Finally, this book may be of interest to large industrial companies, even those that are state-owned, which create their own wastes but only sometimes process or recycle them. It may encourage them to use them more imaginatively and to use other peoples' wastes instead of more costly raw materials. For their interest a few high cost technologies have been described, such as for reclaiming rubber and plastics, because no less complex processes exist at present.

Structure of 'Work from Waste'

The book is divided into two main parts. Part I contains details of the wide range of materials that can be recycled and the processes involved. A list of equipment suppliers is given at the end of each chapter. It is expected that this part will be used as a reference book rather than as a text to be read right through so there is a full index at the back of the book. The only important materials not covered are the organic wastes from agriculture, animals, forestry and fishing. These had to be left out to keep down the size and it is planned to include them in a second volume.

Part II describes how to set up and run a small business recycling wastes. To help understanding, it has been illustrated by two case studies which, while imaginary, are typical of thousands of actual small businesses. The only difference is that the imaginary businesses are being run so that they will succeed. The lessons that lead to success are summarized in thirty-two short and simple rules which are repeated at the end.

Also, in appendices at the back of the book, are details of sources of further help and information and a list of books covering certain subjects in more detail.

Ethics

Finally, it is necessary to comment on ethics. In many countries, the scrap reclamation industries have been regarded by the public and by the police as activities bordering on crime. This is often true; many of the people who have helped me with information for the book were part-time waste collectors/part-time thieves. The more important truth is that it is poverty, not scrap trading, that causes crime because many poor people see crime as the only road to escape from their poverty. Where a practice is commonly fraudulent, I have tried to explain but not to judge; to suggest the possible consequences of dishonest dealing but not to preach against it. Nobody is entitled to interpret this as meaning either that I approve of crime or that I condemn those whose poverty leads them to practise it.

'Work from Waste' is the first book to be written on this subject and it is far from perfect. Corrections, suggestions and new information from readers in developing countries will be very welcome and should be sent to the author at the publishers' address.

Jon Vogler

Introduction

Employment is, in the words of the World Employment Conference of 1976, "... one of the most effective means of ensuring a just and equitable distribution of income and of raising the standard of living of the majority of the population." The only objection to its widespread use as a solution to economic and development problems is that there is rarely enough of it, especially in those countries that need it most. Unemployment and underemployment (employment for too little reward or in a 'marginal' activity such as crime or scavenging) are features of underdevelopment as common as poverty, illiteracy, bad housing or disease. Worse, it is in the countries that lack the resources for social security that unemployment means not just boredom and spiritual demoralization but, in addition, abject poverty, destitution and even starvation.

This book is about one field of employment opportunity: the exploitation of waste. Waste is one of the world's largest industries, although you could not discover this from any book of statistics, because its activities cut across the normal divisions into which industries are placed. If you buy a bottle of medicine it may have a metal top and be protected by plastic foam padding, in a cardboard box. To recycle these parts after the medicine has been taken you will need to sell the bottle to a glassmaker, the top to a foundry, the plastic to a moulder and the cardboard to a paperboard mill. Recycled materials are only a small part of the materials used by most of those factories; yet add up all the bottles, tops, packaging and cardboard cartons and you have an enormous quantity of material. Then add wastes from agriculture, animal and meat industries, mining and quarrying, industries that make iron and steel and other metals, textiles, rubber, chemicals and oils and it is even bigger. Finally, include all the activities of local government in collecting and disposing of household and other wastes and the huge size of the industry becomes apparent.

Why, when employment is so difficult to create, should it be easier to do so in the waste business, an activity in which hundreds of thousands of people are already scratching a living. There are several reasons and they will be discussed in some detail. By persuading the reader that waste offers unique opportunities for creating jobs, it is hoped to encourage him to read further and then to consider whether he can apply some of the ideas to his own business or to the group of poor people with whom he is working or just to pass on the ideas or the book to others. This book is of no value until someone, one day, uses it and finds work and earns money when previously they were idle.

The reasons are these:

Waste is plentiful In most towns and cities of the world it is not only heaped in huge quantities on refuse dumps but also lies in piles around the streets and in small illegal dumps on any piece of waste ground. Most Third World cities are worse than those in industrialized countries which have the money, the technical abilities and the public attitudes to control their waste to some degree. They are usually growing more rapidly with an increasing population of middle and upper social classes. These are the people who can afford packaged goods, processed goods, new furniture or a car or clothing, who take a daily newspaper and cultivate a garden.

Waste is free or if not free then very cheap. It is thrown away because it is either impossible or not worth the time or trouble to sell. Any process that uses materials to make a product has to pay for those materials and, worse, has to pay for them before being paid for the product itself. This need to finance raw material stocks with working capital is, as much as any other, a requirement that hinders the setting up of small industries. If the materials are free or very cheap this hindrance is removed.

Waste is flexible Even if the material is free, there are other expenses in making a product to sell for money; even if only that of feeding one's family while doing so. Waste is flexible in the amount of work it needs. A weaver cannot sell a half-finished piece of cloth. A collector of waste, however, can either process it into something more valuable himself or can sell it immediately to someone else for the price of his next meal.

Waste is labour-intensive It needs people to collect and sort it. This is because it comes from so many different places; from thousands of different homes, each eating slightly different foods, wearing different clothes, living in different kinds of houses down different sorts of streets. Although it can be collected and sorted by machines, no one has yet produced a machine that can do these two things as cheaply and effectively as a human with eyes, hands and legs. In the industrialized countries, where wages are high and fewer and fewer people are willing to do dirty jobs, machines are being used where possible to collect and sort waste but often the result is a cost so high that the attempt to recycle or re-use the waste is abandoned altogether. This will not happen in the Third World while so many people earn a very low income. Waste lends itself to the kind of sub-contracting by big firms to small that helped the 'economic miracles' of Japan, Singapore and Hong Kong.

Waste needs little capital It can be collected and sorted and sometimes processed with very little equipment, buildings or supplies. Of the many industries that need only simple tools and equipment, few lend themselves to such a range of different levels of capitalization, as does waste. To collect waste paper, if you have no lorry you can use a van; if you have no van you can use a donkey cart; if you have no donkey you use a hand-cart; if you have no hand-cart then use a sack and if you cannot even buy or find a sack you can tie it in a bundle. If you have nothing whatever you can carry it loose. However, the less the capital or equipment used the smaller the profits that can be made and the more the effort needed to earn them. You can collect a tonne of paper in an hour with a lorry. With a van it may take two hours, with a donkey cart half a day, a hand cart, a day, with a sack two days, four days with bundles, and loose in your hands it will take a week!

Waste sells for cash which, once the collector and his family have eaten, *may* be used to buy the equipment needed. The first bundle of paper sold can buy half a loaf and a length of string; the next, larger because it is tied, can buy half a loaf and a sack; a week's collections with the sack can yield the price of four second-hand wheels and some scrap wood with which to make a simple cart. If the collector is lucky or sensible or hard-working he can (in theory) continue until he has bought the lorry.

Waste is familiar Even if ways of processing it are technical or complicated, the fact that the simplest person knows what paper or glass is, what it is used for, whether it burns, where it is bought and sold, helps him to develop the confidence to work with it. No one who is unfamiliar with farm crops will try and make his living as a farmer; no one who grew up away from sea or rivers will suddenly seek his employment as a fisherman; yet there is no mystery about waste; we are all brought up among it, wherever we live. The most important requirement to start a small business is the confidence that you will be able to do it and succeed, and familiarity with the raw material helps to achieve this.

Recycling of waste is approved If you decide to obtain your living as a pickpocket there will be many people trying to prevent you succeeding, for reasons that have nothing to do with whether you are good at it or not! If you try to become a cleaner of shoes only your clients are at all interested in your work and if you are ill tomorrow they will go to someone else. If you collect waste, however, a whole range of people and organizations benefit and, if they are wise they will help you or at least not obstruct you. Your customers need the material for their business. The householder or factory that produces the waste needs to get rid of it. The local council will have to collect what you do not, they will have to find somewhere to put it. The government may have to find foreign money to import raw materials if local waste is not collected and used instead. More imported coal or oil or electricity will be needed to process those raw materials than are needed to recycle the waste you collect. Finally, the wastes you do not collect may drift around the streets as litter and spoil the town for tourists, attract flies or rats and block up the drains if there are any. So the community has an interest in your success; provided always that you do not create more litter than you save, or cover the neighbour's washing with thick black smoke or do other things that will quickly lose everyone's sympathy.

Finally, and this is important to the person who wants not just to survive today but also to prosper tomorrow, *waste provides a route for success* in the same trade. The son of a man who, in the nineteen twenties, pushed a cart around the streets of London, collecting waste paper, recently retired as Chairman of the largest waste paper company in Europe, with thousands of employees and offices and depots in five or six countries. Yet he never had to stop being a waste paper seller; never had to learn a new profession or new product. The reason for this is that the waste industry is so large, so varied and so organized. And, not only is waste plentiful but it is multiplying.

These then are the reasons why waste offers the kind of job opportunities that the World Employment Conference outlined. It is a free, plentiful, familiar and flexible raw material, suitable for labour-intensive processing in informal or sub-contract industries, using appropriate technology and little capital and providing a cash income plus other environmental and community benefits.

Part I
Technologies for Recycling Waste Materials

Chapter 1. Waste Paper

In the Third World, more people are self-employed collecting waste paper and board* than any other waste material. There is great scope for waste paper re-use. The following aspects will be studied:
1. The processes used to make different types of paper.
2. The types of waste paper that a collector may find and the markets that exist for each one.
3. Where to find the different types of waste paper.
4. How to collect and process them.
5. What to do if no industry exists nearby to buy them.
   First, an explanation of what paper is and how it is made.

HOW PAPER IS MADE
Fibres and wood pulp
   Fibres are the fine, thread-like wisps from which paper, textiles and many other materials are made. Tear a piece of paper and the fibres can be seen at the torn edge (clearer with a magnifying glass). Paper fibres consist of 'cellulose'**, the material of which many plants and especially trees and stalks, such as wheat, rice and sugar cane, are made. These materials can be used to make paper by breaking them down until the fibres are loose and free of the substances that bind them. In the simplest form of paper-making, still used to make umbrellas in Thailand and China, the fibres are released from strips of tree-bark by boiling in water with ashes, then pounding with a wooden mallet. The process of releasing the fibres is called 'pulping' and the mass of fibres, no longer held together

---

In this chapter the word paper will be used to mean paper and board, and waste paper to mean waste paper and board. Board means the same as cardboard.
**All difficult words in the book have been put within quotation marks (' ') and their meanings appear in the glossary.*

3

but ready to be suspended in water for making paper, is known as 'pulp'. Softwood or coniferous pulps are used for tough wrapping and packaging papers because of their long fibres; deciduous or hardwood pulps provide 'filler' for printing and writing papers. There are three principle types of 'primary wood-pulp' used in paper-making; mechanical, 'Kraft' sulphate, and sulphite pulp.

Mechanical pulp

This is made by pounding or grinding cellulosic material such as wood. It is used for printing newspapers. Newsprint is very weak and loses its strength altogether if wetted – this is characteristic of mechanical pulp. It is ideal for newspapers because it is highly absorbent and liquids, such as printing ink, are soaked up and dry very quickly. Mechanical pulp often contains tiny particles of wood which have not been reduced to fibre and are visible to the naked eye. Thus paper made from mechanical pulp is often described as 'woody'.

Chemical pulp

A strong paper product is most cheaply achieved by pulping cellulose fibres so that they are not weakened by mechanical damage. The wood or stalks are mechanically reduced to small chips and then cooked at high pressure with certain chemicals that attack the bonds between the fibres and release them to form pulp. The most common chemicals used are:

  i) Caustic soda and sodium sulphate which produce coarse, very strong fibres known as Kraft, suitable for sacks and boxes to hold heavy weights, and

  ii) Various sulphites (such as ammonium and calcium) which produce fine fibres suitable for making high quality printing and writing papers (usually bleached white); these are fine and strong but expensive.

There are many variations to pulping processes, but only one point needs to be made here: all types of pulp start out the colour of the cellulose (usually a wood-like colour) and can be bleached white and later tinted (coloured) to other colours.

Use of waste paper in paper-making

The phrase primary wood-pulp was used above to distinguish it from 'secondary pulp' which is made by vigorously stirring waste paper in water (usually in a 'hydra-pulper', a

4

cylinder containing rotating blades), to separate the fibres bonded during the original paper-making process. As these bonds are weaker than those of the original cellulose plant, hydra-pulping is a more gentle process than wood-pulping and consumes less energy. Even so, paper cannot be repulped an indefinite number of times without becoming much weaker. Secondary pulp can never, therefore, have as high a quality as the primary fibre from which it was made, although it can come close *provided* pure waste paper of the same type is used. For example, pulp made by hydra-pulping clean Kraft sacks will make new sacks of only slightly lower quality, particularly if mixed with a proportion of primary Kraft pulp. If, however, the secondary pulp is made from material which contains newspapers or some other weak mechanical pulp product or dirt, dust or clay, it will not be strong enough to use instead of primary Kraft; its value to the paper-maker (and the price he is prepared to pay for it) will be much reduced. This leads to the first important rule of waste paper collecting: pure, clean material is of far higher value than dirty or impure waste paper.

Coated papers

In some cases the matted, absorbent, dull surface of the paper is coated with a material which makes it appear brighter, shinier and harder, and makes printing on it sharper and more contrasting. Coated papers are particularly used in magazines that are financed by the advertisements they print. In the process of hydra-pulping waste coated paper, the coating is washed out: thus the weight of fibre obtained from a tonne of coated paper is less (often by 20%) than that obtained from a tonne of uncoated. The value to the paper-mill and the selling price will also be lower.

Moreover, if the coating is plastic, tar or other material which will not dissolve in water, then the waste paper is not suitable for paper-making and has no value at all. Indeed, it may even reduce the value of other, good paper with which it is mixed. The same is true of polythene film, 'cellophane', glued papers, string, and any material which will not break down in water.

Printed and coloured papers

As well as variations in how the paper is made, waste paper

may be printed or tinted. Both reduce its value: print because it makes both the pulp and the paper made from it dull grey in colour unless bleached (which is expensive); tinting because the tints colour the pulp which must then either be used for a limited range of similarly coloured products (or cheap, grey products) or must be expensively bleached.

Therefore it is important to remember that white waste paper is more valuable than similar material which is coloured, and unprinted waste paper is of greater value than the same material printed.

The paper-making industry

The manufacture and use of paper is one of the world's biggest industries; there is little hand-making or small-scale manufacture. The following types of factories are involved:

Pulp mills that process timber or other materials to make pulp.
Paper mills (and board mills) which use pulp or waste paper to produce finished paper and board.
Paper converters that use paper or board and produce items from them such as boxes, tubes, rolls of toilet tissue, boxes of blank office paper, stacks of printing paper cut to standard sizes, etc.
Printers who usually buy from converters, although larger firms such as newspaper presses may buy direct from the paper mills.
Integrated mills are those that make pulp and then use it to make paper themselves.

TYPES OF WASTE PAPER AND BOARD AND MARKETS FOR THEM

Because the market is so important to waste paper collection, the different types of waste paper will be considered in relation to their markets, starting with the most valuable and going on to those of less value. For values, see Table 1.

Printing and writing papers

This category contains the best quality, most expensive papers which fetch the highest waste paper prices and are mainly made from bleached sulphite pulps. They are, in descending order of value:

    i) *Computer printout (or C.P.O.).* Printing does not

Table 1 Values of different kinds of waste paper

Main grade	Sub grade	Value (compared with old cartons)
Printing and writing	Computer printout	3–4
	Computer cards	2–3
	Printers trimmings —	
	white, unprinted	2½
	white, printed	1½
	coloured, unprinted	1½
	coloured, printed	¾
	Mixed office papers	1½
	Sorted office papers	As printers trimmings
	School and letter papers	¾–1
	'Pams' (pamphlets and magazines)	½
Kraft sacks	Resale as sacks	10
Corrugated cardboard	Waste paper	1½–2
Cartons	Sale as cartons	5
	Waste paper	1
Newspaper	Unprinted	5
	Printed (for sale to a de-inking plant)	⅔
	Printed (no de-inking plant)	⅓
Mixed waste paper	Clean, free from 'contraries'	⅓–½
	Dirty, with contraries	1/10

Note: The comparative values of waste papers are approximate and will vary between different places.

reduce its value, provided it is sold to a manufacturer of high quality printing and writing papers.

ii) *Computer punched cards (sometimes called tab-cards)*
These may be buff-coloured (the most valuable) or coloured. Printing does not reduce their value. They can be sold to makers of high quality printing and writing

papers but are also widely used by the makers of tissues, good quality boxboards etc.

iii) *Printers' trimmings*. These are the edge trimmings left when a printer, box-maker or converter cuts his product to its final size. Their value lies in cleanness, lack of print and quality of material and it is increased if the wise printer has kept different grades separate. If not, it is worthwhile for the collector to sort the paper into different grades and separate printed material from unprinted. This is a labour-intensive activity, widely practised in India, that needs no investment but may create jobs. However, it is tedious work and may cause eye-strain. White trimmings should be sorted from coloured, but different colours need not be separated. All may be sold to makers of printing and writing papers.

iv) *Office papers*. Invoices, ledgers, letter-papers and record cards are amongst these. Those printed or written on are separated from blank paper and whites are separated from coloureds. Carbon paper, self-duplicating paper, plastic coated papers, file covers and bookbindings, metal file clips, string and other office materials should be removed. For sales to a big mill it is unnecessary to remove staples or paper clips as the mill will remove these with magnets; smaller mills may insist, however, that you remove them.

Tear the backings and covers from catalogues with glued bindings. Only a very large quantity justifies an expensive guillotine to do this.

Envelopes, including a few of the cheaper manilla variety (light brown) can be mixed in with whites, as can cream-coloured envelopes and papers in any quantity. Adding machine rolls are usually good, white and unprinted. They may be sold to makers of printing papers and high quality board.

v) *School and letter-papers*. Letter-papers may be of good quality, but school exercise books are low in value, although they often contain little ink which increases their value (feint ruling does not count). They can be sold to makers of printing and writing papers.

vi) *Pamphlets and magazines (known in the trade as Pams)* These are the lowest grade of printing papers other than

8

newsprint. They are often coated, have heavy printing and large amounts of colour; sometimes they may be printed on newsprint. They are not worth sorting unless a paper mill has a particular demand. The advantage is that they are heavy and it is easy to collect a great weight quickly. They are best sold to makers of low quality board.

vii) *Kraft sacks.* Kraft paper is recognized by its strength and brown colour. It is used for large sacks, in two or three ply (thicknesses), or for smaller bags and wrapping papers. (Occasionally, whitish, bleached Kraft is used.) Watch out for sacks with polythene linings, often used to protect chemicals from damp, which should be ripped out. Remove heavily-sewn bottom seams, which are often reinforced with canvas or similar material. Tarred papers (waterproof) are unsaleable and reduce the value of a load. Empty remaining contents from a sack, for example, plastic granules or fertilizers. If collected in any quantity, these may be resaleable.

The important decision is whether a greater profit can be made by selling Kraft for re-use as sacks, or to board or Kraft paper mills for pulping. Re-use may entail repair or more sorting, transport and selling costs, but usually pays off.

viii) *Corrugated cardboard.* This is a brown board made of three layers (Fig. 1). The flat top and bottom layers are

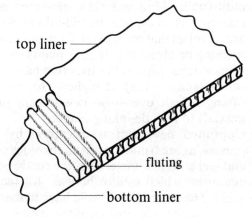

Fig. 1 Corrugated board.

called liners and the corrugated (wavy) centre is the fluting. The liners are often made of primary Kraft, sometimes with secondary material (e.g. Kraft sacks or old corrugated cartons) mixed in. The fluting is made from lower quality material, as its function is only to give stiffness. Pulp for fluting manufacture may have a high proportion of mixed waste paper (see below).

Corrugated board is used to make packing boxes or cartons and these are in demand everywhere. If there is no board mill in your district, they can often be sold for re-use, either in the flattened or made-up state at a value up to five times that of old cartons. They are rarely contaminated with impurities or contraries. They need to be flattened before transporting, otherwise space will be wasted. Printing on cartons has no effect on the price paid by board mills.

ix) *Newspaper.* In some countries, newspapers are little in demand due to their low strength; likewise telephone directories and magazines made from newsprint. Their principal uses are as mixed waste paper for the manufacture of cheap flutings, grey board (cheap cardboard), or the middle layers of 'multilayer boards'. There are three important exceptions:

a) In poor countries where little packaging or newspapers are thrown away, even low quality raw materials are in short supply.

b) Some countries, usually those which are heavily industrialized but lack their own sources of papermaking materials, operate 'de-inking plants'. These are factories that remove ink from old newspapers by washing or bleaching. If such plants exist, or if it is economic to ship to countries that have them, prices for newspapers may be higher. However, there are often enough over-issue newspapers (unsold and unread) to feed de-inking plants.

c) Unprinted newsprint is discarded by newspaper presses, as are trimmings from the sides of the paper and reel ends (the material at the centre of the reel of newsprint which cannot be used for technical reasons). The former can be sold back to manufacturers of newsprint and low quality writing paper. The latter is clean and large enough to be cut up and sold at a high price for food wrappings.

x) *Mixed waste paper.* This is the lowest usable grade and may have almost any composition: grey board or multilayer board and similar packaging materials not acceptable in any other grade, as well as mixed, unsorted materials from other grades. This is the material often collected from municipal (town) refuse by scavengers on refuse dumps or at specially built composting or refuse sorting plants. In a district of offices, factories or wealthy homes it may contain valuable grades, worth sorting out for separate sale if labour costs are low or if the collector is underemployed with time to spare. This must be done with the market in mind: if the only market is a mill making cheap grey cardboard, it is worthless to sort out grades which will then be mixed together again by the mill. It is important to realize that the material left after better grades have been removed may fetch a lower price because it is made up principally of newspapers, packaging and cheap cardboard. However, if there are mills nearby making corrugated board, toilet tissues and cheap grey board, then separated Kraft sacks, brown paper and old cartons can go to the first and printing and writing papers to the second, at good prices which will not reduce the price of the remainder for making grey board.

This point is covered at length because, while merchants may have cornered supplies of high quality materials such as Kraft, corrugated cartons and printing and writing papers, quantities of these may still be extracted from municipal refuse by those who understand what is valuable and what is not. Opportunities exist here for creating extra jobs. Once the principles of sorting have been taught, the work requires neither capital money, skill, nor bodily strength and may be undertaken by the disabled or mentally retarded.

Mixed waste paper is worth half or a third of the value of old cartons, and this value is reduced if it is dirty, such as most material extracted from refuse dumps. By sorting out the higher grades and selling to the right market, a value equal to that of cartons may be achieved; the gain, however, has to be compared with the cost (or, for the self-employed collector, the time) of

11

sorting, selling and transporting to several markets instead of only to one.

xi) *Packaging and wrapping papers.* These follow mixed waste paper in the order of value because of the problems they cause with contraries. Much modern packaging mixes plastics, metals, and other materials with paper and board, and it is difficult or uneconomic to separate them. Greaseproof, cellophane and 'wet strength' papers do not break down in water, cannot be pulped, and are difficult to recognize and remove. The main material is cardboard, containing a high proportion of cheap grey board (sometimes inside an outer layer of good quality). The amount of colour printing is high, too. Therefore, although such papers or boards are expensive to produce, their value as waste is no higher than that of mixed waste paper and may be lower due to contraries.

Table 2 Keep these out of waste paper
The following contraries harm its value because they are unsuitable for paper-making.

Plastics of all sorts, especially those that look like papers such as:
    Polythene
    Expanded polystyrene foam
    Cellophane, greaseproof and wet-strength papers
    'ABS' (used for plastic coffee cups, cream and butter cartons etc.)
    Paper and board coated with plastics
Sanitary towels, babies nappies ('diapers');
String, rope, wire;
Tarpaper, any tarry substance, oilcloth, bitumen roofing papers;
Metals, especially thin foils that look like paper;
Paper and board coated with metal;
Stones, grit, earth, sand, dust, pottery, etc;
Textiles, yarns, carpets, sacking;
Wood, leather, bone, glues;
Organic materials: food, peelings, agricultural waste;
Binding and book covers containing glue, plastic, cloth, oilcloth etc.

Note: The following are not contraries and may be included in mixed waste paper:

- Egg boxes made from paper (but not those made from thin rigid plastic or expanded polystyrene foam);
- Paper tubes or cones used in the textile industries.

SOURCES OF WASTE PAPER

Having established what sort of waste papers can be collected, and where they can be sold, where does one find them? Paper can be collected from the following places, starting with that which is likely to be the most profitable:

Computer offices produce the most valuable of all waste paper.

Printing shops usually sell the trimmings themselves or else they are collected by a merchant.

Newspaper presses almost always sell the edge-trimmings and reel-ends themselves.

Offices throw out quantities of blank paper as well as office records, letters etc. If offices are small or located away from the city centre they may not have made arrangements to sell their waste.

Warehouses receive goods in sacks and cartons and often discard these after unpacking. Quantities may be large.

Factories may also have large quantities of packaging which they do not want. These will get dirty on the factory floor unless rescued.

Shops receive goods in cartons but supermarkets and food stores often give or sell these to their customers. Small shops may not produce enough to make a visit worthwhile unless there are other shops nearby.

Householders may allow their servants to sell any waste paper. It may be dirtied by food waste or ashes and not be in large enough quantities to make a visit worthwhile. Still, thousands of people in many countries make a living by collecting household waste paper, sometimes by paying the householder a small sum.

Refuse dumps and disposal plants receive the paper which no-one has thought worth collecting. Refuse collectors often keep saleable material but quantities of good quality waste paper continue to arrive on refuse dumps all over the world (Fig. 2). By regularly visiting the local dump you may be able to discover which factories or offices discard good quality material and arrange to collect it direct from them.

13

Fig. 2   Good quality waste paper continues to arrive on refuse tips. Kenya.

WAYS OF COLLECTING WASTE PAPER

The cheapest way in which to collect paper is by putting it into a sack, but this does not hold enough to be profitable. The next step is a hand-cart, small enough for one person, or a bigger one for a larger enterprise. The following is a description of a collection project which could be carried out by a team of four to six members. To work as a team, every member should undergo training before starting as a collector. This should cover:

   i) Why waste paper is collected, and how it is used.

  ii) What grades of waste paper are wanted.

 iii) What materials are not wanted or are harmful.

 iv) Terms and conditions of employment.

  v) The importance of punctuality for teamwork.

 vi) What to say when entering a client's premises.

vii) The notion of the project's public image and the need

for honesty and politeness to clients and the general public.
viii) The necessity of avoiding litter and the penalty for failure in this.

Once the project is making a profit it is desirable to adopt a distinctive uniform, the same colour as the cart.

Method of operation
i) One member always stays with the cart, preferably the leader.
ii) The other members call at each office/factory as directed by the leader, with their hessian or woven poly-propylene sacks. Waste paper is collected in the sack until it is full and then emptied into the cart.
iii) The team leader has a route card and ticks off each client visited. It is a good idea to send the same person to collect from the same client each time so that they get to know one another.
iv) Instructions to clients should make it quite clear that only paper and cardboard are required. Unwanted materials should be either rejected on the client's prem-ises – politely – or sorted out on the cart. A sack for con-traries should be hung on the cart and emptied where convenient and *tidy*.
v) At the end, the cart is wheeled to the pick-up point, material is transferred to a vehicle and the cart parked in an agreed location. (More about this in Part II.)

Specifications of a cart to hold 300–400 kilos of paper (Fig. 3)
i) Large wheels for free movement with ball or roller bearings.
ii) A push-bar for two to three people at the front.
iii) Legs so that it can be parked horizontally.
iv) A cage of wire mesh over the top, with a hinged opening for loading.
v) The back drop on hinges for easy unloading.
vi) Some means of measuring loads.
vii) Painted a distinctive colour with a sign giving the name, address and telephone number of the collector.
viii) Dimensions: 1.5 metres long, 1.2 metres wide, 50 cm wooden sides, cage top 1.5 metres above cart floor.

15

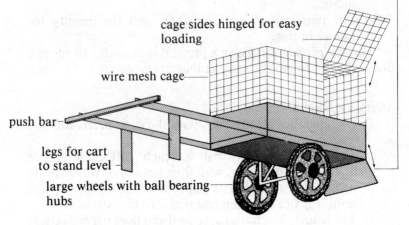

cart back drops for unloading

cage sides hinged for easy loading

wire mesh cage

push bar

legs for cart to stand level

large wheels with ball bearing hubs

Fig. 3   Waste paper collection cart.

Collecting with a vehicle

In the industrialized countries waste paper is often collected in a van or a lorry fitted with a wire mesh cage over the top. This holds a great deal of paper but is expensive to run, particularly for stop-start collections from small shops and offices. For collecting from large warehouses and factories it may be economic. It can be more profitable if it draws a trailer, also fitted with a cage on top. When collecting cartons and boxes it is necessary for someone to tread the load down. Some factories will flatten cartons and tie them in bundles but may charge for doing so. A cart drawn by horse, donkey or bullock is cheaper than a motor vehicle if distances are short, for example in a dense town area.

Cost of waste paper collection

When costing out a waste paper collection scheme take account of:
  i) Wages for collectors and supervisor.
  ii) Cost of letters or visits to clients.
  iii) Cost of publicity – leaflets or advertisements.
  iv) Interest on any loans for handcart or other vehicle.
  v) Wear and tear on hand-cart or other equipment.
  vi) Costs of the vehicle collecting from hand-carts.
  vii) Payments to clients.

16

See also chapter 18 on costing.

It may be more profitable to pay a factory a small sum for a load of boxes that can be collected in one journey than to spend hours and walk miles collecting free, low quality, household waste paper.

BALING

Importance of baling waste paper
To make a profit from collection and sale of waste paper it is usually necessary to bale it, that is, squash it and tie it up. Usually the bale is a square-shaped bundle, densely packed and tied in two or three directions with wire or string.

Reasons for baling
Baling makes transport cheaper. If waste paper is loose, a lorry load will overflow before it reaches the weight limit that the vehicle can carry. Baling paper makes it denser and the weight limit is reached before the vehicle is full. The paper is sold by weight but the lorry costs the same, fully laden or not, so the transport cost *per tonne* is reduced.

Baling makes storage cheaper. Baled material is not only denser but can also be stacked much higher (Fig. 4). Because both seller and customer can store more, a larger vehicle can be used (cheaper per tonne) and a larger quantity sold (higher price per tonne).

Baling adds value to the product. The customer will find baled material cheaper to transport, store and use and will therefore pay more for it (except in one case – see below). He will regard the seller of baled material more highly than the seller of loose paper, and may reflect this by entering into a trade agreement or by continuing to buy when the market is slack (depressed).

Baling reduces fire risks. Fire is a serious and ever-present risk in waste paper processing. Baling prevents air reaching the inside of the bundle, so even fierce flames only char the outside. However, this does not mean there is *no* fire risk where paper is baled, particularly if there is unbaled material lying around. Note, too, the danger from fire if wet paper is baled. The paper 'ferments' and the temperature can rise high

17

Fig. 4 Baling permits high stacking of wastepaper, improves tidiness and reduces fire risks. Photo: courtesy of Oxfam.

enough to burn. Wetting waste paper to increase its weight is dangerous as well as likely to annoy the buyer and lead to trouble for the seller.

Cases when baling is not desirable
   i) If the buyer has no means of lifting the bales, unless it is possible to make a smaller, lighter bale that can be lifted by hand.
  ii) If buyer and seller are located close together and neither stores the material for a long time. The cost of baling cannot be recovered against savings in transport or storage. Work out the cost and the likely savings and improved prices before you start a baling operation. In Third World countries where labour is cheap, where the

one-man firm has lots of spare time and transport gets dearer each year, baling usually pays off.

BALING PROCESSES AND PRESSES

The simplest process is to stand on a pile of paper while a friend ties it! This, however, is more like bundling than baling. Baling is most efficiently done in a press, a strong box equipped with some means of compressing the material and holding it while it is tied.

Treading box

The simplest, cheapest baling press is shown in Fig. 5. It may be used for paper or thin metal scrap. It is a strong, hinged, four-sided wooden frame with no top or bottom but a joint at one hinge. To operate:

   i) Lay string or rope in the empty box.
  ii) Fill the box with paper, treading down each layer.
 iii) Tread down and tie the string ends while still standing on top.

Fig. 5 Simple baling box, full and ready to tie. Note the steel hinges on the near corner. India.

Baling wastepaper in a simple press.

Fig. 6a With one side down, material is laid flat in the press, treading down if necessary, until it is nearly full. The sides are latched into place and the latches tied to prevent the sides from springing open under pressure. Mexico.

Fig. 6b The box is filled and the platten placed on top, followed by the beam. A hanger is placed over one end of the beam and hooked a few teeth down the toothed rack. A second hanger is placed, loose, on the end of the beam, followed by the lever stirrup.

Fig. 6c The lever end is fitted under a low tooth and force applied. The hanger is slipped over the nearest tooth and the force is released. The operation is repeated at the other end, so that the hanger already in place can catch a lower tooth.

Fig. 6d With one person working on either side the latches are released and the sides removed.

Fig. 6e Wires are inserted, using the long wiring needle, and twisted together.

Fig. 6f When wiring is complete, the hangers are jerked off, the beam and platten removed and the bales pushed out sideways.

21

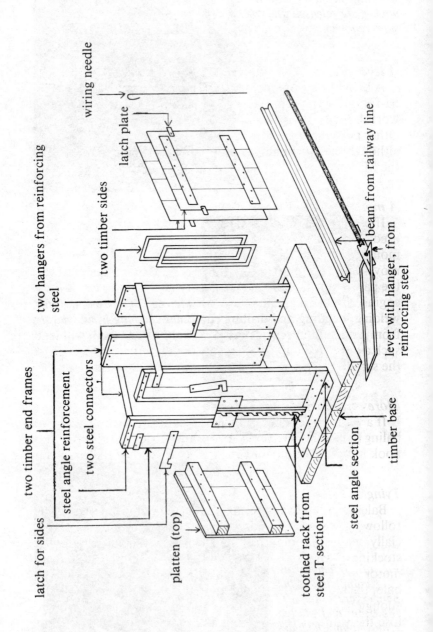

wiring needle

latch plate

two hangers from reinforcing
steel

two timber sides

latch for sides

two timber end frames

steel angle reinforcement

two steel connectors

platten (top)

toothed rack from
steel T section

steel angle section

timber base

lever with hanger, from
reinforcing steel

beam from railway line

Fig. 7   Parts for waste paper baling press.

22

iv) Open the box joint, swing the sides away and remove the bale.

A treading box can be made by a carpenter with hinges and catch bought in a hardware store.

A lever press

A better hand-operated baling press is used in Mexico, Figs 6a-f show how it is operated. Its manufacture requires a metal workshop as well as a carpenter. The parts are shown in Fig. 7. Other designs of simple baling presses are available (Fig. 8), although these probably would not be as simple to operate as the Mexican unit.

A motorized screw press

If electric power is available then a motorized press can be used. The press has a strong vertical steel frame on which is mounted an electric motor that turns a vertical screw which moves the press platten (the strong, flat board that compresses the paper) up and down. This kind of press can be made in an engineering works equipped with a large lathe, and cutting, welding, bending and drilling equipment, or it can be bought from a manufacturer of presses. Often, a paper mill will lend such a press to their waste paper supplier, although this will tie the supplier to the mill and may result in lower selling prices.

More complicated baling presses

If a waste paper operation increases in size a whole range of baling presses are available. These are outside the scope of this book but see **Equipment suppliers** at the end of the chapter.

Tying of bales

Bales should always be tied two ways and often three. The following waste materials are useful for tying: string, especially made of polypropylene, rope, wire, ladies tights or stockings, strips of sacking and strips of rubber cut from motor tyres. The higher the pressure applied when making the bale, the stronger the tying required. If you do not tie tightly enough or in enough directions and the bale breaks, you will lose the value of the material and have to pay the transport operator as well!

Fig. 8   Hand-operated baling press using screws and capstan nuts. India. Photo: courtesy of Oxfam.

Two useful tools for tying bales while they are in the baling press are a needle made from thick wire, about a foot longer than the width of the bale, and a pair of stout pliers.

Machines also exist for strapping bales, using steel strapping (a flat, thin steel strip) but unless a source of second-hand strapping is available it is usually too costly for waste paper. For details see Chapter 2 on steel scrap.

BINS AND BUNKERS

Bins or bunkers can be made to store waste paper while it awaits baling or transport, or to help in the sorting process. Their advantages are:

- Floors, gangways and working areas are kept free of waste for safer working.
- The waste is kept clean and its value maintained. Mixing of different grades is prevented.
- Fire risks are reduced.
- More material can be stored on a given floor area.
  Storage bunkers have side and rear walls (and floor) only. A

24

front wall would increase the amount that the bunker could hold, but make loading and unloading more difficult. A roof may be used to keep out rain but this, too, can make loading difficult. A floor sloping steeply down to the front could make unloading easier but the angle of slope (necessary for paper to slide under its own weight) would be so large that either the volume of the bunker would have to be much reduced or its height much increased.

MARKETS FOR WASTE PAPER

The two most common markets for waste paper are:

i) *Paper or Board Mills* may make any or all the products described earlier in the chapter. It is best to sell to them direct if possible. They are final users and will pay the best prices. If you can sign an agreement with them they may take material from you when the market is slack and they stop buying from merchants.

ii) *Merchants* buy from printers, converters and small collectors and sell at a profit to the mills. They can only make a profit if they buy at a lower price than they sell so both you and the mill make a bad bargain if you sell through a merchant. The only situation that may be better when selling through a merchant is when quantities are so small that the mill would not buy them, but this is rare. Sometimes mills set up their own merchanting department to buy waste paper and the seller has no choice.

Chapter 15 explains why you should avoid selling to a merchant if possible and always try to sell to a final user.

What to do if no markets exist nearby

In some places it is not possible to sell waste paper at all because:

- Many other people are collecting and the market is flooded.
- No paper mills exist in the district.
- Paper mills exist but are so far away that transport costs would be too high.
- Paper mills exist but use rice straw, kenaf or bagasse as raw materials.
- Middle men control the market and offer prices that are too low.
- Not enough space is available for storage.

In such cases one of the following may be considered if you are capable of the necessary processing operations.

SMALL-SCALE PAPER-MAKING

Hand-making process[1]

Pulp is made by beating waste paper or fine cotton rags, and suspended in a large volume of water with constant stirring. A wooden frame or 'mould' bearing a fine wire mesh is dipped in the 'suspension' and brought up in the horizontal position. The water drains away evenly to leave a uniform layer of pulp on top of the mesh. This is gently stripped off and laid on a rectangle of felt on a solid board. Other pieces, interleaved with felt, are stacked above it. The pile of felt and sheets, topped by a wad of several layers of felt, is pressed to expel most of the water. The baling presses described earlier would be suitable for this, but a higher pressure is desirable. The felts can then be safely removed and the paper dried on canvas or hessian trays. As it dries, the paper wrinkles and requires a second pressing.

Further treatment may be applied, depending on the use to which the paper is to be put. For writing paper, dipping into a bath of gelatine or starch solution, followed by further drying, provides a coated surface which will resist ink penetration. To obtain a much smoother surface, sheets may be interleaved with perfectly smooth metal plates and pressed or passed through heavy rollers.

A small-scale (one tonne per day) paper-making plant

This Indian plant is simple to operate and can use a wide range of raw materials from waste paper to agricultural wastes such as sugar cane, sisal, banana or bamboo. Cotton rag, widely available in India, is also used. The raw material is first passed through a chopper, then cooked with caustic soda or lime in a digester (this is unnecessary when recycling waste paper). Next, it is broken down to basic fibres in a 'Hollander beater' (Fig. 9a) which takes one-and-a-half to eight hours, depending on the raw material, and can include washing and bleaching.

This pulp is diluted with plenty of water and fed into the cylinder mould machine which forms the paper. A wire-mesh covered cylinder revolves in a vat full of pulp. Water is sucked

26

Fig. 9a   Hollander beater used with the Indian one tonne per day papermaking machine.

Fig. 9b   One tonne per day papermaking machine. The paper is peeled off the cutting roll, cut and stacked for callendering.

27

out through a drain in the cylinder, leaving a layer of pulp on the wire-mesh surface.

At the top of the cylinder an endless band of woollen felt (Fig. 9b) picks up the pulp and conveys it to the cutting roll where an operator peels off the pulp in sheets which are stacked for squeezing in a hydraulic press. Finally, the sheets are dried and calendered (squeezed between smooth rollers).

Each sheet is 86 × 56 cm and the weight of paper ranges from 65 grammes per square metre (gsm) for writing and printing, to over 300 gsm for packaging. Amongst many applications are envelopes, file covers, file cards, insulating and filter paper.

Most of the water used in the process is recovered but there is a net consumption of about 46,000 litres in 24 hours. The plant includes a number of three-phase electric motors. It employs 12–16 workers per shift, plus management. It is available complete (apart from local civil engineering construction) for between £20,000 and £30,000 CIF. This compares very well with conventional paper machines, which have a capital cost of at least £100,000 per tonne of daily production without counting the cost of ancillary equipment such as beaters. For the suppliers of this plant and others see **Equipment suppliers** at the end of the chapter.

Costs of one tonne per day plant

These are late 1979 prices, 'FOB' Bombay, as a guide to current prices. Some equipment is not necessary if the plant is to be used for recycling waste paper without agricultural wastes; in this case about $ 17,500 can be deducted from the total price.

	$ U.S.
Hollander beater: Roll dia. 91 cm, width 76 cm. with washing drum. Capacity 200 kg rag, 250 kg waste paper. Trough to be constructed locally from concrete. Two required.	6,500
Hydraulic press: Capacity 150 tons. 1 m × 1.25 m platform with 46 cm loading height.	3,500
Calendering machine: Two rolls, 30 cm dia, 91 cm length, speed 10–15 rpm.	3,500
Paper cutting machine: 1 m cutting width, two sets of knives. Motor and manual operation.	2,400
Couching trolleys: Two needed plus two tables.	200

Cylinder mould and vat: Hand or power operated.
Cylinder mould of 1.06 m dia., 1.0 m length.
Overhead gravity flow tank, continuous felt, couch
roll, press roll, set of squeeze rolls, guide rolls,
tension rolls, cutting roll.   6,600
Knife grinder: To sharpen paper cutting machine
blades.   300
Rag chopper: Stationary knife and three revolving
knives.   1,200
Vomiting digester: 1.22 m high, 1.68 m dia. to hold
250 kg rags or jute. Volume 2 cu. m.   1,000
Drying chamber: Wheeled trolleys (16), rails, blower,
compressor for kerosene heating. Tunnel to be made
locally.   3,200
Baby beater: For experimental purposes. Roll dia. 30
cm, width 20 cm, with trough and washing drum.   1,000
Motors: 2 × 22kW for beaters; 7½kW for calender;
5½kW for cylinder mould machine; 2 kW for
hydraulic press; 1½kW for paper cutting machine;
2kW for rag chopper; 1kW for drying chamber
compressor; 1kW for knife grinder; 1kW for baby
beater; 4kW for drying chamber fan; motor pump
sets for water, three sets.   8,500
Agitators: Two units consisting of 2kW motor,
reduction gear and rotating paddle (pulp tanks dia.
2.13 m, height 3 m, to be made locally).   1,000
Pulp pump: with 2 kW motor, 3 off   1,100
Switches and starters   4,000
Accessories and foundation bolts   1,000
Spare parts   4,400

Total FOB Bombay	49,500
Estimated ocean freight	3,100

OTHER MARKETS FOR WASTE PAPER

Use of paper for animal bedding
Banks, government and other offices often 'shred' waste

paper into thin strips to prevent 'confidential' information from being read. Some experience has been gained in England of using this material for bedding animals and one commercial company, Shredabed Limited, markets both the material and machinery for making it. They claim that:

- Pigs bedded on this material keep cleaner.
- Poultry gain a little more weight and suffer less mortality than birds bedded on woodshavings, straw or sand (Fig. 10).

Fig. 10   Use of shredded waste paper for animal bedding. Photo: courtesy of Shredabed Ltd. U.K.

- Other livestock suffer less from respiratory (breathing) problems when bedded on paper instead of straw.
- Shredded paper is much easier to 'muck out' from pens and stables after use. It spreads easily on fields and breaks down to form excellent manure.

30

Shredded waste paper is easy to bale, thus costs of transport and storage are low. However, efficient shredding machines are expensive and hand tearing is tedious. Some anxiety has been expressed over the heavy metals contained in printing inks that might cause sickness among animals bedded on waste newspapers, but no evidence of this has been reported.

In cities where livestock fetch high prices but straw or other bedding materials are hard to obtain, this business may yield good profits, particularly if combined with an operation to sell the manure to gardeners. Sadly, few Third World pig breeders obtain the benefits of bedding them on anything other than earth.

Manufacture of egg and fruit boxes from old cartons
In rural areas there may be excellent markets for these. They can be produced from old corrugated cartons with a small amount of hand operated equipment, namely:
  i) guillotine or paper shears;
 ii) folder;
iii) punch for slotted tray pieces; and
 iv) stapling machine.
The old cartons are cut down to accurate size, refolded and stapled. It is important that the trays fit exactly and do not move during transportation. The off-cuts from the boxes are

Fig. 11 Egg trays and fruit cartons are made from offcuts of old cartons, using a hand-made punch. The punch is welded steel plate, 4mm thick, hinged along the bottom. The lower plate is slotted to match the punch which is hand-operated with a long handle. The edges of the punch cutters need to be kept sharp. Colombia.

31

the materials for the trays which are guillotined to a standard size and punched (Fig. 11).

Fruit and egg cartons from waste paper

Another system makes egg cartons from paper pulp using a small-scale paper plant called the Super Melbourne. Waste paper is first soaked, then pulped and refined. The pulper, derived from a domestic washing machine, breaks the waste paper down in water and the refiner completes the job of reducing it to basic fibres.

The slurry which results is poured on to a sheet of mesh stretched over the forming tank of the Super Melbourne and a valve in the tank is opened. The water draining from the tank sucks moisture from the layer of the pulp, which is then pulled from the tank on its sheet of mesh.

The layer of pulp is folded over once and pressed between specially shaped dies. After forming, the egg tray is laid out to dry in the sun or in a heated room. These egg trays look a little different from the usual type but they are just as strong and serviceable. Fruit and vegetable trays can also be made.

The process employs four people but labour economies can be achieved when several Super Melbourne machines are batched together for greater output.

Flat sheets: By substituting a press for the egg carton dies, Super Melbourne can be made to turn out flat sheets of paper suitable for cutting and creasing into cartons.

Statistics:

Output: 60 egg trays per hour, or 60 sheets of paper size 84 × 66 cm.

Electricity: Pulper and refiner – 300 watts.

Water: Most of the water used is recycled.

Floor space: About 2 sq. m for the machinery and 5 sq. m for drying.

Shipping: The machinery is shipped in a 0.97 cu. m container, weight 150 kilos. Shipping costs to Africa and Latin America are about $ U.S. 330.

Price: FOB London was $ US 2000 in 1979. Flat sheet version with a press but without dies is the same price.

Another example of a paper pulp moulding system was originally developed by ITDG in conjunction with Tomlinsons.

Manufacture of paper bags and funnels

In many countries, small traders use these for the sale of nuts, sweets and many other items of food. There are serious risks to health from contact between food and unprocessed waste paper which may have been in contact with poisons or diseases.

Use of waste paper as a building material

All over the world the very poor use waste paper to construct their homes. It is cheap and will keep the wind out and the sun off but there the advantages end. It does not resist water, is highly inflammable, it is eaten by rats, is weak and tears easily and rots or becomes brittle after quite a short time. It is an unsuitable material that demonstrates the desperate condition of those who have no alternative. A great improvement is:

Manufacture of asphalted roofing sheets (Figs 12a & b) Low quality, low cost roofing sheets with a life of about five years can be made from the very lowest grades of mixed waste paper; grades which would not be acceptable for paper-making due to the amount of dirt and contraries present.

A factory with three moulding machines, costs about $ US 200,000 for plant and machinery and can produce about 8,000 sheets daily, each about one square metre in area, or over two million square metres per annum. About 35 people are employed and 50 tonnes of paper per week are used. In India, the roofing material retails at around $ US 0.25 per sheet; in South America, at about $ US 0.6 per sheet. The manufacturing process is as follows:

i) The waste paper is washed and pulped in a hydrapulper. A mechanical hammer mill or a Hollander beater may be used instead.

ii) The pulp is passed through a 'screen' to remove dirt, grit or other impurities, and on to a board-forming machine similar to that already described, to produce a continuous length of board that is cut to lengths as it comes off the machine.

iii) The board is spread on the ground and dried in the open air. Next, the edges are trimmed on a rotating slitter.

iv) The board passes through an oven at the end of which are corrugating rolls. The corrugated sheets are then trimmed again and stacked in cradles.

Fig. 12a   Manufacture of asphalted roofing sheets. Dipping in asphalt. Note the use of a steel cradle and chain-operated hoist. The operators wear gloves to protect their hands but their bodies are covered in asphalt due to working stripped to the waist in the heat. A wise employer would insist on light cotton shirts and provide a laundry service.

Fig. 12b   Finished asphalted sheets in position.

34

v) Next, they are dipped in a bath of hot asphalt. (Asphalt is inflammable so the means of heating must be carefully chosen.) The asphalt dries rapidly at air temperature and the sheets are unloaded and stacked.

vi) When quite hard they are taped in bundles for sale as third quality or sprinkled with mineral chips on soft asphalt prior to packing as second quality, or hand-painted and packed as first quality.

Alternatively, the board may be made on a cylinder mould type of board-forming machine. The board forms on the cut-off roll, a metal cylinder whose circumference is the length of sheet required. When the required thickness of sheet has formed, it is cut along a groove in the roll and the sheet is then peeled off. Peeling requires skill and smoothness as the board has little strength.

Waste paper as an insulating material

In Canada and the U.S.A., there has been some experience of using shredded waste paper as a thermal insulation material, that is to say, a material that keeps warm houses warm and cool houses cool. The thermal efficiency (i.e. the effectiveness in doing its job) of shredded and fluffed-up waste paper is almost as good as glass fibre. To guard against fire, the paper is soaked in a solution of borax, and dried. Such material is much cheaper than other thermal insulators and could be used widely where no straw is available, provided each batch is tested to ensure that the fire-resistant treatment is effective.

By sandwiching a 15 cm layer of shredded waste paper between two sheets of corrugated, galvanized steel, a roof can be made that provides a cool interior in intense sunshine. The material should be treated against fire as above and possibly against pests.

Waste paper as a fuel

Waste paper is the world's most commonly-used kindling material (material for starting a fire). It can be used as a fuel if it is screwed or rolled up tightly, as it will burn more slowly than when spread out in thin sheets. It burns with a sooty flame and is not ideal for cooking.

In a number of developed countries, city refuse is being processed into pellets of Refuse Derived Fuel (RDF) which contains plastic, textiles and a high proportion of paper. A calorific (heat) value between half and two-thirds that of mineral coal is reported.

References

1. Sweetman, J., 'Making Paper by Hand', *Appropriate Technology* Vol. 3 No. 4 (Intermediate Technology Publications Ltd).

Equipment suppliers

Motorized screw baling presses
- Harris Group, Fiber Baler Division, 63 South Robert Street, St. Paul, Minnesota 55107, U.S.A.
- Edwin Mills and Son Ltd., Firth Street, Huddersfield, U.K.
- Dell Balers Ltd., Hightown Road, Cleckheaton, W. Yorkshire, BD19 5JT, U.K.
- Vanesco Ltd., 165 Garth Road, Morden, Surrey, SM4 4LH, U.K.

Paper Machinery
- Paper Mill Plant and Machinery Manufacturers Ltd., 181 S.V. Road, Jogeshwari, Bombay 400060, India.

Small-scale papermaking plant
- Third Scale Technology Ltd., Melbourne Bury, Royston, Herts., SG8 6DE, U.K.
- Tomlinsons (Rochdale) Ltd., Newhey Road, Milnrow, Rochdale, U.K.

Animal bedding manufacture
- Shredabed Ltd., 11–12 Bridford Road, Marsh Barton, Exeter EX2 2QX, U.K.

Chapter 2. Iron and Steel

Metal scrap is one of the world's largest industries with regard to the number of companies and people employed, weight of material handled and value of equipment used. Iron or steel which has reached the end of its useful life is called 'scrap' or ferrous scrap to distinguish it from non-ferrous scrap metals which do not originate from iron. The latter will be discussed in Chapter 4. This chapter is divided into two sections:

A. **Iron and Steel Scrap** looks at the sources of ferrous scrap; how to collect it; the different grades; how to sell or re-use them and the reclamation of motor cars.
B. **The Forge and the Foundry** describes how to produce, from ferrous scrap, finished goods that can be sold to the public.

Before examining the iron and steel scrap trade, it will be useful to understand a little about the production processes and the uses of iron and steel.

The production of iron

Iron is a natural element, usually found as an 'oxide' of iron mixed with other minerals and called iron ore. This is reduced in a blast furnace to produce metallic iron called pig iron (so-called because the moulds in which it used to be cast were arranged around a central channel like piglets suckling a sow). Pig iron is impure and contains 3 or 4% carbon as well as other chemicals such as manganese, phosphorus, sulphur and silicon. Some of these chemicals burn in the blast-furnace to form 'slag', a layer of oxides on top of the molten iron. Slag can be recycled in many ways – see Chapter 9 on mineral wastes.

Pig iron has two uses. It can be melted in a 'foundry' where it is cast into moulds to produce solid, heavy, often brittle objects such as manhole covers, pipes, pulleys and objects with complicated shapes such as valve bodies or cylinder blocks for engines. It can also be made into steel.

Sometimes iron ore undergoes a 'direct reduction' process to produce small pellets of sponge iron, so-called because they are porous and spongy. These, too, can be used for steelmaking, but they are unsuitable for foundry work until they have been converted in an electric arc furnace (see p. 43 and 72).

The production of steel

Steel is iron with less carbon and steelmaking is simply the removal of the carbon by burning. This makes the steel stronger, more flexible and easier to cut than iron. The other impurities in pig iron are removed by burning them in the steel-making process and again the slag produced can form valuable by-products.

There are many different processes for making steel from pig or sponge iron and all produce molten steel which may then be cast directly into a shaped mould in a steel foundry to produce an end-product. Steel castings are not as common as iron. Steel may be cast into ingots for forging, the process of hammering hot steel, to make items of extreme toughness and strength. It may also be cast into 'slabs, blooms or billets' for rolling. Rolling is the most common process for shaping steel. The billet is heated until it glows yellow, then passed forwards and backwards between powerful steel rollers of the correct size and shape to produce the cross-section that is required. Steel sections in turn may be cut, cold-rolled, forged, welded, electroplated or treated in many other ways to form the huge variety of steel components in use in the world today.

A. Iron and Steel Scrap

Before entering the steel scrap business, it is necessary to find out exactly what kind of iron and steel industry exists nearby. The local Chamber of Commerce or the Ministry of Industry will be able to help you, and a glance through the classified telephone directory will also be very useful: look under 'Iron', 'Steel', 'Foundry', etc.

Ferrous scrap can be fed back into the iron and steel manufacturing processes already described at any of a number of stages:

Foundry scrap. Scrap iron or steel may be melted in a 'cupola' or rotary furnace to make iron or steel castings. It is usually mixed with pig iron.

Steel mill scrap. Scrap steel, but not cast iron, may be melted in a steel-making furnace and cast as billets for rolling. Usually, the scrap is mixed with pig or sponge iron.

Rerolling scrap. Large pieces of scrap steel may be cut to regular shapes and hot-rolled into new sections of a smaller size. Rerolling is practised widely in parts of Asia, but less elsewhere.

Re-using scrap. Steel may be used as a raw material and cut, formed, forged or treated in any other way to fabricate new objects.

Rerolling and re-use yield far more value from a given weight of scrap and should be tried wherever possible.

Where and how to locate ferrous scrap

Before collecting any scrap make sure that it does not belong to anyone. In some countries, traders in scrap have to register with the police and it might be a good idea to write to the local police station stating your name, address and intention of setting up a metal scrap business. This helps if you are later invited to accompany a policeman who finds you with a bundle of reinforcing steel on a building site one dark evening! It is cheaper to buy material than to steal it and pay a fine or go to prison. The owners of scrap metal rarely know its value, so it will not be difficult to agree on a low price. If you buy material be sure to get a receipt. Ferrous scrap can be found at the following locations:

Construction sites. Off-cuts of reinforcing steel rods and mesh, wire and nails.

Demolition sites. Poles, girders, joists, steel doors and windows, drain covers, pipes, railings, grills etc.

Engineering workshops. Offcuts, swarf (turnings and chips from lathes, drills etc.), disused parts and machinery.

Garages and depots. Disused motor parts, scrap cars.

Factories, mines, quarries, drilling sites, farms, technical colleges etc. Disused machinery, construction steel, partitioning, drums and containers, pipes, tanks, carts, motors, in fact – anything!

Streets, parks and waste land. Disused railings, manhole covers, pipes etc.

39

Households. Domestic appliances (cookers, refrigerators etc), tin cans, broken bicycles, perambulators (prams), toys, tools, furniture etc.
Refuse dumps. Any of the above.

Unlike waste paper, scrap metal does not always arise in regular quantities; a demolition site, for example, may suddenly yield a large tonnage in a district from which only tin cans have emerged for years. So, rather than going from house to house or shop to shop regularly, scout rapidly around a district and investigate 'For Sale' notices, builders or shop-fitters' trucks, the presence of cranes, scaffolding, air compressors and similar signs of construction and demolition.

The most profitable way of locating scrap is to write to and visit local factories and sources that are likely to produce scrap regularly, and to convince them that you can collect regularly, promptly and tidily in response to a telephone call.

Another source of scrap, which will be looked at in detail later, is that of abandoned or crashed motor vehicles. Often, local traffic police will enter into an agreement or a commercial contract with a scrap metal dealer, whereby they inform him of such a vehicle and he, in return, removes it promptly so as to avoid danger to other traffic. However, the economics of removing scrap cars, particularly in country areas, are not always profitable, so first of all work out costs and profits.

Frequently, the money from the sale of scrap goes directly to the owner, the manager or the foreman of the fabrication shop and does not pass through the firm's books. Collectors should ask themselves whether they are partners in fraud, and can be prosecuted if they agree to such an arrangement. Failure to agree to it may well mean that another dealer gets the scrap! It is difficult to be a virtuous and a successful scrap dealer but it has been done!

Collecting scrap metal
A strong cart or vehicle is essential. It will need to be a little larger than that used for collecting paper and should, if possible, have folding, low sides and, if desired, extra-high lattice sides above them.

As cuts from rusty steel can cause septic wounds, leather gloves should always be worn (cheap, serviceable gloves are made from trimmings of leather). Boots with steel-reinforced toe-caps are an added protection. Never handle scrap metal in bare feet or stripped to the waist.

Items of scrap metal may be very heavy and serious injury can result from lifting them. Always keep your back vertical when lifting, bending at the knees. If it is not economic to travel with an assistant, then either persuade a friend to come and help with heavy items at short notice or learn how to set up a tripod and borrow or buy a block and tackle. Check the block and tackle and any ropes or chains you use. If they are worn or damaged do not use them. If you use them, stay out from under and keep your friend, your donkey and your children out from under too!

Often, scrap items can be handled more easily if sharp or outstanding or awkward parts are removed. Carry on your cart a hacksaw, spare blades, a pair of pliers or wire cutters or, even better, a pair of 'bolt croppers', as well as an axe. Make sure the police agree you need them for your work and not for crime.

SORTING FERROUS SCRAP FOR SALE AND RE-USE

If you have read the introduction to this chapter you will understand why scrap has to be sorted into different grades. You *can* leave this task to the person who buys from you, but the chances are that you will be paid less. In every country the grades required will be a little different: they will often differ between two towns in the same country. The following list of ferrous scrap grades should serve anyone selling scrap in a Third World country that has one or more steel rolling mills, usually with electric arc furnaces, and a number of small or large iron foundries, plus workshops of different kinds:
1. Cast iron.
2. Heavy melting scrap, also known as HMS or No. 1.
3. Medium scrap or No. 2.
4. Light scrap or No. 2 bundles or No. 3.
5. Swarf.
6. Rerollable pieces (only if rerolling mills exist).
7. Re-usable pieces.

1. *Cast iron* (Fig. 13)
    Cast iron can be identified by its dull grey colour, comparative weakness (it can often be broken by a hammer blow), and

Fig. 13   Cast iron scrap. Kenya.

complicated cast shapes, sometimes with numbers or words cast 'proud of' (higher than) the surface. It is one of the most valuable, highly-priced forms of scrap and can be sold to a local iron foundry at much lower cost of transport than to a steel mill which may be hundreds of miles away. Cast iron borings (chips from a factory that machines cast iron) can be sold alongside it, but probably at a lower price. If possible mix them in with the heavy material.

Depending on the size of your customer's furnace, very large pieces may need to be broken with a sledge-hammer or cut with an oxy-acetylene or oxy-propane cutting torch, described below. It might be worthwhile breaking all pieces down to the size required by the customer, possibly as small as 15–20 cms maximum dimension, but only if you are sure that the customer will pay for this extra service.

Fig. 14   Heavy melting scrap, also known as No. 1 or HMS. The drum in the foreground should not *have been included!*

2. *Heavy Melting Scrap (HMS)* (Fig. 14)

Whenever possible, steel scrap should be sold direct to a steel mill. In Third World countries these are mostly 'mini mills' using electric arc furnaces. A first charge of scrap is melted, the glowing electrodes withdrawn, the top cover swivelled away and a second load of scrap discharged into the furnace from the charge basket. Flames and smoke arise when the new scrap touches the molten metal within. It is the necessity for a second and sometimes a third or fourth charge of scrap to produce a full furnace load of molten metal that determines the economics of furnace operation. Valuable time and energy are saved by reducing the number of times the furnace has to be recharged. For this reason, steelmakers will pay far higher prices for smallish pieces of solid, heavy scrap more than 6 mm thick which will form a heavy, dense charge. Scrap that fills this requirement is HMS and fetches the best price of all.

Obviously, large furnaces can accept much longer pieces than can mini mills. In Britain, the maximum length of HMS is 1.5 m. Elsewhere, mini mill furnace diameters are often not more than 2 m and charge baskets 1½ m, in which case material of about two-thirds of a metre in length is preferable.

Other dimensions should not exceed half this or less, and pieces should be free of awkward 'projections' that will prevent close packing in the charge. If you have substantial pieces that are longer than this or have projections you should either cut them with a hand shear or an oxy-acetylene cutter, or keep them separate to be cut at the steel mill. The important thing is to concentrate in one load all the HMS that the mill operator can use without his having to process it first.

Use of cutting torch

Oxy-acetylene or oxy-propane cutters are a vital tool for the scrap metal operator. A complete kit consists of:
- 1 pair of cutting goggles and 1 pair leather gloves.
- Leather apron and gaiters.
- 1 cutting torch (not to be confused with a welding torch).
- 2 long rubber pipes, one red and one black.
- 2 gauges to control and measure gas pressures. The oxygen gauge is black, and that for propane or acetylene is red.
- A cylinder of oxygen (black) and one of propane or acetylene (red).
- A special trolley on which it can all be mounted.

The companies which sell the gases (known as industrial gases) usually sell the rest of the gear and should supply you with full details of the operation. Never try to make your own, as there could easily be a fatal explosion, nor should you try to repair it yourself unless you are *very* skilled. Make sure that you understand *fully* how the torch works before putting it to use.

Operation is as follows. The gauges are mounted on their respective cylinders, taking care to match the red components and the black. The pipes and torch are connected and both taps on the torch closed. The cylinder gauges are adjusted to the pressures recommended by the torch manufacturer. Often the cylinder gauges have two dials – the second tells you how much gas is left in the cylinder. The red gas tap on the torch is opened and a match applied to the nozzle to produce a bright, smoky yellow flame. Then the black oxygen tap is opened slowly; the yellow colour gives way to a blue heating flame with a slight roar. The heating oxygen comes out in six small blue cones, about 8 mm long. Open the tap until all the yellow has disappeared but no further. Squeeze the trigger. A fine line of blue down the centre of the flame is the cutting oxygen. It makes a

44

roar. If the flame goes out you have too much oxygen in the heating flame; turn the tap back a little. Always turn off the oxygen before relighting.

To cut a steel plate. Mark the cutting line in chalk. Lower the goggles over your eyes, hold the torch in your right hand and support the metal tubes of the torch on the back of the left glove so the torch can be moved smoothly along the line without altering its height above the steel. Start at the very edge of the plate, keeping the blue heating flame vertical and the height such that the tips of the oxygen cones touch the surface. After about twenty seconds the steel will start to melt; squeeze the cutting trigger and the jet of oxygen will blow the molten metal out of its path. Slowly and steadily advance the nozzle along the line, keeping it perpendicular to the surface and the cut will advance with it. If you go too fast, the metal will not be molten under the nozzle and cutting will cease: too slowly and molten metal will drip off leaving a messy edge, besides wasting expensive industrial gases.

Plan where the piece will fall at the end of the cut, so as to avoid injury. Beware of hot edges. Shut off the torch at the acetylene tap, then close the oxygen tap. To avoid leaks, close gauge valves when work is finished, even for a short period.

If you have no edge at which to start cutting (e.g. when cutting pipe into lengths) you have to blow a starting hole. Proceed as before, heat until the steel melts but, as you press the cutting oxygen trigger, withdraw the torch a few inches to prevent molten metal from splashing on the nozzle and stopping the jet of cutting oxygen.

DANGER! Flame cutting can be dangerous if not correctly done.

Never – cut without wearing protective clothing, especially goggles.
  – cut near inflammable materials – wood, paper, petrol, oil, grease etc.
  – open oxygen cylinders near lighted fires, cigarettes etc., or near oil or grease, as an explosion can result.
  – cut cylinders or tanks that may have contained petrol, gases, chemicals, explosives etc.
  – allow molten metal to fall on clothing, gas pipes etc.
  – allow gas cylinders to be heated.
Always – check that gas has not leaked into or under pits,

drums, containers, etc. before lighting the torch. The explosion from a leak can kill.
- ensure that all taps and valves are off at the end of the day.
- tie gas bottles if they are standing vertically.

Typical costs of gas cutting gear in a developing country

Torch, pipes, gauges and safety clothing	$330
Bottle trolley (optional)	$150
Deposit on one pair of cylinders	$120
Recharge – oxygen	$ 14
– acetylene	$ 45

3. *Medium Scrap (No. 2)* (Fig. 15)

This includes material which is thinner than 6 mm but is reasonably free from rust, dirt and any metals that cause difficulties in steel-making, especially tin and copper. Medium

Fig. 15 Medium steel scrap. Note that the workman is wearing leather gloves to handle this material. Mexico.

scrap may be sold to a foundry or steel mill, or to a merchant (who will pay less).

The pieces should be cut to lengths which will make a dense furnace charge easy to obtain. Ask your customer what size he needs and will pay for. Remove projections and any material that is not iron or steel. It is not economical to cut No. 2 scrap with expensive industrial gases; a hand shear should be sufficient. Of course, once money starts to come in from your business, you can buy an industrial shear that will cut through thicker material. (It is possible to buy Alligator shears that will cut HMS of 20 cm thickness, but they are very expensive.)

If you have no shear and cannot make one, you can cut No. 2 scrap with a hacksaw, but this takes a long time. Often, you can reduce long pieces of No. 2 to length by bending them double or treble. Make sure you wear gloves or you will damage your hands and a steel scrap man who cannot use his hands is out of business!

4. *Light Scrap (No. 2 bundles or No. 3)*

This is the lowest acceptable quality and fetches the lowest price. It contains sheet material which is not able to be included in No. 2 because:
- It is too thin – in most cases anything less than 3 mm is not accepted for No. 2; check this either by asking the user or by including it and waiting to see if it is rejected.
- It is too rusty. A surface coating of rust is acceptable in No. 2 but not if it is very deep;
- It is coated or contaminated with tin, i.e. tin cans (see Chapter 3);
- It is heavily coated with paint or oil or is mixed up with other material such as rubber or plastic.

Light scrap may be sold to a foundry or steel mill or, again, to a merchant who will pay less.

Baling of light scrap. Light scrap such as large, rusty sheets of galvanized (zinc coated) steel are the worst forms of furnace feed, but even they can be made more acceptable (and that means a better price!) by baling them. Baling steel is not in principle different from baling paper, except that more power is needed to attain a really tight bale. However, this does not mean that steel cannot be baled without a motor-driven machine. The baling operation used in Colombia produces

Fig. 16 Hand baling of light steel scrap: tamping down with half-shaft of a lorry to get a compact bale. Colombia.

surprisingly good bales (Fig. 16). The sequence of operations is:

i) Position wire (or even better, if you have a strapper, flat steel strapping strip) in a cross at the bottom of the baling box. Line the bale with a square of sheet metal or even thick cardboard.

ii) Charge the box with light scrap and 'tamp' down, using the 'half shaft' of a lorry or similar tool, and treading on it at the same time.

iii) Cover the completed bale with sheet metal or cardboard.

iv) Wire or strap in a cross, taking care not to overtighten the wire and break it.

v) Open the baling box and unload the bale.

Any of the baling presses described in the section on baling paper (p. 19–24) can be adapted for baling light scrap by tamping down as you load. Any type or size of more expensive press can be purchased as your business develops and this should be one of the first items to consider as an investment of profits. (See **Equipment suppliers**).

The advantages of baling are again:

- More weight can be loaded on a lorry so transport cost is cut;
- More material can be stored in your yard so you can negotiate a better price for the larger quantity;
- The buyer finds storage easier so will pay a little more;
- Handling and loading are easier, quicker and cheaper; and
- A denser furnace charge is obtained.

Some scrap dealers think it an advantage that they can hide poor material (or even stones) in the centre of a bale. However, the buyer will usually find out before he has paid for the load, and, if not, he will probably do so before he has paid for the next load, and will either reduce the payment or never buy from that supplier again.

5. *Swarf*

Swarf is the name given to cuttings and chippings produced when metals are machined, for example on a lathe. They are thin, light and arise in spirals and other awkward shapes, and must be compressed if they are to form an economical furnace feed. If no baling or 'briquetting' press is available this may be done by tamping them down inside a can or drum. A can of tinplate will, of course, slightly reduce the value of cuttings of pure metals.

Swarf is often covered with cutting oil from the machining process. Not only is this a contaminant in the metal, it is also a valuable liquid which can be resold to the machine shop or factory from which it came. It can best be recovered by squeezing or baling above a pan.

DANGER Swarf cuts horribly! Handle with leather gloves or a piece of bent reinforcing rod.

6. *Rerolling of steel scrap*

In some countries there exists a small branch of the steel scrap industry that rerolls scrap into sections. Heavy gauge material is flame cut into parallel-sided slabs which are heated in an oil-fired reheating furnace (but not melted, so the furnace is simpler and cheaper than that used in a steel mill and less energy is used). It is then rolled in a four or five stand mill (a stand is one pair of rollers) of 20–30 cm diameter. Indian rerollers are notable for their ingenuity in adapting second-hand (often belt-driven) machinery and for the skill with which this labour-intensive operation is carried out. Capital costs of the plant may be as little as $ US 180,000 (or even less for used plant).

Material needs to be at least 60 cm long and a maximum thickness of 100 cm and 1 m wide is common. A favourite material is 'ladle skulls' from the integrated steel mills, (mills which make *and* roll steel).

Rerolling is very suitable for thick plates cut from ship-breaking (cutting up of old ships) an industry being adopted by many Third World countries short of heavy scrap. It requires a very high degree of technical and manual skill and is not recommended as an activity to anyone without previous rolling mill experience.

7. *Re-use of steel scrap*

One of the most obvious ways to recycle steel is to use it to produce another object (Fig. 17). In general, this can be done with knowledge of the basic methods of metalwork, as taught in technical schools the world over and fully described elsewhere. However, two waste materials justify special mention because they are so commonly used – oil drums and reinforcing steel. A third material, tinplate, will be covered separately in Chapter 3.

Fig. 17 Gate made from steel scrap uses the attractive pattern left after stamping electric motor parts from steel strip. Peru.

Oil drums

The standard 45 gallon (200 litre) oil drum is a most valuable object in any country; it can be used as a container for liquids or solids; as a waste bin; converted into a small (but short-lived) furnace; mounted on a cart or lorry or cut open to make an animal feeding trough. However, as a source of raw material it is even more widely used.

Re-use of oil drums. Drums sell for a higher price if they are clean, painted and free from dents and damage. Dents can be removed by hammering. A piece of railway line makes an anvil. Ensure that caps, tops or taps are not lost or damaged, and try to display your wares.

Some drums might previously have contained toxic (poisonous) chemicals so try finding out where they have come from and, if in any doubt at all, clean thoroughly, in case they may next be used to hold drinking water.

Use of oil drum material. A 45 gall. drum makes a rectangular sheet of steel 180 × 90 cm, plus two circular pieces 57 cm in diameter. The large sheet is often flattened by throwing it under the wheels of passing heavy lorries on a flat stretch of road (Fig. 18). These flat sheets are widely used for cladding shanty houses, or the sides of carts. When cut down they are used to make buckets, dustbins, stoves etc.

Fig. 18   Flattening oil drums under passing lorries — a potentially dangerous activity.

51

Fig. 19   Manufacture of cooking bowls from oil drums ends. Kenya.

The circular ends are a convenient material from which to manufacture large, general purpose washing/cooking bowls (Fig. 19). The centre of the circle is hammered to spread and bulge the metal, usually against a sandbag or sandy floor. The amount of spreading is reduced further out towards the rim of the circle and there is none at the rim. The resulting bumpy bowl shape is then hammered against a smoothly hollowed cast iron mould, specially machined on a lathe, to produce a smooth bowl but with a wrinkled rim. The rim is marked with dividers and trimmed off.

Use of reinforcing steel

Concrete is usually combined with steel to increase its strength and steel rods, known as reinforcing bars, are widely produced and used. They are often made in standard lengths and cut to the required size on the construction site. The off-cuts are a useful material which can be cut with an ordinary hacksaw, bent across the knee or heated in a simple charcoal forge to flatten or shape an end. Note the earlier comments about suspicions of theft if you remove such material from a site without having written permission or a receipt.

52

In Kenya, a number of workers have developed an industry using reinforcing bars and similar materials, which justifies further description. The hand shear has already been mentioned in the section on No. 2 scrap. In addition, these enterprising men have made hand-operated punches, folders and other metal-working machinery (Fig. 20) all from scrap metal. From these they manufacture such products as heavy duty bicycle carriers, stands and foreguards (strengthener between front forks and handlebars), small agricultural tools and metal working tools.

Fig. 20 Hand-made metal forming machines: this workshop included a shear, a punch, a bending machine and a machine for cropping reinforcing bars, all made with a hacksaw, hand drill, etc. Note how the machines have been mounted on wooden trunks, hammered into the ground in the absence of a concrete floor.

RECLAMATION OF MOTOR CARS AND SIMILAR VEHICLES

This is included in this chapter because most of the material recovered is iron and steel. However, other metals may also be recovered. The reclamation of motor vehicles can be considered in three parts:

1. *Recovery and resale of components*

The important principle here is that parts are worth much more when re-used rather than scrapped. Every city in the world has dealers in second-hand car parts and in some towns a complete commercial district is devoted to nothing else (Fig. 21).

Fig. 21   Resale of used car parts. Note the car 'shell' in the front of the picture, and the neat racking of parts. Egypt.

Here are a few principles on dismantling a car for spares (often known as 'breaking'):

i) It is often easier to cut or break the bodywork on which a part is mounted and then unbolt the part at a bench, instead of unbolting the part from an awkward position on the vehicle. Never use a flame-cutting torch near the petrol tank, feed pipes, carburettor etc. The explosion could kill you.

ii) Parts sell more quickly and for higher prices if they are
   - kept in sets;
   - labelled by make and model of car;
   - cleaned (use paraffin);
   - made as good as new by fitting new bushes (small bronze bearings) linings (e.g., brakes and clutches,) seals, electrical contacts or by repairing (e.g., radiators, motors and generators, gearboxes etc.)
iii) When selling used car parts it is a good idea to:
   - display them on the counter or at a stall so that buyers can easily find the part they want;
   - group all the parts of a similar type (e.g. all the brake shoes) or all the parts for a given model of car (this is more difficult as sizes vary);
   - advertise in the local paper;
   - have a handbill printed describing the range of parts you stock and the models of car for which you can supply parts. Placing these under the windscreen wipers of elderly cars of this model could bring you many customers.

2. *Recovery of unsaleable parts for scrap*

If parts are unsaleable, some value can be recovered by selling them for scrap. It is worth sorting them into different materials, and the following list is a guide to this. However, some parts may be made of different materials from those listed and it is useful to learn how to distinguish them.

Cast iron.   Note, however, that any of these may be made of cast steel. To tell the difference, note that steel is shinier and will not shatter under a hammer blow, whereas iron is grey, and thin sections will shatter. If in doubt, put it on the iron pile: steel castings will not spoil cast iron scrap but iron will spoil HMS.

Cast iron

Cylinder block (crank case)	Clutch housing
Cylinder head	Steering gearbox casing
Sump	Brake drums
Gearbox casing	Flywheel
Differential casing	Wheels

Starter and generator casings (after removal of copper)

Heavy steel

Pistons and rings
Con rods
Crank shaft
Cam shaft
Gears
Clutch parts
Half parts
Timing chain
Diesel injectors

Brake shoes
Steering linkage parts
Shock absorber cylinders
    and pistons
Transmission shaft
Brake discs
Leaf or coil springs
Lorry chassis
Generator and motor shafts
    (after removal of copper)

Light steel

Body
Doors
Lids
Valve cover
Fan

Bumpers
Hub caps
Headlamps
Air filter

Aluminium

Fan
Cylinder head (a few
    models)
Crank case
Pistons
Starter motor and generator
    casing (after removal of
    copper)
Steering wheel

Zinc

Carburettor
Hydraulic cylinders
Door handles
Lamp sockets
Small gear boxes (e.g.
    windscreen wipers)

Copper

Generator armature
    ″   stator
Motor armature
    ″   stator
Radiator
Electric cables

Small electric motors (e.g.
    windscreens wipers)
Distributor points
Electrical switches
High tension coil

Bronze

Bearings from:
— crankshaft
— gearbox

— differential
— steering gearbox

| — wheel hubs | be steel (ball or roller) |
| (but any of these may | bearings) |

Non-metallic parts such as glass, rubber and plastic are difficult to reclaim, although Fig. 22 demonstrates an unusual use (see also under appropriate chapters).

Fig. 22 Unusual use for headlamps: decorating a religious statue by the roadside. Colombia.

3. *Recovery of the shell*

The shell is all that remains of the car when the above parts have been removed. Shells abound in many parts of the Third World, not only in cities and suburbs but also in rural areas. They are a hazard to traffic and to children and serve as breeding areas for mosquitoes and other pests. However, their large size and low weight of metal makes them uneconomic to transport to a distant steel mill or foundry. Neither are there sufficient numbers to justify investment in huge car-crushers such

57

as those used in the industrialized countries (the apparent large numbers are usually accumulated over many years). Because people in some Third World countries are so resourceful in repairing and obtaining used spares, their cars often run for thirty or forty years, also diminishing the scrap supply.

Where large numbers of shells are accumulating, a simple, labour-intensive cheap method is needed to reduce them to pieces small enough for economic transport to the scrap buyers. The following system has been developed:

Equipment:
  10 cm (4″) brick bolster chisel
  1 kg (2–2½ lb) hammer
  Pair of leather gloves
  Hand-cart
  Wire cutters
  Boots

Also useful:
  Axe
  Hacksaw
  Bolt croppers
  Rope

A team of about six strong youths can wheel the hand-cart around the district and cut car shells into manageable pieces by hand. Thick pieces may need cutting with a saw or bolt croppers. The size of the piece depends on the size of the hand-cart and the needs of the buyer. When the cart is full it can be taken to a secure place and the contents collected regularly by lorry on a round.

Before cutting up a car shell, make sure that it doesn't belong to anybody; it may form part of a house or wall of a compound. Find out if this is the case before you touch a shell or you may be asked to pay for it. If you are considering paying for car shells remember that the average car contains about two-thirds of a tonne of ferrous metal and two-thirds of this may have been stripped out so the shell will probably not contain more than 150 to 200 kg of saleable scrap. The value of your work in breaking it down and the cost of the transport must be deducted from the sale value of the material, so do not pay too much. If you do not buy it is most unlikely that anyone else will!

Car shells are dirty and painted, and the material is thin. If not baled, the price per tonne will be low. Against this, large quantities may be available and there are good prospects for recovering components that have been missed by strippers, so the operation may well be profitable. The author plans to write a book on this in the near future.

B. The Forge and the Foundry

The forge and the foundry are two processes that use ferrous scrap to produce finished goods for re-sale. If no such industry exists locally it may be possible to set one up on a small scale to produce goods that are not cheaply available locally. Both processes can be fed, mainly or completely, on scrap metal, which creates not only skilled workshop jobs, but also work for unskilled people, collecting and processing scrap. The forge is much simpler and will be described first.

Fig. 23a Simple forge. Note the hand-turned fan to provide the draught, the workpiece placed across the hottest part of the fire, and the flat tray of fuel and tools. Egypt.

THE FORGE

In order to flatten or shape a piece of solid steel, heat it to red (or yellow) heat, at which point it becomes softer and more workable. The finished product will be far stronger than steel that has been 'cold worked': this becomes hard and brittle and may crack or break in use. The furnace in which pieces of steel may be heated is called a forge and the word is also used to describe the complete workshop in which forging is done. For working with reinforcing steel and similar sizes of mild steel, this may be very small with simple requirements, namely:
- a bed of coal, coke or charcoal
- a source of draught (wind) through the bed
- an anvil
- tools for handling and hammering the hot workpiece

The bed can be constructed of bricks or concrete blocks, but a mild steel or cast iron bed, lined with bricks will last longer. A pipe embedded in the bottom, with a grill placed across it to prevent entry of fuel, will carry the draught. The bed should be at a convenient height for working (Fig. 23). If indoors, a hood and chimney will also be needed to remove the fumes which are poisonous.

The draught is best produced by a fan driven by a small electric motor. If no electric power is available the fan can be driven by a bicycle wheel and a rubber belt made from the inner tube of a car tyre (Fig. 24).

The anvil is often made of railway line, cut and strapped to a heavy trunk of timber. The anvil has to absorb heavy blows and should not be made of cast iron which will shatter.

Tools. The most important tools are the hammer and the tongs. These should be of various sizes so that work of different sizes and shapes can be comfortably held. Long tongs are needed when two men are working together, one holding and one hammering. For heavy work such as flattening a bar or driving a wedge to pierce an eye hole, a sledge-hammer is used, with a head weighing 6 kg or more. For lighter work a hand-hammer of 2 kg is sufficient. For a single man operation short tongs are needed. Special chisels have a thick wire handle so they can be safely held when struck with a sledge-hammer, and also a short stout shaft that will not bend or flatten under heavy blows. Different chisel shapes are used for cutting,

Fig. 24 Bicycle wheel forge draught. The wheel has been mounted on the pedal axle of a broken bicycle and an old inner tube is the belt to drive the fan. The draught goes under the ground to the forge bed in the bottom right of the picture. The work, pieces of bicycle carriers made from reinforcing bar, can be seen at the left of the picture. Kenya.

bending, notching or piercing, and chisels must be kept cool with water when in use or they will lose their cutting edge.

Operation of the forge

The coal or charcoal is lit with kindling close to the air pipe. The draught will help it to light. About 10–15 cm depth of coke is needed for the smallest workpieces, more for larger ones. The draught is maintained until there is a region of intense, glowing fuel and the workpiece is thrust into this and withdrawn, using the tongs, when it is bright yellow. The draught is stopped to conserve fuel.

The workpiece can be worked only when it is hot enough. The yellow colour will turn to red but continue to work until the red colour dies, indicating a temperature too low for hot working. The piece is then returned to the forge and the draught restarted. Do not overheat the workpiece or you will weaken it.

Metals can be successfully welded by hammering together two pieces both of which are at brilliant white heat (emitting sparks). The metals must be perfectly clean at the start – grind or file off scale and rust. Forged items may be placed in water to cool them only if they are then tempered by reheating to just below red heat and cooling in air. There are various other ways of 'heat treating' steels to make them tougher, harder or more easily workable, but they are beyond the scope of this book.

A small hand-operated forge

Alternatively, a bellows forge, as illustrated in Figs 25a & b may be constructed. The air blows both on the downstroke and the upstroke, thus helping to keep the forge heat constant.

The bellows top, bottom and centre are all made of wood and the walls of soft leather. The fuel tray is specially made from stout steel sheet, although an old steel or stainless steel sink basin could be adapted. It is lined inside with fire clay or bricks. The grill is made from a standard sink waste and the piping is standard plumber's pipe, tee and elbow. The handle is made of reinforcing bar and the joints in the linkages are nuts and bolts with washers.

Operation

The centre of the bellows is fixed to the steel legs. Starting with the handle up, the lower bellows is full of air. As the handle is pressed downwards the linkage pulls the bottom of the lower bellows up, forcing air through the open upper valve into the upper bellows and along the pipe to the fuel tray. Some of the air fills the upper bellows. The pressure of the air in the lower bellows keeps the lower valve closed so that no air can escape.

When the handle is pumped upwards, the upper bellows collapses under its own weight (or an extra weight may be placed on top), the air pressure closes the upper valve and the air is forced along the pipe to the fuel tray. The lower bellows expands, the lower valve being forced open by air pressure to allow air to enter and fill it ready for the next downstroke.

An even simpler forge can be made from a standard oil drum[1].

Fig. 25a   Small, hand-operated bellows forge. Note the operating handle made of reinforcing bar, the link connecting the fixed bellows centre to the front leg and the shallow tray with coal or charcoal. The handle is just returning from the down position and the upper bellows has just started to collapse. Peru.

63

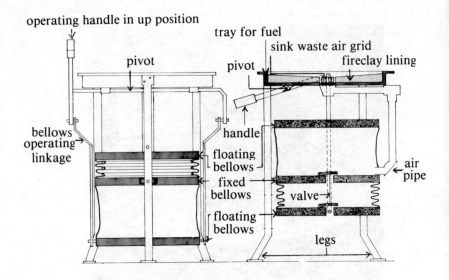

operating handle in up position

tray for fuel

sink waste air grid

fireclay lining

pivot

pivot

bellows operating linkage

handle

floating bellows

fixed bellows

floating bellows

valve

air pipe

legs

Fig. 25b   Diagram of hand-operated forge. Front view with bellows in down position (handle up). Section side view with bellows in up position (handle down). Peru.

CAUTION Due to the presence of hot metal, people engaged in forging operations should be provided with the following protective clothing: leather gloves, leather aprons, boots (preferably with steel toe caps). A medical kit for the treatment of burns should be kept available, and in tropical climates a fan provided for each workman.

Products that can be made by forging include

Agricultural tools of all types such as hoes, rakes, mattocks, axes and plough blades.
Axles for carts, trolleys and trailers.
Carpenter's tools such as hammers, pincers, screwdrivers, chisels, adzes and drill bits.
Mason's tools such as stone chisels, trowels, hammers and crowbars.
Garage equipment such as ramps, brackets and tow hooks.
Rowlocks and *cleats* for boats.
Horseshoes
Machine parts of all sorts, especially for the many items described in this book, such as baling presses, shears, furnaces, fans etc.

64

A SMALL IRON FOUNDRY

Many Third World towns do not have a local foundry or steel mill and the nearest is often many miles away. Not only is there no market for scrap metal, but all types of iron and steel objects have to be brought in and are very expensive. This situation may justify setting up a small foundry locally which will create employment, provide a market for scrap metal (and employment for scrap collectors and sorters); and provide cheaper iron and steel goods with less delay and difficulty.

However, it is necessary to be realistic about such a project, as the quality of locally-produced goods may be much lower, until skill and experience are obtained. Even then mass produced goods may still turn out cheaper despite the distance factor. Such an activity can only be done by people with organizing ability, practical skill and determination.

The following notes are not intended to provide a complete guide to setting up a foundry (that needs a book on its own) but to outline the processes and equipment needed so that the idea can be seriously considered and studied, the requirements discussed with suppliers of equipment and the size and nature of the market for castings researched. The need to obtain experienced assistance and advice, especially for melting operations, must be emphasized. Standard equipment exists for the purposes shown and advice even on small-scale operations is obtainable from manufacturers.

Equipment needed for a small foundry

- storage space for scrap metal and means of carrying and loading
- furnace for melting the metal
- patterns or a workshop for making patterns
- moulding equipment including sand preparation
- casting equipment
- finishing equipment
- safety equipment

Scrap metal storage

Scrap can be stored in the open as long as it is reasonably close to the furnace. Enough space is needed to keep three or four grades separate. A strong wheelbarrow will be useful for carrying and a shear will be necessary to reduce the size of large pieces.

FURNACES FOR MELTING FERROUS SCRAP

Table 3 Furnaces for melting ferrous scrap

Type of Furnace	Fuel	Other charge material	Product	Size	Capital cost
1. Cupola	Coke or hard charcoal	Solid pig	Cast iron	Medium	Low
2. Rotary furnace	Oil	Solid pig iron	Cast iron	Medium	Medium
3. Crucible	Gas, oil or coke	None	Steel and cast iron	Small	Low
4. Electric arc furnace	Electricity	None	Steel and cast iron	Small medium or large	Medium or high
5. Induction furnace	Electricity	None	Steel and cast iron	Small	Medium or high
6. Air or Reverberatory	Pulverised coal or oil	Molten or solid pig iron	Cast iron	Medium or large	Medium or high

The furnace size given in Table 3 will also indicate the size of scrap that the furnace can accept. A good combination for starting a small foundry would be a cupola for cheap, large volume casting plus a small electric arc or induction furnace for small quantity work required quickly. Only the smaller size furnaces will be described here.

1. *The cupola furnace* (Figs 26a & b)

The cupola is cheap to build and operate but too laborious to use for small quantities of material. A unit of the size shown melts about 4½ tons of metal in half a working day. It may be operated daily if required, or less often, casting moulds being stockpiled in preparation. Larger or more efficiently run cupolas may achieve production of up to 20 tons per hour or more. The cupola is not unlike a small blast-furnace. It is a vertical cylinder of steel plates, lined with bricks or other refractory (heat-resistant) material to protect the steel from the intense heat generated.

The cupola illustrated has a steel shell diameter of 1 m and the diameter of the inside of the lining is about half this. The air holes are just over 1 m above the bottom door. It can produce just over 1 tonne of iron per hour and the charge is 140 kilos of iron and 20 kilos of coke in each layer, although other

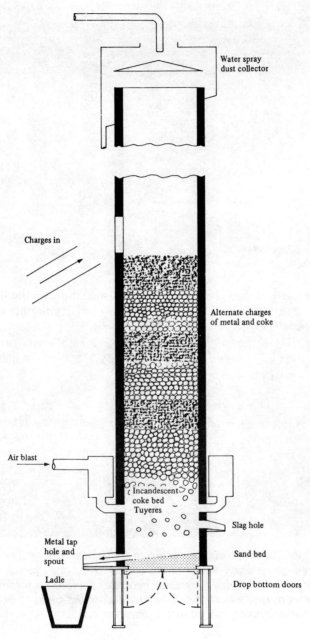

Water spray
dust collector

Charges in

Alternate charges
of metal and coke

Air blast

Incandescent
coke bed
Tuyeres

Slag hole

Metal tap
hole and
spout

Sand bed

Ladle

Drop bottom doors

Fig. 26a   Diagram of a cupola.

67

Fig. 26b View showing the pouring spout of a cupola. The mica-covered observation windows are clearly seen, one open and one closed. The dark tinted goggles are necessary for looking through the windows during a heat. Note the rack below the spout to hold the ladle while tapping molten metal. Peru.

users of cupolas have reported more economical ratios of up to 10 of iron to 1 of coke. Charcoal can be used if coke is not available but difficulties have been reported. One kilo of lime or sea-shells is added to 'flux' the iron – prevent oxidation and allow slag to drain away more easily through the slag hole at the back, which is opened from time to time. More lime is needed if the scrap is rusty or dirty.

Operation of the cupola

Before starting, it is necessary to clean out the slag from the previous heat, particularly around the air holes. Broken lining can be repaired with a mixture of fire clay and sand. The spout opening of about 2 cm diameter is made either with a specially drilled brick, or moulded with sand and fire clay. The semi-circular bottom doors are propped closed and a layer of moulding sand not less than 10 cm deep placed on them, rammed down and sloped towards the spout.

Firing begins three hours before molten metal is required. The cupola is charged with a little coke which is ignited with kindling wood. When it is burning well more coke is added to rise 80 or 100 cm above the air holes. When this is at red heat, alternate layers of iron and coke are charged on top. The iron may be scrap only or a mixture of scrap and pig iron.

Charging is done either through the top of the cupola or, if a spark arrester is fitted (a prudent measure if other buildings are near the foundry), through a door in the chimney. When charging is up to the door or top the iron soaks in the heat for nearly an hour. A blast of air is blown into the cupola, entering through holes around the shell above the base which are fed by a circular air chamber, supplied in turn by a pipe running from an electrically driven fan. After a few minutes molten metal builds up on the hearth. The tap hole is then closed with a cone-shaped clay plug until enough molten metal has accumulated for pouring to begin. During operation, the cupola is refilled to the charging door or top as the material inside settles lower.

Tapping requires the removal of the plug and the molten metal pours into a fire clay ladle held by two men using the carrying handle. The man at the split end can tilt the ladle to pour smoothly and accurately into the prepared sand moulds. The ladle is made from a steel bucket with a wide pouring lip lined with fire clay or with a heat-resistant material made of ground fire brick mixed with 'marl'. At the end of the heat the blast is stopped and, whilst the coke is still hot, the prop is knocked from under the bottom doors to allow them to swing open and the remains to fall to the floor. These are quenched with water and removed to avoid damage.

One problem with cupolas is that they emit smoke and carbon monoxide fumes. It is possible to fit equipment to reduce the air pollution but expensive not to reduce melting efficiency. Check the level of smoke permitted with your Municipal Authority.

2. *Rotary oil fired furnace* (Fig. 27)

The rotary furnace is the logical next step for the foundry that has successfully operated a cupola. Because it reaches higher temperatures it can be used to cast steel but requires a higher standard of refractory lining, using better quality bricks and special cements. It is more flexible than the cupola and can be conveniently used for small quantities.

Fig. 27 Rotary oil-fired furnace. The furnace rotates on rollers to constantly move and speed up melting. The oil burner at the right-hand end is fed with pre-heated air by the large fan and pipe above. Molten metal is tapped through the spout in the front centre of the furnace drum. Lifting lugs allow the furnace drum to be lifted by crane and replaced with another for melting a different metal. Charging is through the left end of the drum (hidden).

It consists of a steel cylinder with conical ends and the point of the cone cut off to leave a hole about half the diameter of the cylinder. The cylinder is mounted inside circular turning wheels that run on slow electrically driven rollers. The turning agitates the scrap and speeds melting. Scrap and pig iron are charged in through one circular end hole. At the other end is the oil-burner which uses No. 5 residual bunker oil blown through a nozzle with air from a powerful fan. Pouring is done through the spout in the middle of the cylinder wall. Slag is removed through a spout in one end. A separate cylinder is used for each different type of metal to prevent contamination. The furnace shown, operating in Peru, casts about 50

Fig. 28   Crucible furnace — turning wheel and gearbox for tilting to pour metal. Note the strong tubular stools on which it sits. Peru.

tonnes of iron a month but much higher production than this is possible.

3. *The crucible furnace* (Fig. 28)

The crucible furnace is used for small-scale operations, more often with non-ferrous metals but also for cast iron and steel. It differs from the two furnaces just described in that the fuel and the metal are kept totally separate, giving much better control over purity and composition. This is achieved by holding the metal in a fire clay crucible which is seated inside the bucket-shaped furnace. Although the furnace can be coke-fired, oil or gas are more convenient as they heat more quickly than coke, are more widely available and are simpler to use in a tilting furnace.

The furnace and its lid are lined with fire brick and mounted on strong bearings at the centre of gravity. The oil burner flame enters through a hole in the bottom while the burner pump is behind a screen to prevent damage from slag or hot metal during work. The crucible is suspended in the centre so that it is surrounded on all sides by a jacket of heated air. Tilting is by a hand wheel acting through a reduction gearbox; the crucible spout is blended into the furnace spout with fire clay. For higher temperature work, crucibles are made from graphite mixed with the fire clay. They are fragile when cold but strong when heated. Each crucible should be used only for one type of metal.

4. *Electric arc furnace*

This is not the huge electric arc furnaces used in mini-steel mills but a tiny furnace, such as that shown in Fig. 29. It comprises a cylindrical pot of alumina brick and magnesite, held within a steel hoop mounted on a shaft that rotates in simple vee-blocks. The lid, also of fireclay held by a steel band, is penetrated by two graphite electrodes which in turn are held in copper clamps mounted on a tilting and lifting mechanism. A pair of parallel connected D.C. (direct current) arc welding generators (such as manufactured by Lincoln Electric Co.) provide current of up to 1000 amps each at low (40) voltage, by thick flexible copper cables to the electrode clamps. The generators can be powered by a small diesel engine or can safely be run off 3 phase mains electric supply. This furnace is rather complicated to make and operate and for this reason will not

Fig. 29 Note the steel band, mounted on a turning axle, which holds the furnace body of this tiny electric arc furnace. Colombia.

be described in great detail here. It is charged with small pieces of scrap and the lid is lowered. The arc strikes from one electrode to the scrap and back to the other electrode. As the charge melts the electrodes are lowered by handwheels. It takes about one hour to melt a charge. The electrodes are used up in the course of operations and have to be renewed. For this reason and because of the consumption of electric power (or diesel fuel) the unit is not cheap to run, compared with other types of small furnace described. On the other hand, it is flexible, handy to use for small batch work and of comparatively low capital cost (especially if second-hand welding generators can be bought, for example at the conclusion of a large welding construction project such as a pipeline).

5. *Induction furnace*

This is similar to the crucible furnace except that the crucible is set permanently in the furnace, surrounded by a water-cooled electric coil. A high frequency (1000 cycles per second) alternating current is applied by a special generator. The coil creates a magnetic field which 'induces' electric currents in the charge to generate heat and melt the scrap. A large unit can contain up to 4 tons of scrap and takes a little over an hour to heat, but much smaller units are commonly used, even down to laboratory models holding only a few pounds. However, they are expensive for their size.

Induction furnaces are very clean and there is no possibility of chemical changes due to contact with fuel or the high temperatures of the electric arc furnace, so they are very suitable for non-ferrous metals and alloy steels. Another advantage is that cast iron can be made from steel scrap without the need for imported pig-iron. The process is called recarburizing and requires graphite charcoal and ferro-silicon additions.

FOUNDRY MOULDS

The making of complicated moulds for casting metals demands great skill, although many products can be cast using simple methods. It is not intended to do more here than outline possible methods so that the reader can judge whether it is within his capabilities, in which case he will wish to obtain one of the many books which describe the operation of sand-casting in detail.

The first requirement is a spacious floor area, which need not be concreted but is usually of sand. Also:

   i) A large number of *mould boxes* of sizes to suit the

products to be cast and in numbers, depending on whether metal can be melted in small quantities, such as in an induction or electric arc furnace or in large quantities, as in the cupola. The boxes are usually made of thin steel plate. They have no bottoms but are made with locating pins so that they will stack accurately one on top of another, with each pin fitting into the hole in a bracket on the box below. Each box has carrying handles on each side.

Frequently, castings only require two mould boxes but a deep casting, such as the body of a large valve, may need several.

ii) The *pattern* of the product to be cast. This is made in wood if it is to be used many times, or in clay or wax if only once. It is the same size and shape as the outer surface of the product to be cast except that it has changes in size to allow for shrinkage in the metal as it cools after casting. A pattern-maker needs to understand clearly these allowances.

Often, the pattern is made in several pieces, for example, one for the top half of the product and a separate one for the bottom. The joint surface between them is perfectly flat. If the shape is such that it will be difficult to withdraw it from the finished mould, other pieces of the pattern are made separately.

iii) *Cores* are a form of expendable (able to be used up) pattern made in sand to create holes in the final casting. If wooden cores were used they could not be withdrawn from the casting after it set; the cores of sand can be crumbled out. Cores are often made using sand mixed with water glass (sodium silicate) which can be moulded in a wooden pattern and then hardened by gassing with carbon dioxide.

iv) *Sand*. Ordinary silica sand is suitable for making foundry moulds; it is cheap, readily-obtained and can withstand high temperatures. Fine grain sizes make smooth, accurate castings. However, it needs a 'binder' to maintain its shape during manufacture of the mould and casting of the metal. Clay, added in between 8% and 15%, is suitable and cheap. Many small foundries use naturally clay-bonded sand, too. It is important that moulding sand be even, of uniform moisture and free

75

from hard lumps or impurities. Usually, a power-driven mixing mill is used; hand-mixing is possible but laborious.

Making the mould

The mould box is placed on the level floor, or on a stout movable moulding board. The lower pattern half is placed inside with its flat joint face down. Ready-mixed sand is packed carefully around it and pressed into any hollow corners. The mould box is filled, with the sand well rammed up during filling, then levelled off accurately to the top edge of the mould box.

The first mould half is then turned over and the moulding board removed, displaying the flat bottom of the lower pattern half. The top is sprinkled with fine dry parting sand to ensure that the two halves of the mould separate easily after they are made. The upper pattern half is positioned on top of it, with short dowel rods in one half and fitting holes in the other to ensure an accurate position. A second mould box is placed round it, positioned to pins on the first mould box and the second half is rammed up with sand in a similar fashion. A pin is put in to form the 'sprue' through which metal will be poured (Fig. 30a). The two halves are separated again and a channel or 'gate' made in the lower half, so positioned to match the sprue. If there is more than one part to the casting, then they can be connected by further gates. A riser will also be made; a long hole in the top half that can be filled with molten metal which will flow back into the main mould cavity as the metal cools and top up shrinkage. Small vents are made to within a short distance of the pattern to allow the escape of gases after pouring molten metal.

The patterns are finally withdrawn from the sand by vibrating them very slightly sideways and pulling them out with a spike, taking care not to disturb the sand. Cores are inserted, the halves repositioned, and with a weight placed on top to hold them together against the pressure of the molten metal, the mould is ready to pour.

Pouring is done from a ladle which is held by two men using a forked carrier (Fig. 30b). The ladle is filled from the furnace, carried to each mould in turn and tilted by the man holding the forked end of the carrier. Pouring should be steady and

76

Fig. 30a Making the mould. The mould on the left is complete and ready to pour. Note the pouring sprue and riser at the corners of the top half (standing up) and the corresponding gate at the corner of the bottom half, running into the actual mould. Peru.

Fig. 30b Pouring molten metal into the mould. Note the weights on top of each mould so that the top halves are not forced off by the pressure of the liquid metal. The flames are caused by inflammable gases given off. Peru.

77

continuous. Often, gases given off in the mould explode during pouring, but this is normal and need not cause alarm.

Finishing of castings

After pouring the metal and allowing a suitable time for it to solidify, the mould is broken open and the casting withdrawn. Attached to the casting will be solidified metal from the various tunnels referred to above, and these must be removed. Hand files, hammers and chisels may be sufficient for small castings: if not then an oxy-acetylene torch or a grinding machine will be necessary. Next, the casting is 'fettled' to smooth any small knobs and edges of metal. When using grinding machines, goggles or a visor must be worn to protect the eyes, in case the wheel shatters.

Finally, any embedded sand is smoothed away from the surface.

Further developments

Moulding machines exist for high production. There is also a continuing mixer filler process for chemically-bonded sand moulding. Although the cost of chemical binders is high, this process is so flexible and so suitable for varied production that it has proved to be viable for small foundries in many countries.

Safety equipment

Scrap handlers must always wear safety boots (with steel toe caps) and leather gloves. Anyone handling hot metal should, in addition, wear leather gaiters or leggings, gloves and goggles or face visors.

A medical kit, well stocked, for the treatment of burns, scalds, cuts and eye injuries is essential. A stretcher should also be kept close by. When electrical equipment is being used, a notice should describe treatment for electric shock (see Chapter 17).

Products that can be made in a small foundry

This is a list of products that can be made in a ferrous foundry. It is taken from a report on the foundry industry undertaken by a developing country in the South American Andes and may be regarded as typical. No other process can produce complicated shapes so readily (Fig. 31).

Fig. 31   Bench ends made in a small foundry. These are typical of the complicated shapes that can easily be made in a foundry. Peru.

Spare parts for industrial and agricultural machines
Sand mixers
Moulding presses
Coffee grinders
Coffee de-pulpers
Grinders, vibrators, mortar mixers
Shears
Woodworking machines
Suction pumps
Elevators
Weigh scales
Defibrilators
Forging dies
Millers
Ventilators
Spares for textile machinery
Burners
Sugar and other food processing equipment
Stoves and heaters
Shoe lasts
Manhole and drain covers
Valve bodies
Fans and turbines
Pipes
Motor casings
Weights and counterweights
Couplings
Bench ends
Car and lorry parts
Shelving brackets
Well tops and covers
Bells, discs and shoes
Wheels
Bearings and pedestals and many more.

References

1. *Oil Drum Forges* (Intermediate Technology Publications Ltd.).

Equipment suppliers

Foundry Equipment
- Pioneer Equipment Co. Ltd., Old Padra Road, Akota, Baroda, Gujarat, India.

Gas cutting torch
- British Oxygen Co. Ltd., W. Pimbo, Skelmersdale, U.K.

General suppliers of metal scrap machinery
- J. McIntyre (Machinery) Ltd., Acorn Park Industrial Estate, Harrimans Lane, Dunkirk, Nottingham, U.K.
- Vanesco Ltd., 165 Garth Road, Morden, Surrey, SM4 4LH, U.K.
- Hydraulic & Engineering Works, 10066, 1st Floor, D.B. Gupta Road, Pahar Ganj, New Delhi 110055, India.

Induction and Electric Furnaces
- Hindustan Brown Boveri Baroda Ltd., 264 Dr Annie Besant Road, Bombay 430025, India.
- G.E.C. of India Ltd., Chitarajan Avenue, Calcutta, India.

Rerolling Mills
- Mukand Iron and Steelworks, Belapur Road, Kalve, Thana, Maharashtra, India.
- Davy Ashmore India Ltd., Kharagpur G-19, Middleton Street, Calcutta, India.

Rotary Furnaces
- A.C.C. Vickers-Babcock Durgapur Ltd., Express Tower 18th Shahabad Floor, Nariman Point, Bombay 430021, India.

Chapter 3. Recycling of Tin Cans

DETINNING OF CANS

Tin cans are actually made of steel coated with a very thin layer of tin, and often with lacquer as well. They are a problem to steelmakers as the tin, which has a lower melting point, causes zones of weakness in the hot steel, leading to 'hot shortness' and other problems. For this reason, cans are not used by steelmakers in the industrialized countries unless the tin has been removed (or at least reduced) by 'detinning'. Alternatively, their use is restricted to the production of low-quality products such as reinforcing steel.

In many developing countries where there is a shortage of steel scrap, cans are accepted, provided they form less than 10% of the total scrap charge and are evenly dispersed throughout: one steelmaker claims to use up to 50% cans to make reinforcing bars! Some steelmakers prefer cans rusted in the weather for some weeks before use.

In the original manufacture tin is applied to the steel sheet by either of two industrial processes. The more modern is 'electrolytic deposition' which results in an extremely thin layer of tin (thickness 0.0015 mm) and weight 0.5% to 1.0%. In the older process, the steel was dipped in a bath of molten tin resulting in a much thicker layer of tin by weight 1.5% to 7.0%. Not only is the percentage contamination of hot dipped steel higher, creating the need to remove it, but the amount of pure tin recovered by detinning is larger, which benefits profitability.

As a guide, the sale of pure tin, one of the world's most valuable metals, pays for the cost of a detinning operation so that the increase in value of the steel is free. Detinned steel with less than 0.05% tin fetches a price double that of scrap tinplate.

Three types of detinning process have been observed in

Third World countries: the alkali process, the alkaline electrolysis process and the acid process. All three will be described here. The choice of process will depend on raw materials and energy costs in the proposed location.

THE ALKALI DETINNING PROCESS

The tinplate material must be clean and open. Used cans need treatment before detinning (see p. 88).

Description of an alkali detinning operation (Mexico)

Plant capacity: 24 tons per three-shift day is claimed.

Equipment: –

- 3 steel tanks of 3000 litres capacity each, coated with 4 mm plastic and fitted with filling and draining pipes.
- 7 steel baskets to fit snugly inside tanks each fitted with 'lifting eyes' and able to safely hold 2 tons of material.
- 1 overhead crane of 3 ton capacity.
- Heating system to maintain tanks full of liquid at 95°C – may be electric immersion heaters or gas, oil or solid fuel-fired but should be designed to avoid naked flames playing on plastic-coated tanks.
- 1 baling press for thin gauge steel (see p. 47).

Operation

At any time that two baskets are being loaded, two more are detinning in hot solution, one is full of cold rinse water for rinsing and two are being unloaded. Baskets are loaded fully but material is not compressed (Fig. 32).

The detinning solution consists of 15% caustic soda and 5% sodium nitrite (an oxidizing agent). Sodium nitrate could also be used. Each charge of fresh tinplate is detinned for two hours, during which time the detinning liquid should be constantly stirred or agitated to speed up the process. The number of charges that can be treated with a given batch of solution will vary with the nature of the material being detinned. Electrolytic tinplate, for example, will exhaust the detinning solution more slowly than hot dipped. The solution should be tested for alkali concentration from time to time and further caustic soda and sodium nitrite added as necessary.

Fig. 32   Alkali detinning. Heated alkali baths with charge baskets in the foreground. Mexico.

At the end of each day, the tin is recovered from the solution by adding six kilos of calcium carbonate (chalk, limestone or seashells) for every tonne of steel that has been detinned. Again this quantity will vary with the material and should be adjusted in practice. The tin forms a solid 'precipitate' of calcium stannate which is allowed to settle at the bottom of the tank before the liquid is drained off or filtered. The solid is dried and put into bags ready for transport to a tin smelter where tin is extracted chemically or electrolytically. The tin-free steel is rinsed and baled prior to sale to a local foundry or steel mill.

The latter part of the process might be modified to use 'quicklime' instead of calcium carbonate. The quicklime would regenerate the solution of caustic soda with substantial economies, as its cost is only one-third that of caustic soda.

DANGER All processes using caustic materials, especially hot ones, are hazardous and this is no exception. Employees should be trained in the correct use of protective gloves, aprons, face visors and gaiters, and should wear safety boots with steel-reinforced toe-caps. A clean wash-basin should be available by the lavatory and the manager should keep, ready-to-hand, a medical kit containing an eye-bath, eye-rinse liquid and jelly for treating scalds. Should any caustic solution fall on the skin it must be washed off in cold water immediately.

THE ALKALINE ELECTROLYSIS PROCESS

This is chemically similar to the alkali process but is more complete in that the end-product is metallic (if impure) tin.

The process described is in use in Bombay, India and handles 50 tons per month, although its full capacity could be far higher than this. Dirty or rusty tinplate cannot be treated.

Equipment: – 2 brick built natural draught furnaces, each equipped with a 10 m high chimney, a coke-burning hearth and two lines of ten cells, each designed to hold a steel tank at the temperature of 70°C to 80°C (Fig. 33).

– 40 unlined steel tanks, each 1.2 m diameter and 1.2 m deep, connected electrically in series by copper 'bus-bars' to the negative terminal of a 50 or 60 volt dc transformer/rectifier. This is powered by the 400 volt mains to give a voltage drop of about 2½ volts per cell. The tanks should be removable (but only for maintenance purposes).

– Mobile pump and hose.

Fig. 33 Alkaline electrolysis detinning: the furnace with cells. Note how the charge basket rests on wooden blocks to prevent electrical contact with the tank, the lifting lugs on both baskets and cells, the anodes and bus-bars and the tiled furnace top. India.

- 40 steel anodes, hinged so that they can be retracted when a charge basket is lowered into or raised from the tank, connected to the electrical supply and in contact with the scrap charge.
- 50 steel charge baskets, fitted with lifting lugs, designed to hold 300 kg of loosely-packed steel sheet scrap, and to fit snugly into the tanks without electrical contact with the (cathode) tanks.
- 1 overhead crane of 2 tons capacity
- 1 steel baling press
- 1 reducing furnace, ingot casting moulds, tools etc.

Operation

The process is slower than the previous one but is very economical. The tinplate is submerged in pure 9% caustic soda solution at 70 to 80°C while an electric current is passed through the solution. The tin is deposited at the cathode. The caustic soda needs only occasional replacement, but should be

85

topped up with water to replace 5% evaporation every 24 hours. The baskets are replaced every four to eight hours, the actual time depending on individual experience.

To discover when detinning is complete, observe the voltage drop across the cell, which kicks upwards at this stage. Another way is to watch for changes in the colour of the scrap to various shades of blue, black and red brown. The steel is rinsed and baled as soon as detinning is completed.

Every five days the tanks are drained and the 'sponge tin' scraped from the sides and bottom. It is kept moist to prevent oxidation, then washed and passed over an electromagnet to remove any steel particles. It is then dried and smelted with high purity pinewood charcoal; 60% of the tin is reduced to the metallic state and is cast into ingots. The remaining 40% is embedded in the 'dross' which is ground, and again reduced with charcoal. The ingots may be purified by melting in a reverberatory furnace and skimming the dross from the surface.

In addition, there will also remain tin-bearing slimes at the bottom of the baths, slimes from the various washing processes, and oxides of tin from the regeneration of the electrolyte. All these can be collected together, dried by centrifuge or other means, and smelted to recover the tin.

THE ACID DETINNING PROCESS

This process has been developed by the National Research Development Corporation (NRDC) of India, who claim that it is three to four times as fast as the conventional alkaline process, so that tin can be released from a batch of scrap in only 30 minutes to an hour. Also, because the scrap can be six times as densely packed in the charge basket, a production rate twenty times faster is achieved. Rusted metal and shredded used cans can be treated. Full details of the process were not disclosed to the author, although the following information was provided on raw material and equipment requirements to produce steel with 0.05% residual tin content and tin of 99.5% purity. Those interested in the process should contact NRDC.

In general, acid processes are more difficult to control than alkali and there are obvious hazards from the emission of chlorine gas.

Size of the plant The plant, for processing approximately

86

4000 tonnes of tin scrap per annum (12 to 15 tonnes per day) is of batch type with two sets of processing tanks for 'leaching' the tin coating from the parent material and a set of dilution tanks etc.

Raw materials – Tin scrap (both hot dip tin scrap containing 1.5–7% tin and electrolytically-coated tin scrap with a tin content of 0.5–1% tin). Tin recovery will be greater if hot dip material is used.

– Hydrochloric acid – approximately 40 litres per kg of tin metal leached. If electrolytic tin scrap is used the acid consumption may increase by 20%.

– Aluminium scraps.

Plant and machinery

– 2 fibre-reinforced plastic (frp) tanks of 4.5 m³ volume, with PVC lining.

– 2 sets of fume exhaust equipment, each of 6–8 kW leading to the atmosphere with pipework fabricated from frp.

– 4 frp process tanks of volume 4.5 m³, PVC lined, for recovery of residual liquor from the detinned scrap bundles after removal from the process tanks.

– 8 wooden tanks of volume 4.5 m³ used as dilution tanks for recovery of sponge tin, reinforced with angles, protected with frp lining and coated with acid-resisting paint inside and outside.

– 2 sets of travelling lifting equipment (crossbar type) with pulley blocks of 2 tonnes capacity and 5 metre chains for hand operation.

– 1 hydraulic power-operated press with 4 kW motor for dewatering the sponge.

– 1 platform weighing scale of 1 tonne capacity.

– 1 tilting furnace of 100 kilos capacity with necessary motor, blower and burner (1.5 kW capacity).

– 1 acid tank of 5000 litres capacity with all fittings and pumping facility.

87

       – Other equipment such as electrical wiring, temperature recorders, pipe with fittings, nylon rope, foundry tools and mouldings, etc.

Land and building. The total area required will be about 2500 sq. m, out of which 1000 sq. m is required for the process hall and 1500 sq. m for the laboratory, office, storage etc. The height of the process hall is about 7 m.

Manpower requirement. The total manpower requirement is 15, with one supervisor, four skilled workers, six semi-skilled labourers and four unskilled labourers. Office personnel will be needed as well.

Total installed hp. The total installed power for this project will be about 33 kW.

Preparation of used cans for detinning

The processes described above have rarely been employed for detinning used cans from household refuse. Normally, new, bright tinplate scrap from can and box-making factories is used. However, used cans have been successfully detinned in Britain for many years. All that is required is that they are clean and shredded, or at least unfolded. Cleanliness is vital as food remains and dirt etc. will contaminate the detinning solution, block pipes and prevent the solution from coming into contact with the tin-bearing steel. Rinsing well in cold water is usually sufficient.

Cans designed to be liquid-tight have tightly folded and sometimes soldered seams; often two circular and one straight seam per can. Up to a quarter of the tin is contained within the seams and the detinning solution can only reach this if the seam is opened or cut. In industrialized countries this is usually done by feeding the cans through a shredder which chops them up by sheer destructive energy. This process is expensive, the machinery unreliable, and only huge plants have proved to be economic.

In certain Third World countries (notably Egypt) cans are cut by hand shears, like a larger version of those used for cutting grass and hedges (Fig. 34). The can is reduced to flat circles and rectangles which can be densely bundled to reduce transport costs and are ideal feedstock for detinning. The process is tedious and rewards depend on the price that can be obtained.

Fig. 34 Shearing open used cans. The thin strip contains solder. If the material were sent for detinning, this would be removed. Egypt.

The thin seams are separated from the flat sheets. So far no process has been developed to recover the tin, lead and steel from the seams as pure metals. It might be worth detinning these but only if the vat could be kept separate and not used for other detinning (as the resulting tin will certainly be contaminated with lead and only able to be sold for solder manufacture). The steel will also be contaminated. The total quantity of material is small unless done on a large scale so it may be best to ignore the seams altogether.

Aluminium cans. The other metal used in cans is aluminium, usually in 'rip-top' beer and beverage cans. Although this wasteful and expensive form of container is mainly used in rich countries, it may be found in tourist and wealthy districts of poor countries (where for some people clean drinking water is an unobtainable luxury, let alone beer in expensive containers!). Aluminium tops and ring-pulls can be removed by hand during the shearing operation described above, and the aluminium, which is of high quality, sold.

As an alternative to hand-shearing, cans may be shredded or 'granulated' in a suitable machine (called a shredder, granulator or pulverizer). At Oxfam Wastesaver,* a 50 hp granulator designed for shredding plastics was successfully used. The only problem was a rather high rate of wear on the cutting blades, but this could be overcome by using a larger and more powerful machine.

OTHER MARKETS FOR TINPLATE CANS AND CAN-MAKING SCRAP

Use of skeletons

In the process of manufacturing cans and crown corks (metal tops for fizzy drinks), circular pieces are stamped out of large rectangular sheets of tinplate. The remainder, known as a skeleton (Fig. 35) may be sold for the:
- manufacture of air conditioners and filters. The skeletons are used as the frame to support wire wool stuffing; and must be packed flat for transport.
- manufacture of animal pens and cages.

Use in the copper industry

'Precipitation iron' is used for the extraction of copper from low grade ores. Some companies use detinned cans for this, others use can manufacturers' process scrap or even used food cans. The copper is leached from the ore in an acid solution into which the cans are loaded, so that the copper precipitates out as a solid at the bottom of the container.

For this market, consult any local copper mine or smelter. They will probably require the material loose (i.e. unbaled) and free from dirt, or they may require it shredded or opened as described above for detinning.

---

* A recycling factory developed by the author for Oxfam in 1975.

90

Fig. 35   Tinplate skeleton used for air conditioner manufacture. The material is scrap from a factory producing "crown cork" bottle tops. Mexico.

Use by iron founders

The quality required of iron castings such as manhole covers is often much lower than that required by the steel industry, and foundries may be willing to accept a percentage of tinplate, depending on the type of product they are producing. It should be baled to the highest density possible.

Use for production of refined pig iron

This is the raw material for steelmaking and iron-founding and in most countries is the largest market for used tinplate cans. They should be baled to as high a density as possible to reduce transport and melting costs. Cans which have been burnt (e.g. in a refuse incinerator) are acceptable.

Use for control of chromium plating wastes

Small-scale chromium plating workshops in Third World countries rarely treat their waste chromium acid solutions because to do so is complicated and expensive. These solutions are highly poisonous and dangerous. It is reported that rusting

Fig. 36   Tools for ornamental tinplate working: all the punches were home-made from reinforcing bar, and hardened in the forge shown in Fig. 25a. The circular pad is made of lead and is placed under the object being embossed. Note the completed pieces in the foreground. Peru.

Fig. 37 .Embossed casket made from tin cans. Peru.

tin cans may be used to reduce the chromium prior to precipitation.

The chromic acid waste solution is held for 24 hours in a tank containing heavily-rusted tinplate cans. Reduction is known to have been completed when the characteristic orange colour of the waste disappears. Calcium carbonate is then added in excess quantity to precipitate the chromium, which can be chemically processed for re-use.

To treat 100 m^3 per day of waste liquid (containing 5 parts per million excess sulphur dioxide and with a pH value of 3.0), 25 Kg of cans and 330 kg limestone (or similar) per day are required. After six or seven fillings the cans are used up and have to be topped up. The cost of this method of treatment in the Philippines was reported to be about half the cost of the conventional method of treatment, and savings in raw material costs were significant.

RE-USE OF TIN CANS

As well as recycling, cans can be used as raw material to manufacture items for resale. They can be cut with household scissors (although sheetmetal workers' 'tinsnips' are better), they can be bent, folded, rivetted, joined by a folded seam, soldered, nailed, punched and embossed. In Fig. 36, the tools

Fig. 38   Lamp, funnel, jug, flyspray and brush made from tin cans. Objects: courtesy Mr Tony Tigwell, India Alive Project.

used by a metal worker in Cuzco, Peru, to produce, at home, enchanting jewel caskets (Fig. 37) from tin cans, are shown. Many other items can be made by the less skilled (Fig. 38).

Equipment suppliers

Acid Detinning Plant
–   NDRC, 61 Ring Road, Lajpat, Nagar 111, New Delhi 110024, India.
–   The author.

Chapter 4. Non-ferrous Metals

Metals other than iron and steel are described as non-ferrous. The most interesting as regards scrap are aluminium, copper, brasses and bronzes, zinc, lead, silver and other precious metals.

HOW TO TELL THE DIFFERENCE

One problem facing the collector is how to identify all these different metals. This is important because they are used by quite different markets and the best prices are paid by the final users, normally foundries or refiners who will not buy mixed or unidentified metals. If you cannot separate them, you will have to sell to a middle man who can, and he will pay less than the final user. Here are simple tests to identify a metal:

   i) *Find out where it came from.* Manufacturers use only certain raw materials, therefore others can be ruled out.
  ii) *Consider the size, shape and former use of the item.* This chapter will give you an idea of the products made from various metals.
 iii) *Test it with a magnet.* Ferrous metals are attracted (pulled) by or to it; non-ferrous metals (with the exception of chromium and nickel and their 'alloys') are not.
  iv) *Look at the basic colour*
   v) *Drill or take filings.* Examine the clean cut surface in a good light (but not direct sunlight) immediately, before an oxidation film forms and makes identification difficult. The following effects should be seen:

Aluminium	– silver grey
Copper	– reddish-brown
Brasses	– golden yellow
Bronzes	– golden yellow to reddish-brown
Lead	– dull grey
Zinc	– yellowish
Nickel	– silver

Table 4 Chemical spot tests

Material	Chemical spot test
Copper	No reaction.
Red brass	Silver nitrate will turn a black colour in solution.
Yellow brass	No reaction.
High grade bronze	Silver nitrate will produce grey colour in solution.
Manganese bronze	No reaction.
Cupro-nickel	Nitric acid will produce an immediate green colour.
Nickel silver	Nitric acid produces an immediate green colour, plus a vigorous reaction and a puff of brown smoke. Specimen will develop a pink colour after acid is washed off with water.
Silver plated metals	Nitric acid and hydrochloric acid will produce a milky-white precipitate in the solution on the plated surface. After removing plating, if base metal is a copper base alloy, nitric acid will turn green; if aluminium the specimen will be light in weight. If the base metal is steel the specimen will be magnetic.
Aluminium	Silver nitrate will remain clear in solution.
Magnesium	Silver nitrate will produce a dark grey to black colour in solution. Filings will flare with a white flame.
Lead	None. Weight and softness are a useful guide.
Zinc	Nitric acid applied to filings will produce fizzing and immediate brown smoke. Solution will remain clear with no precipitation.
Die cast zinc	Nitric acid applied to filings will produce an immediate light brown smoke similar to, but lighter than, zinc. Solution will appear greenish with no precipitation.
Tin	Nitric acid applied to filings will produce yellow smoke and yellow colour on surface of solution; white precipitation will remain in solution.
Silver	Place a drop of nitric acid on the sample and allow it to react for one minute. Then place a drop of water on the acid spot. A drop of hydro-chloric acid or a couple of crystals of common salt placed in this liquid will produce a curdy white appearance if the metal is silver.
Gold	One or two pieces of the plated metal are placed in a small beaker with nitric acid, then heated. If the samples remain gold in colour they actually contain gold.

96

vi) *How hard and heavy is it*? Lead is very heavy; so is copper but not as heavy as lead. Most brasses and bronzes are heavier than steel. Cast iron is a little lighter than steel. Zinc is light but aluminium is even lighter. Lead is extremely soft; aluminium is soft and can readily be scratched with a knife, as can zinc and copper. Some brasses and bronzes can be softer and some harder than mild steel. Yellow brass is soft compared with manganese bronze which is hard, brittle and coarse. Cast iron is very hard and some alloy steels can be even harder and cannot be cut with a hacksaw.

vii) *Use chemical spot tests*. Thoroughly clean the surface with a *clean* file or grinding wheel and apply a drop of the chemical. The metal temperature should be 15° – 25°C (i.e. not exceeding normal temperatures) for the test. The following chemicals are required:
   - nitric acid concentrated (HNO_3)
   - hydrochloric acid concentrated ($HC\ell$)
   - silver nitrate 0.5% solution ($AgNO_3$) dissolved in water.

The tests are given in Table 4.

COPPER

Copper is the perfect material for recycling. It is valuable, easy to identify, easy to clean, heavy and can be readily sold to small foundries or larger companies which refine and produce copper sheet, wire or bars. It has many important alloys, particularly bronze (which contains copper, tin and zinc) and brass (which contains copper and zinc only): scrap from either is easy to sell. To discourage theft, pack the scrap in oil drums and hammer the ends over. Copper can be graded as follows, although a merchant may pay the same price for ungraded copper provided the brass and bronze are kept separate. Make sure the prices for each grade are better than those for ungraded.

i) *Pure copper* may include scrap from factories that make copper products, although they usually reclaim it themselves; ends of copper tubes used in water systems in houses and other buildings; pieces of electrical machinery; wire and heavy cables.

ii) *Copper cables with plastic covering* can be found in electrical installations; house wiring; electrical machinery;

car electrics and overhead cables. When collecting copper wire, be careful that it is not carrying live electric current; a fatal shock could result. Also, make sure that the material doesn't belong to someone else (see Iron and Steel, Chapter 2). The plastic or rubber covering has to be removed and this can be done in one of three ways:

a) By hand with a sharp knife or wire strippers (which can be bought from any tool store).

b) By burning, although this creates black smoke and poisonous fumes. It may also be against the law because it makes the air foul and should never be done near other people or animals, nor where the dust from the smoke can fall on land used for growing crops. It burns the copper, lowers its value and fails to recover the plastic.

c) Using a cable stripper. This is a machine that chews off plastic, leaving the copper wire unharmed. The machine has two toothed rollers, driven in opposite directions by an electric motor, which chew the soft plastic without cutting the slightly harder copper. A variation of the design uses a single toothed roller of deep vee profile and a slitting roller in line with the throat of the vee. The cable covering is slit along its length at the same time as it is chewed from the other side. Like all machinery, it is expensive to buy and run, and is faster than the other methods but creates fewer jobs for unskilled workers.

The advantage of using a knife or a cable stripper is that the plastic as well as the copper can be recycled.

iii) *Copper contaminated with tin* may be found in electrical cables, tools, and food and drink machinery. The tin is very valuable so this scrap can be sold, and used for the production of bronze. It must, however, be free from lead (e.g. solder) or zinc.

iv) *Copper contaminated with solder* is very common in plumbing scrap: pipes and pipe joints; ball valves, copper cylinders; boilers and water heaters. These may have brass or gun-metal (a kind of bronze) fittings attached to them, which should be removed and graded separately. If the solder is melted down with the copper the melt will need purifying or refining. To avoid this, it

98

is best to cut off the soldered joints (elbows, tee pieces, connectors etc.) and add the pure copper to grade (i). The solder contaminated material may be sold to a refinery or to a factory that makes objects from gunmetal.

The solder will normally be silver in colour and easy to distinguish from the copper, but dirty scrap may need cleaning, scratching or filing before solder is revealed.

Certain scrapped car radiators are examples of solder-contaminated copper scrap, but they should be kept separate from plumbing scrap as they may be made from a different alloy of copper.

v) *Electrical machinery* may contain a mixture of all the above types of copper scrap. It is probably worth breaking it down into the separate grades.

vi) *Chromium plated copper* has a bright, shiny silver finish. Test it with a file and keep separate from other copper scrap. It can be sold to a refiner.

Refining of copper

This needs specialist skills and will only be described briefly. The copper is furnace-melted and molten sand added to form a slag. Air is blown into the molten mixture and iron, tin and lead are all oxidized and float on top in the slag. 'Cadmium', sulphur and other impurities are then given off as gases. Some of the copper also becomes oxidized and has to be reduced by 'poling' with green tree trunks in the molten copper (as in the smelting of copper ore).

Casting of copper into ingots

Pure copper can be melted in any of the small furnaces described in Chapter 2, and can be cast into ingots. A foundry is necessary for this, equipped as for iron and steel. If the copper is to be cast into ingots for resale it is worth investing in cast iron moulds (Fig. 39). Special equipment to measure the furnace temperature is necessary and specialist advice should be obtained if possible.

ALUMINIUM

Sources of aluminium scrap

Aluminium is one of the most widely used metals because it

Fig. 39   Cast iron mould for billets of aluminium, copper, etc. The furnace is of the type shown in Fig. 40. Photo: courtesy of Chine Furnaces, U.K.

is cheap to produce, lightweight, and very easy to work. The main sources of scrap are:

- cooking pots, saucepans, kettles
- car parts (see Chapter 2)
- aeroplane parts: aeroplanes are made almost entirely of aluminium alloys
- domestic appliances including vacuum cleaners, washing machines, dryers
- tubes, boxes, containers for medicines, bottle tops and other packaging
- camping equipment
- door and window frames
- scrap from factories manufacturing aluminium products
- electric cable is often made from aluminium as it is cheaper than copper – it is normally heavy gauge only
- some drink cans, mainly those imported from the U.S.A.
- cooking foil, mainly obtainable from hotels.

Aluminium and its alloys can be identified by their light

weight and the surface which is shiny when new but turns dull when oxidized in the air (unless coated or anodized when it will remain permanently shiny). Aluminium-based metals can usually be distinguished from zinc because zinc is mainly used in castings which shatter easily under a hammer blow, whereas aluminium does not, (although there are some exceptions: aluminium alloy castings which shatter and some zinc alloys which do not at room temperature).

Aluminium usually occurs in much smaller quantities than ferrous scrap but is worth about ten times as much. It is not usually baled except for foil and drink cans made of very thin material that is uneconomic to transport unless baled and burns when charged uncompressed into a furnace. These materials can be baled in the same way as paper, but cardboard ends must be added to the bales and plenty of string or wire used to avoid losing material.

Markets for aluminium scrap

In developing countries the largest market will be small foundries, but there may also be mills that melt the scrap to produce ingots for conversion into sheets, extrusions, castings etc. Most of these will buy aluminium scrap if its composition is known, but may refuse to buy foil unless baled. Foil may also be sold to steelmakers, who use it as a deoxidant: it is ground and thrown into the crucible to reduce slag. If no foundry exists nearby, you may be able to sell to a merchant who transports regularly to another town, but his prices will be lower.

Grading of aluminium

When collecting, keep known alloys separate from commercially pure aluminium. Thereafter, the main task is to remove all non-aluminium materials such as plastics, oil, iron or steel, copper, dirt or the contents of containers. Cooking pots or saucepans often have handles of plastic or steel and these may be held on with steel rivets. It is easier to cut off the aluminium than the steel but essential that all steel is removed to get the best price! *Small* amounts of paint or paper labels etc. are harmless and will burn off in the furnace, but aluminium bonded to vinyl or other plastic is unsuitable.

The aluminium is then graded to: clean heavy, dirty, foil and other thin material such as cans and containers. Small quantities of the latter can be mixed in among the clean heavy without the price dropping.

Manufacture of ingots

Your market for aluminium scrap can be improved by casting your own ingots. A furnace is needed with a sloping hearth (Fig. 40) capable of reaching temperatures 200 – 300°C above that at which aluminium melts, 660°C. The aluminium will melt before any ferrous metals and will run down the furnace hearth into a holding well from which it may be poured into open sand moulds. The ferrous metals remain on the hearth, avoiding the need to remove them from the scrap beforehand, but low melting point contraries such as plastics must be removed.

Fig. 40 Furnace with a sloping hearth, suitable for aluminium and other non-ferrous metals. Note the oil burner on the right, the fire-brick lining to the furnace and door and the sloping well for the molten metal underneath. Photo: courtesy Chine Furnaces, U.K.

An aluminium foundry

Once you have successfully cast aluminium ingots, you may consider casting finished products. Their value will be far greater than that of the raw scrap. This is not, however, an easy process and some knowledge of foundry operations is vital. You will also need to establish that:

i) Markets exist for the product you are able to make with your skills and equipment.

ii) No other aluminium foundry in the same district is making these products or, if so, the market will support two manufacturers.

iii) You have access to equipment; fuel or power; skill in mechanical matters; some knowledge or advice on casting aluminium; and sufficient scrap material.

iv) You have the time and determination to work on a rewarding but difficult venture.

v) The product is not available locally, made from another material such as steel, stainless steel, aluminium sheet, enamelware, pottery, plastic etc. If so, will your product be cheaper, stronger, better or more beautiful, so that you can still achieve sufficient sales?

Products in cast aluminium

Here is a list of products that can be cast in aluminium:

Saucepans	Lids
Kettle spouts	Burners for stoves
Cooking pots	Car parts
Ladles	Door and window handles
Spoons and scoops	and fittings
Moulding boxes	Ventilators
Filters	Knife scabbards
Furniture fittings and	
handles	

Equipment for an aluminium foundry

Of the furnaces described in Chapter 2, the rotary, reverberatory or crucible may be used for aluminium. The Jamaican foundry shown in Fig. 41 uses a tiny oil-fired crucible furnace and, because the aluminium can be ladled out with a steel ladle, it does not need to tilt. The linings of furnaces used for melting aluminium should be made of bricks containing not less than

Fig. 41 Aluminium foundry. Note the oil-fired crucible furnace and the steel die (on the stool, right centre). The electric cables running across the floor are dangerous.

40% alumina. This is because it is preferable to melt the aluminium under a flux to prevent it oxidizing, and the fluxes used most, i.e. sodium chloride (common salt) with potassium chloride, attack brickwork without alumina.

The procedure for melting

   i) Sufficient metal is melted and fluxed in the furnace to cover the scrap as it is charged in.

  ii) Only when a sufficient pool of molten metal has formed under the flux can scrap be added more quickly. Do not cool the contents so much that they solidify again.

 iii) The aluminium may be blended at this stage, which involves adding various solid chemicals and gases: this is a complicated process and will not be discussed here. Refining should not be necessary before manufacturing the objects listed above, provided clean scrap is used. If products crack or develop other faults on casting or cooling, first check the purity of the scrap and only then seek specialist advice on refining.

iv) It is often necessary to stir or agitate the molten metal to speed up the melting of newly-added scrap and reduce fuel use.

It is possible to sand-cast aluminium in a manner similar to cast iron, but, as aluminium is often used to make smaller components in far larger numbers, it may be economic to use 'die-casting'. This replaces the sand mould with one of steel, accurately machined and expertly finished – the die. It opens to release the solidified casting and can be used thousands of times; some parts may wear, but they can be replaced. Like a foundry pattern, the die has to be expertly designed, so that the metal will flow, solidify and shrink correctly. Therefore dies can cost thousands of pounds. The Jamaican foundry obtained second-hand dies of common objects like saucepans and lids to save money. Friends or contacts in an industrialized country will be able to obtain second-hand dies (or other machinery) more easily and cheaply than they can be found in the Third World, and aid agencies may help, too.

CAUTION Some developing countries ban the import of second-hand machinery!

Metal dies require a special coating before use to prevent the casting sticking to the die. A fairly simple bone-meal type dressing may be used. Dies also need degassing – a tablet can normally be obtained from coating suppliers. The supplier of the die should be able to advise on both these matters.

The simplest process is 'gravity die-casting': the metal is ladled into the heated die and the only pressure is from its own weight. A more complicated but faster process uses a 'pressure die-caster' that forces the molten metal into the die, ejects the finished casting and closes the die ready for the next cycle. Use of a machine of this type will enable high rates of production to be achieved but will cost a large sum of money and create little employment. It has more complicated machinery to go wrong, requires a wide range of spare parts and may be out of use for long periods if parts cannot be obtained. Complex and costly dies are needed for each component. As with all complicated machinery, when considering its use, look carefully at your ability to maintain and repair before investing large sums of money. It is also important to examine the market for the product you plan to make. Will you be able to sell enough to 'amortize' the capital costs of the machine, or could you satisfy a limited local market by doubling your equipment for gravity die-casting, or running a night-shift using the same equipment?

ZINC

Zinc is a cheap, easily-cast material used for castings where strength is not important. It melts at 420°C so can be melted in the same type of furnace as that used for aluminium. It is widely used for galvanizing (protecting steel from rusting) and to make brasses (alloys of copper and zinc). Zinc casts fairly well and is widely used for 'die castings' but not all factories with die-casting machinery can use zinc scrap. Metal of high purity is required and is alloyed with carefully controlled additions of aluminium (and sometimes copper).

Products made from zinc include
- Parts for cars (especially door handles, brackets, casings for small gear boxes, carburettors etc); washing machines; refrigerators; slot machines and meters; radios and televisions; oil burners, and some printers' plates and type.

Because zinc is a weak metal, zinc castings often contain inserts of steel, to receive screws or bolts. These inserts must be removed before use and this can be done by the collector himself by shattering pieces with a hammer.

Dry cell torch batteries have a casing made from zinc, but it is rare for these to be recovered. It does happen in Cairo, however, both for the carbon electrode rod and the zinc casing which is cleaned of the acid paste with a suitable tool. Take care that the acid does not touch the skin, eyes or mouth!

Galvanizing is a process during which iron or steel objects are covered with a thin layer of zinc to protect them from rust. The process may result in dross, ash and other wastes that may be treated to recover the zinc.

Zinc can easily be melted in a furnace at 400°–500°C with a chloride flux, but the metal obtained may not be pure. Almost pure metal can be obtained by evaporating the metal in a controlled atmosphere and collecting the vapour in a condenser (a steel drum, cooled by water will do) from which it may be remelted and cast into ingots.

LEAD

Lead, like copper, is an easy material to recycle if only you can obtain enough of it. Its grey colour when oxidized, great density, softness and flexibility make it easy to identify. These same properties make it valuable, easy to store, transport and work into its final shape. Because it melts at a low temperature (325°C) no special furnace is needed and it is cast by any industry that uses it. Thus, the sources of lead scrap are also the markets into which you can sell it:

Car battery plates
Pipes for plumbing
Gutters and spouts for rainwater
Weights and counter-weights
Bearings of 'white metal' (lead and tin)
Lead covered cable

Solder
'Flashings' for roofs to make a watertight joint at a junction in the roof
Wine bottle tops and 'seals'
Printing metals
Furnace flue ducts

Melting lead

Although it is easy to melt, care is needed to ensure that as little lead scrap as possible is lost as fumes and dross. This can be achieved by using a flux and a reducing agent.

The scrap is first washed in a concentrated solution of sodium carbonate to remove sulphur and then smelted in a reverberatory furnace at 800–900°C, using coke as the reducing agent and a flux of soda ash, borax and fluorspar. Although at these temperatures metal losses are higher, a 5% loss is acceptable and recovery is made by:

(a) putting the fumes through a wet washer and recovering the sludge;

(b) adding this to the dross for recovery as above.

Dross can be skimmed off and saved for future treatment to recover the lead. This can be done in a reverberatory furnace by heating with caustic soda.

DANGER Lead is a poison and can cause fatal illnesses if you eat after handling it or breathe the fumes given off when melting lead. Any workshop handling molten lead should have hoods and extractor fans fitted and employees should wear effective face masks and have regular medical examinations.

107

It should *never* be taken home where, for example, small children may suck it.

RECOVERY OF SILVER FROM PHOTOGRAPHIC MATERIALS

The high value of silver, even in small amounts, makes this activity one of the most profitable covered in this book. A small hospital taking 100 X-rays a day could recover silver worth $ US 6,000 a year. However, a certain understanding of chemistry is necessary for this activity, so non-chemical readers will excuse a brief explanation of the *chemistry of photography*:

Black and white negative film is a thin sheet of transparent plastic covered, on one or both sides, with emulsion, a layer of silver bromide grains in gelatine. When acted upon by light, each grain decomposes to silver sulphide. The film is 'developed' by treatment with an alkaline solution of an organic reducing agent, (usually hydroquinone), called the developer. The developer converts the silver sulphide grains to metallic silver, while leaving unchanged those grains unaffected by light.

Fixing is the removal of the undeveloped grains of silver bromide by making them soluble in water and then washing thoroughly. The fixer is usually sodium thiosulphate (hypo) and the chemical reaction is:

$$AgBr + 2S_2O_3^{--} = Ag(S_2O_3)_2^{---} + Br^-$$

The soluble salt (that is washed away) is silver thiosulphate. The remaining photographic negative is thus darkest (i.e. it has the most silver) where the most light has fallen.

A positive print can be made by exposing print paper, likewise coated with silver bromide emulsion, to light that has passed through the negative and developing and fixing in the same way. The development of colour films is a far more complicated process but, in the end, a similar operation occurs; metallic silver, deposited in the developing process, is washed away, this time in a bleaching solution.

It will be evident that much (up to 80%) of the silver that was originally contained in the emulsion of the new, unexposed film is wasted in the process of developing, fixing and printing a photograph or an X-ray. Prices for silver move rapidly up and down but it is almost always worth recovering this material and it is also possible to recover the silver from unwanted photographs and X-rays.

First, methods will be described for reclaiming the silver from spent fixing solution and then the recovery from old film will be described. It is impossible to avoid the explanation being a little technical but the rewards, in terms of valuable silver recovered, should make it worthwhile!

RECOVERY OF SILVER FROM USED FIXER SOLUTION

Three methods will be described but there are many others.

1. *Electrolysis*

In this process, silver is removed by passage of an electric current. Ready-made equipment can be bought.

Home-made unit

Alternatively, a home-made unit can be simply constructed (Fig. 42). *The container* should be a large, good quality plastic bucket with a well-fitting lid. Holes are cut in the bucket for plastic inlet and outlet connectors to plastic hose, and in the lid for mounting a few simple electrical parts as follows:

Electrical circuit
- Rheostat (variable resistance) 0–10 ohms
- 3 amp fuse
- 5 amp on/off switch
- Ammeter, 0–3 amps. d.c. (direct current)
- Transformer/rectifier to reduce the mains electrical voltage (usually 120 volts or 230/240 volts a.c.) to 5 volts d.c.

Electrodes. The anodes are carbon or graphite rods mounted on an inner plastic lid so that they dip into the solution. The cathode is a pair of stainless steel sheets, curved into two cylinders and mounted. A strip of stainless steel connects them together and also to a single bolt through the bucket side which acts as the electric terminal. To remove the cathodes for scraping off silver, it is thus only necessary to remove one nut.

Operation

The bucket is filled with spent fixer solution until the cathode is completely covered. The lids are replaced (making sure the anodes and cathodes do not touch) and the current

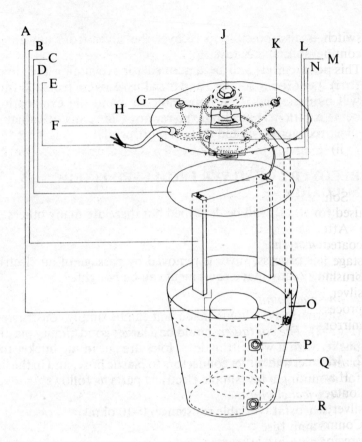

Key

A. Stainless steel cathodes
B. Graphite anode rods
C. Plastic lid
D. Stainless steel anode
   connecting strip
E. Mains input cable
F. Ammeter
G. Fuse
H. Plastic lid

J. Variable resistor
L. On-off switch
M. Connector to cathodes
N. Lead to anodes
O. Connector to cathodes
P. Hose outlet connection
Q. Plastic bucket
R. Hose inlet connection

*Fig. 42   Diagram of simple equipment for electrolytic recovery of
silver from photographic wastes*

Note: parts hidden by other parts are shown dotted

switched on. Silver metal is deposited on the cathode. This continues until all silver has been plated out of the solution. This point can be ascertained by either:

i) Dipping a bright copper coin or other object in the solution for a few moments. If it comes out silvered, the solution still contains silver. If not, the solution is exhausted, or

ii) Dipping in a special test paper strip which can be obtained from the companies listed at the end of the chapter.

Solution from which the silver has been removed can be re-used for fixing.

After several fillings of fixer solution the cathode will be coated with silver metal to a thickness of over 1 cm at which stage it should be removed. The silver can be recovered by brushing or scraping or by gently bending the cathode. The silver is 96% to 99% pure and can be sold without further processing to an electroplater, a jeweller, a manufacturer of mirrors or photographic materials or to a merchant.

2. *Metal exchange method*

If an active metal such as iron, zinc or aluminium comes into contact with a solution containing a less active metal such as silver, it will replace it in the solution and precipitate the silver. Commonly used are zinc dust, 350 grammes of which will precipitate all the silver from a 60 litre fixer tank in 24 hours. However, zinc dust can harm photographic materials, so it must only be used well away from the dark-room area. Other materials used are steel wool (as used for cleaning pots and saucepans) and aluminium chips, obtainable from a factory that machines aluminium.

Operation

The process can be done very simple as a batch operation by placing steel wool in a bucket, covering it with the spent fixer solution, and stirring for ten minutes. The mixture is left for 24 hours for the reaction to take place, then the solution is tested to see if any silver remains using the tests described above. If the solution is clear of silver, the liquid is carefully poured off to leave a sludge of silver which can be put in shallow pans and dried in the sun or in an oven. It is then packed in plastic containers and sent to a refinery for the pure silver to be

111

extracted. The solution cannot be re-used for photographic work as it now contains metal impurities.

3. *A continuous flow unit*

A simple unit can be made with two buckets, one larger than the other, and set up as shown in Fig. 43. The inner bucket is loosely packed with steel wool pads and stands on blocks about 4 cm high inside the outer which has a drain pipe fitted near the top.

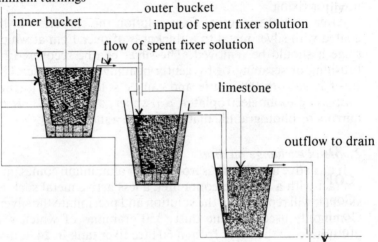

Fig. 43 Diagram of equipment for silver recovery by metal exchange method.

Operation

First, the unit is half-filled with spent fixer and pads are placed in the inner bucket so that the top pad is fully covered with solution. After a time, the pads become flattened and their level sinks: new ones should then be added with spent fixer keeping the pads covered all the time. Spent fixer can be added continuously and each new quantity will displace some clear solution through the drain. The liquid coming from the drain should be checked from time to time and, if it contains silver (usually after 1000 litres or more solution have been treated) the inner bucket should be removed, drained carefully and the mixture of silver sludge and squashed pads removed, dried and packed for sending to the refiner. New pads are put into the bucket and the process continues as before.

A slightly improved set-up can also be made using two units, identical to that described above, connected 'in series' so that the drain from the first is the input to the second. The drain to the second flows into a third which is filled with limestone (chalk or sea shells will do as well) and the drain from this flows directly into the municipal drains or into the soil. The object of the second unit is to recover any silver that may escape from the drain of the first when the pads are ready for replacement, and the object of the third unit is to neutralize the acid solution so that no polluting material is discharged into the public drains or the ground.

Aluminium chips or zinc dust may be used in the above system in place of steel wool but may need to be supported on a bed of steel wool layers. Steel wool is likely to be cheaper.

Comparison of the electrolytic and metal replacement systems

Advantages of the electrolytic system are:
   i) Silver is easily and cleanly removed.
  ii) It needs no further processing and can be sold for cash immediately.
 iii) The fixer solution can be re-used.
  iv) No problems of effluent (waste liquid) disposal.
   v) No raw materials need be stocked.

Disadvantages are:
   i) The silver can be easily stolen, although this can be overcome by padlocking the unit lid.
  ii) The cost of the equipment is higher and it is more complicated to set up.
 iii) Electric current is required.

Advantages of the metal replacement system are:
   i) Lower capital cost.
  ii) Simpler equipment which needs no electric supply.
 iii) Silver-bearing sludge is unlikely to be stolen.

Disadvantages are:
   i) It needs careful watching (although this becomes less

important if the two or three tank method is used).
ii) Removal of the pads is a messy process.
iii) The silver sludge has to be sent away for refining. The transport or postage cost may be high as iron, zinc etc. are included in the sludge.
iv) The fixer solution cannot be re-used.
v) Raw materials (pads and limestone) need to be kept in stock.
vi) The process must take place away from the developing area.

Use of silver borohydride

Although the two methods described above should serve most purposes, a third method is worth description because it is cheaper than electrolysis yet still produces silver that requires no further refining. Silver borohydride is a compound that will reduce silver salts according to the chemical equation:

$$8Ag^+ + BH_4^- + 2H_2O = 8Ag + BO_2^- + 8H^+$$

One kg of silver borohydride can produce 22 kg of silver. Equipment could be similar to, but on a smaller scale, than that described for metallic replacement. Check whether you can obtain the material in your locality before considering this process.

Recovery from developer solution

As was explained earlier, it is the fixer solution that removes the undeveloped grains of silver bromide (or, in the case of colour film, of metallic silver). However, it is likely that some silver will also be present in developer solution and also in washing waters. It is therefore recommended that these should be treated in a similar manner to that described for fixer.

Recovery of silver from unwanted film

As previously explained, a large part of the silver remains on the film as metallic silver grains in gelatine. This may also be profitably recovered when the film is no longer required. Although X-ray film, photographic negative, photographic prints and other papers may look different, they all have similar emulsion and the following should be collected wherever possible:
i) *X-ray plates from hospitals and clinics* These have emulsion on both sides of transparent acetate film and

may be very large (often 43×35 cm). A full troy* ounce of silver is contained on only 21 such new (undeveloped) plates and much of that amount may remain on the developed plate. Hospitals often throw out plates after a certain period of time to release storage space, so large numbers may be available.

ii) *Photographic negatives* from chemists, photographic shops that run a developing service, T.V. and film studios, government laboratories, universities, technical colleges etc. As more and more tourists and other amateurs take up photography it will also be possible to collect unwanted negatives from them.

iii) *Photographic prints* from the same places and, in addition, from cutting rooms in television and motion pictures studios where large quantities of film are discarded.

Burning

Unless good equipment is used this process can result in the loss of a large amount of silver. The film is chopped in a shredder, granulator or even by hand, and burnt in a small furnace. The problem is to prevent much of the silver-bearing ash disappearing up the chimney, so precipitators need to be fitted in the flue. These usually take the form of metal rods, charged with static electricity, so that ash clings to them. From time to time the rods are discharged and the ash removed and collected.

The ash from the hearth and the flue is smelted at a temperature of 700–1100°C with a mixture of sodium sulphate and sodium carbonate (not less than 20% of either) with air blowing through. The resulting metallic silver is impure and can either be refined by electrolysis or dissolved in concentrated nitric acid to yield silver nitrate for silvering mirrors, or in hydrogen cyanide for electroplating jewellery, silver tableware etc.

CAUTION There is a danger of explosion from silver nitrate in the presence of ammonium hydroxide. Such solutions should be treated with hydrochloric acid to precipitate silver chloride

---

*Silver is usually measured in Troy ounces: 1 Troy ounce = 31.1 grammes or about 1.1 Imperial ounces.

for recovery, and should be supervised by a competent chemist. Hydrogen cyanide is highly poisonous.

Enzyme treatment

If the enzyme can be obtained, then this is a much simpler operation than burning, with higher rates of silver recovery. An enzyme is a substance that will eat the gelatine that holds the silver grains, thus releasing them from the film or paper. Enzymes from animal stomachs, obtained from a slaughter-house, can be used.

The material is chopped, shredded or granulated and placed in a plastic or wooden vat or large bucket. Enzyme is added with water at about 25°C and the mixture stirred with a wooden paddle until it is apparent that the silver has been removed from the plastic film or backing paper to settle as a silver sludge at the bottom. The film and paper is removed by sieving and the solution filtered to recover the sludge which can be dried in the sun or an oven and sent away for refining, or recovered electrolytically if you have an electrolytic unit as described above. If enzymes are not available, hot water or bleach solution may be used instead to free the silver from the film.

Quantities of silver that can be recovered

The following are estimates and will depend on the efficiency of the recovery operation, the extent of exposure of the film, the type of film used etc. However, they may be used to calculate the profit that can be made from silver recovery. At the time of going to press the price of secondary silver is about US $ 7 per troy ounce; it is necessary to check the current price and to allow for variations when calculating the profits that can be made. In general, it can be said that silver recovery, in the manner described above, will always be profitable if enough material can be obtained for processing.

Other precious metals

Because of its high value, the goldsmithing industry recovers all waste that is economic. Precious metals may be found, sometimes in significant quantities in electronic scrap, but the process of identifying, separating and recovering these are complex and cannot be described here.

In Bangkok, the 'Klongs' or canals contain minute quantities of precious metals from lost jewellery, industrial waste

116

Table 5 Quantity of silver recovered per thousand x-ray films

Film Type	Film Size	Weight of Silver	
		Troy ounces	Grammes
X-ray plate	35cm × 43cm	25	780
X-ray plate	25cm × 30cm	12	370
Dental film	3cm × 4cm	0.35	11

Table 6 Quantity of silver recovered per tonne (1000 kilos) of film

Film Type	Weight of Silver	
	Troy Ounces	Grammes
Medical X-rays	225 to 320	7,000 to 10,000
Photographic Negatives	100 to 400	3,000 to 13,000
Photographic Prints	22 to 160	700 to 5,000
Motion Picture Negative	225 to 400	7,000 to 13,000
Motion Picture Prints	100 to 250	3,000 to 8,000

Table 7 Quantity of silver recovered from used fixer solution

How well used	Troy Ounces per gallon	Grammes per litre
Partly	0.06–0.24	0.5–2.0
Normally	0.5 –0.6	4–5
Fully	0.75–1.0	6–8

etc. A small group of Thai people 'pan' the black mud from these filthy waters to recover them. The hazards to health are great and the returns small and the practice is not recommended!

Equipment suppliers

Cable strippers
- G.L. Murphy Ltd., Imperial Works, Menston, LS29 6AA, W. Yorkshire, U.K.
- Metpro Machinery Ltd., North Road Industrial Estate, Bridgend, Mid Glamorgan, U.K.

Furnace for making aluminium ingots
- Chine Furnaces, Units 4 & 5, New Road, Newhaven, East Sussex, U.K.

117

Silver recovery equipment
- The X-Rite Company, 4101 Roger B. Chaffee Drive, S.E. Grand Rapids, Michigan 49508, U.S.A.
- Photographic Silver Recovery Ltd., Saxon Way, Melbourn, Royston, Herts SG8 6DN, U.K.

Chapter 5. Plastics

THE FUTURE OF PLASTICS RECYCLING

In the industrialized world, vast quantities of plastics are produced from scarce petroleum, but very little recycling takes place. In the Third World, plastics are used much less and most are made from imported raw materials. Their use, however, is increasing rapidly and recycling is widely practised in some countries. A principal reason for this difference is one of quality standards. It is expensive and often impossible to recycle plastics in order to reproduce the qualities of the original material. Economic recycling processes produce material which is usually inferior and always different from the original. The products made from recycled plastic are equally inferior. In the industrialized countries, with complicated laws to protect buyers, and high quality goods to suit the rich, such products are unacceptable. In the Third World, short both of resources and of rich buyers, such products are not only tolerated, but are in greater demand than dearer products made from virgin (unused) materials. As the price of petroleum and its products rises, so do the prices of raw materials for plastics. Price increases of several hundred per cent have occurred over the past few years, reflecting the real future scarcities of energy sources and raw materials.

The purpose of these reflections, at the beginning of a practical chapter, is to draw the reader's attention to the excellent future prospects for plastics recycling. As petroleum becomes more and more expensive, prices for *clean*, *well-sorted* plastics waste will rise, and the number of firms willing to buy it will increase. No material holds better prospects for creating employment; but only if it is approached with the word *quality* uppermost in the mind.

DIFFERENT KINDS OF PLASTICS

There is a difference between thermosets and thermoplastics.

119

Thermosets are plastics that are mixed and moulded to the desired shape and then heated to fix that shape. This process cannot be reversed and these materials cannot be recycled (except by grinding them to powder to use as a filler, but there are cheaper and more suitable materials for this purpose). Common thermosets are: phenol formaldehyde and urea formaldehyde, used for making electrical fittings, and plastic laminates such as 'Formica' for furniture and 'Melamine' for crockery.

Thermoplastics, however, once they are moulded, can be used for any length of time and then heated to change their shape. There are hundreds in common use and new ones are constantly being developed. However, three 'polymers' are most commonly recycled and others will only be discussed so that they can be identified. The three are: polyethylene, polypropylene and polyvinyl chloride (PVC). In addition, urethanes, both rigid and flexible, are very easy to recycle and the end product (and the cuttings) have many uses, for example, as cushion and pillow filling and insulation.

1. *Polyethylene*

This is commonly called polythene and is the most widely-used plastic in the world. It is soft, flexible, waterproof, easily moulded and easily coloured. Although it is not cheap, it can be drawn into extremely thin sheets and sections to produce low cost products. A refuse sack made of jute costs about ten times and weighs about thirty times a sack made of polyethylene. The latter is much weaker but will be disposed of after one use so this should not matter. Polyethylene has two common forms: high density and low density. When produced as film (very thin sheet used to make sacks and bags) high density polyethylene is stronger, harder and crackles in the hand if crumpled. Low density material is almost silent; it is soft and stretches more when torn. The importance of knowing this difference is that the two cannot be mixed in production and wastes must therefore be separated if they are to be sold to a factory.

Low Density Polyethylene is used to make:
- Thin film products: sacks, bags, sheeting, cheap waterproof clothing.

- Food and drink containers, squeeze bottles, bowls, buckets.
- Flexible piping.
- Flexible moulded parts for cars, bicycles, domestic appliances etc.
- 'Jerrycans' and water containers, drums for liquids.
- Childrens toys, sports goods, some cheap shoes.

High density polyethylene is used in the production of:
- Film for sacks, bags and sheeting
- Bottles
- Bottle crates and many other items.

2. *Polypropylene*

This is a very strong, flexible plastic, a little harder and more expensive than polyethylene. It is used to make furniture of high durability (lasting a long time), string and rope, often in bright colours, and moulded parts where strength is important, such as car battery cases. Material woven from fine polypropylene tape has largely replaced jute in the manufacture of sacks, bales, carpet backings etc.

3. *PVC*

It is cheap, easily moulded, has reasonable resistance to wear and is often bonded to textiles or other materials. It is used for children's balls and other toys; pipes (both flexible and rigid); ladies handbags; suitcases and other luggage; plastic-covered textiles and clothing; transparent bottles of very clear quality (used for shampoos, soft drinks, etc. where appearance improves sales); electric cable insulated covering; transparent packaging: shrink wrap (a highly stretched plastic bubble over goods for sale).

Identification of Polymers

The following simple tests will distinguish most of the common polymers so that they may be separated before sale.

Water test. Add a couple of drops of detergent (washing powder or liquid) to the water, then drop in a small chip of the plastic. Does it sink or float?

Burning test. Hold a small piece in tweezers, pliers, or on the

121

blade of a knife to the edge of a flame. Does it burn? If so, what colour?

CAUTION Burning material may drip and give off poisonous fumes. Use a small sample and hold away from the body and feet.

Fingernail test. Can it be scratched with a fingernail?

Table 8 Identification of Polymers
(This includes two more fairly common plastics – polystyrene and cellulose acetate)

Test	Polyethylene	Polypropylene	PVC	Polystyrene	Cellulose acetate
Water	Floats	Floats	Sinks	Sinks	Sinks
Burning	Blue flame with yellow tip, melts and drips	Yellow flame with blue base.	Yellow, sooty smoke. Does not continue to burn if removed from flame	Yellow sooty flame, drips.	Burns like wood or paper
Smell	Like candle wax	Like candle wax, less strong than polyethylene	Hydrochloric acid	Sweet	Like burnt wood or paper
Scratches with finger nails	Yes	No	No	No	No

N.B. To confirm PVC, touch the sample with a red hot copper wire and hold the wire to the flame. A green flame from the presence of chlorine confirms it is PVC.

Problems of recycling plastics

If plastics could, like metals, be melted down and remoulded, recycling would be much simpler. Instead:
  i) Products often contain parts made from two or more different polymers, sometimes strongly bonded together, or to metal or textiles. The temperature at which different polymers melt and flow in a mould or die is not the same, so they cannot be moulded together and must be separated before recycling.
 ii) Coloured plastics can only be recycled into certain other colours.

122

iii) Used products may be dirty, especially if they have been put among other refuse. Oil may affect the chemical behaviour and grit may block moulding machinery.

iv) The physical properties (strength, flexibility, density, transparency, etc.) of recycled polymers are often different from those of virgin material. Recycled plastic may become brittle on the surface if exposed to 'ultra-violet' light, so care must be taken when using recycled material in agriculture, for example. Plastic irrigation hose from recycled material is cheap, but should be buried or covered with earth.

COLLECTION OF WASTE PLASTICS

Before beginning a collection of waste plastics it is important to study the market and find out:

i) Which plastics are used by manufacturers, both locally and elsewhere?

ii) Do these manufacturers use reclaimed material and, if not, would they use it if good quality material was offered?

iii) What price will they pay and for what degrees of cleanliness?

iv) What will transport cost if the user is far away?

v) Are there any types, or quantities of material that they cannot take?

It is a good plan to do a small survey of the plastic waste that arises in the district; especially from factories, markets and other large users. A visit to the local municipal refuse dump will be very informative. Look for a plentiful supply of plastics *for which there is a market*, then find out the main sources of these materials and a suitable means of collection. Suppose, for example, that the best market is for PVC for the manufacture of drainage pipes, and that any colour is acceptable. If the rubbish tip contains large numbers of broken ladies handbags, and a local factory strips PVC insulation from cable ends when manufacturing electrical goods, you could run: a once-a-month, house-to-house collection of handbags, and a more regular collection from the electrical factory.

The following methods of collection may be considered:
- House-to-house collection combined with other materials (e.g. paper).

- House-to-house collection of plastics only, but of all types of polymer.
- House-to-house collection of certain objects only, e.g. handbags and luggage.
- Collection at a central point, e.g. a church or market.
- Collection from street boys in return for payment at the door.
- Regular collections from shops, factories, hotels, etc.
- Purchase from scavengers on the municipal refuse dump.
- Scavenging or collecting oneself.
- Methods of collection, types of cart etc. are the same as for paper (Chapters 1 and 13).

PROCESSING OF WASTE PLASTIC

There are many processes but the most common is a process applied to polyethylene film in many countries:

i) *Sorting and dry cleaning* The material is sorted as follows:
   a) Other materials, for example, shoebuckles, bag handles and catches, canvas shoe uppers, stones, metals etc. are removed.
   b) Other plastics are rejected.
   c) Polythene other than film is rejected (bottles, pipes etc).
   d) Dirt and dust is shaken out.

ii) *Washing.* This is only done if necessary. The water need not be pure, and the material can be dried in the sun and wind, often on a line.

iii) *Baling.* As with paper, this is only done if transport over a long distance justifies it, or if the buyer is willing to pay more for baled material. The methods of baling plastic film are the same as for paper.

iv) *Granulating.* The film is chopped into tiny pieces in a machine called a 'granulator', a drum with a knife at the bottom, passing close over two fixed blades. The bottom consists of strong mesh of the size of material required. Material which is too large to fall through the mesh remains above it until cut into small enough pieces (Fig. 44). A small granulator of about 4 kilowatts can process 100 kg of material per hour, while one of 19 kW can handle 500 kg per hour, large enough for most needs.

Fig. 44 Plastics granulator: close-up of blade of horizontal axis machine. The blades are each held by four bolts and can be adjusted after sharpening as the bolt holes are slotted. There is a fixed blade at the bottom and, below it, a grid through which material falls once its size is small enough. Note the guard over the pulley and drive belt — a wise safety device. India.

Fig. 45 Crumbed plastic film waste. India.

125

v) *Crumbing*. This may be done at the same time as granulating by using a special machine called a crumber, or separately, or omitted altogether. It entails granulating the material rapidly so that its temperature rises and then, when it is just above melting point, introducing a jet of water to cool it rapidly. As a result, the small flakes of granulated film become a coarse, uneven crumb (Fig. 45). Crumbed material is denser and easier to extrude.

vi) *Pelletizing*. This requires an 'extruder' with a special die, a water bath and a chopper. The extruder (Fig. 46) consists of:

- A hopper to hold the material fed in.
- A barrel, often heated with electric elements, although this may only be necessary on starting. Later, friction generates heat and cooling may be needed.
- A screw that rotates in the barrel, drives material (fed by gravity from the hopper) to the other end, and generates heat by friction to melt the material.
- A slow-moving screen or sieve through which the plastic passes to remove grit etc.
- A die: a flat, thick, steel plate with shaped holes through which the molten plastic is forced, coming out of the other side like toothpaste from a tube. If, for example, the die is T-shaped, then the plastic will emerge in a long strip with a T cross-section. For recycling, the die has a number of small holes, about 3 mm dia., through which the plastic is extruded out in a bunch of long strips (sometimes called spaghetti). These pass through a water-bath several feet in length (where water continually flows to prevent the temperature rising) and are cooled to become solid. A pair of feed rollers keeps them moving forwards through:
- A pelletizer which is a sharp edged, multi-bladed rotating knife, which chops the spaghetti into small pellets. Its speed is set to match the speed of feed rollers (which match the speed of the extruder) to give a pellet length of about 4mm. An alternative arrangement mounts a chopper on the back face of the die, so the material is chopped while still soft as it

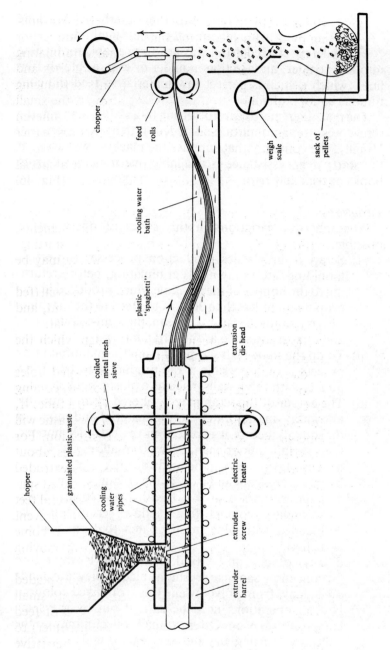

Fig. 46 Diagram of process for extruding and pelletizing plastic waste.

chopper

feed rolls

weigh scale

sack of pellets

cooling water bath

plastic "spaghetti"

extrusion die head

coiled metal mesh sieve

granulated plastic waste

hopper

cooling water pipes

electric heater

extruder screw

extruder barrel

emerges, then falls into the waterbath. Machine suppliers will recommend the best method.

The pellets produced in this way are now suitable for feeding into an extruder, an injection moulder or even a 'blown film line', which demands perfect raw material to feed the continuous balloon of film.

The machinery needs careful setting by a skilled man e.g. the screw pressure, amount of heat added, rate of extrusion, etc. Usually, the company that supplies the machine will assist at the start; if no assistance is available one must work from books or trial and error.

Variations

A number of variations in this series of operations is possible:

i) Scrap from plastics production processes ('injection moulding' etc.) only needs granulating, before returning to the hopper of the machine which produced it, in a proportion of less than 30% of the feed to the machine. This is possible because it is clean, the right colour, pure, and almost the same as the virgin material.

ii) To do the same with scrap *not* from the manufacturing process is only possible if the product is to be of low quality with thick walls, such as a plastic bucket.

iii) The colour of the scrap may be altered by adding a dye known as 'master batch' to the material and mixing it thoroughly before it is placed in the extruder hopper. Only certain colour changes can be made e.g.

a existing colours can be made deeper;

b white or clear can be dyed any colour;

c light colours can be blended to form darker secondary colours (e.g. yellow scrap could be blended with blue master batch to form a green pellet);

d any colours can be dyed black. (This is why refuse collection sacks are usually black; they are made cheaply from polyethylene waste of mixed colours.)

iv) Not all operations need be carried out by the same company or person. Often, a small collector may do the collection, sorting, dry and wet cleaning and removal of non-plastics and sell to a factory who, with their greater technical skills, will separate the different polymers and

granulate, extrude and make pellets which they will sell
to a variety of customers. However, a collector will get
better prices if he can do these operations himself.

Recycling of material other than film There are few differences
except that:
   i) Large rigid objects such as jerrycans or car battery cases
      may need to be cut up before they will go inside the
      granulator drum. A band-saw is the best machine for
      this but a hatchet can also be used.
   ii) A more powerful granulator may be needed.

OTHER PLASTICS RECYCLING PROCESSES

The basic process described is the only one that has achieved
regular commercial success; even then it becomes uneconomic
in industrialized countries with high labour costs whenever the
price of virgin polymer falls. In the Third World the process
seems to have been economically stable, because those with no
alternative employment have preferred to continue it for low
rewards than to have no livelihood at all. There are two other
processes used in industrialized countries that may be economic: cable stripping and moulding of mixed plastic scrap.

Cable stripping
This is really part of the process of recycling copper and is
described on p. 98. PVC cable sheathing is of widely varied
colours but is suitable for the production of dark grey, brown
or black pellets for manufacture of drainage pipes etc.

Moulding of mixed plastic waste – a high cost technology
Some machines use a mixture of all types of plastic wastes in
the manufacture of large, solid objects that do not require
good appearance or strength. The most advanced unit is the
Reverzer machine made by Mitsubishi of Japan. The machine
has been used for making cable drums, pallets for fork-lift
trucks, grids for pig pens and other items as shown in Fig. 47.
   The Reverzer concept could be useful in Third World countries that have sufficient technicians to operate it successfully
because:
   i) It produces agricultural products at lower cost than
      timber, and timber is scarce in many countries;

Fig. 47 Products from the Reverzer machine: drain pipe, gulley, post, fence post and stake, all made from mixed plastic waste.

   ii) It uses plastic, one of the worst causes of litter, river pollution and blockages of irrigation canals;

  iii) It has a huge appetite for material: one Reverzer machine could provide employment for an army of small waste collectors; and

  iv) It is supposed to accept lower quality plastic waste, leaving the higher purity material to be repelletized.

In its present form it is not recommended because of the huge capital cost and reportedly poor operating reliability and economics. The concept, however, is suitable for development in a cheapened, simplified, reliable version, using manpower rather than machines wherever possible, and such a unit might have wide application in the Third World.

Other machines have been designed to produce flat building panels. However, plastic suffers from very poor fire-resistance and is not generally regarded as a safe material for house construction, so these panels may be restricted to agricultural use. In conclusion, it is important to emphasize that the recycling of mixed plastics has not yet proved to be a viable project in Third World countries.

RE-USE OF PLASTIC ITEMS

The following examples have been seen:

130

Polyethylene sheeting is used widely for roofs and walls of shanty houses. It is cheap, widely obtainable, easy to fix, waterproof (but only if free from holes) and windproof. Its disadvantages are that it is ugly, tears easily and so ceases to be waterproof and cannot resist strong winds. The very poor sometimes use it for clothing, for which it is totally unsuitable, but better than nakedness.

Polyethylene bottles are cut to make drinking mugs; drums and containers are used, whole or cut, for carrying water and other liquids. These are cheap and plentiful but may be contaminated with dirt or previous contents (possibly poisonous) and may melt or dissolve with heat or when used to hold certain chemicals.

Polyethylene bags are, in some cities, washed (often in river or even sewer water), dried and used for food. This practice is a serious danger to health.

Expanded polystyrene foam containers make useful plant pots, seed boxes, tool boxes etc. (Fig. 48). Chopped foam is an excellent sound and heat insulator but there is a dangerous fire risk if used in housing.

Fig. 48   Tool box made from polystyrene packaging. Thailand.

Equipment suppliers

Granulators and plastics machinery
- Plasplant Machinery Ltd., Bordon Trading Estate, Oakhanger Road, Bordon, Hants, GU35 9HH, U.K.
- Maheshwari Plastic Engineering Works, 88/1 Dudheshwari Road, Opp. E.S.I.S. Hospital, Ahmedabad, India.
- STD Plastics Machinery Ltd., 19 West Walk, Yale, Bristol, BS17 4AX, U.K.

Plastics Extruders
- R.H. Windser (India) Ltd., Plot E, 6U Road, Thana Industrial Estate, Thana, Maharashtra, India.

Reverzer
- Rehsif S.A., P.O. Box 508, CH-1213, Petit-Lancy 1, Switzerland.

Chapter 6. Textiles

To study the various processes for recycling textiles, it is important to understand how they are made and some of the different fibres used to make them.

TEXTILE FIBRES

These are flexible, hair-like objects, very small in diameter (thin) compared with their length, which may vary from a centimetre to more than sixty centimetres. They come from many different sources; the most important for us are:

1. *Natural fibres* which grow or occur in nature:
   i) *Vegetable fibres* – cotton, for making cotton cloth
      – flax, for making linen, a very fine cloth.
      – jute, sisal, hemp, for making sacking, ropes, carpet backing etc.
   ii) *Animal fibres* – sheeps wool, for making wool and worsted cloth and knitting yarns
      – special wools, like alpacca and mohair, for finest woollen cloths.
      – silk, for making the finest of all natural cloths.
      – hair, normally shorter than wool and mainly used as stuffing.
   iii) *Mineral fibres* – asbestos, used for fire prevention purposes.

2. *Synthetic or man-made fibres (mmf)*
   – nylon, rayon, acetate, acrylic, polyester and other types used for making cloth. These use a variety of raw materials but particularly petroleum and cellulose.

Yarn is a continuous bunch of fibres, usually twisted, made by

133

'spinning' fibres, either by hand or by machine. The type and quality of yarn is determined partly by the nature of the fibre used, and partly by the way it has been spun.

Cloth is made by weaving. Yarn is threaded in one direction in and out of yarn running crosswise to it. Cloth character is likewise decided both by the yarn used (which may be different in the different directions) and the method of weaving. Processes other than weaving can be used, such as knitting or carpet weaving, to produce totally different products from similar yarn.

Garments are made by cutting cloth to pattern shapes and sewing pieces together using fine sewing yarn, of cotton or synthetic fibre. Other objects such as blankets, sacks, boat sails or furniture covers are made in a similar fashion.

Fibre, yarn, cloth and garment are together all known as textiles; all begin with fibre and the basic processes of reclaiming textiles involve turning them back to fibre. At each stage of manufacture of textiles, wastes are created that can be collected and recycled.

The textile industry consists of three types of organization:

i) The handicraft or hand operators who may do any or all of the operations above, from fibre to garment.

ii) The individual workshop or factory that either spins, weaves or makes up garments.

iii) The 'integrated' factory which does several operations all under one roof e.g. spins, weaves and makes blankets.

Any of these may be a market for reclaimed textile material, so may other kinds of factory outside the textile industry.

TYPES OF TEXTILE WASTE AND THEIR USES

Soft wastes do not contain twisted fibre. They include:

Carding waste. Carding is one of the first operations on raw natural fibre. Wire brushes (the cards) are passed through the fibre to disentangle knots, remove foreign matter such as 'burrs', wood, dust, etc., and lay the fibre in a uniform bunch. The material removed during the carding process also includes some very short fibres which have a value as stuffing for pillows, mattresses, cushions, children's toys, and furniture. It may be necessary to remove hard pieces by hand sorting or by machinery such as a fan and cyclone – a box in the shape of one cone on top of another which allows the separation of material from more solid material (Fig. 49).

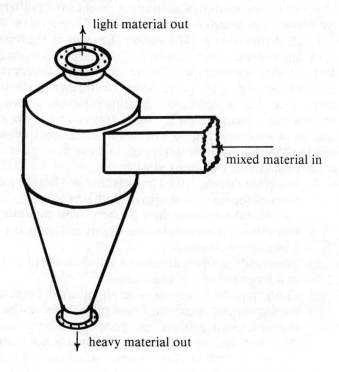

Fig. 49   A cyclone.

Comber waste or 'noils'. Worsted, the pure woollen cloth used to make men's suits, is spun from fibre that has been combed parallel. Only long fibres are suitable: short ones do not remain parallel and are removed during combing. They are called noils and are used in spinning woollen yarn, where the direction of the fibres does not matter. The buying and selling of noils is arranged within the industry.

Finishing waste or 'raisings'. Cloth may be sheared to give a uniform 'pile' or other processes may be used. These produce very short pieces of fibre known as raisings, which are uniform, soft and free from the hard foreign matter found in carding waste. They are suitable for stuffing the very softest pillows or mattresses.

Hard wastes are pieces of yarn from spinning and weaving operations. Before they can be respun the twist must be removed by garnetting. A garnetting machine has rollers and cylinders covered with saw-like teeth which separate the fibres and pull them straight. The tighter the twist in the yarn the more rollers are needed; some machines have four main cylinders and sixty smaller rollers. Such complex machinery is only justified for large-scale production. No further space will be devoted to this specialized recycling operation except to observe that, *whatever* waste comes from a textile operation (and there are others not covered here), someone, somewhere has developed a machine to recover and use it.

Woven material is only wasted when:

i) The colour of cloth on a loom is changed but the pattern remains the same. A length of cloth is produced in which the old colour blends into the new. This may often be very attractive and there is rarely any difficulty in selling it to mill employees.

ii) Salesmen's samples are discarded when the production of a given pattern of cloth ceases.

iii) Cloth may be faulty as a result of error or machine breakdown. It is rare for woven material to become available to an outsider, except at a strictly commercial price, but churches, charities or voluntary groups whose supporters include textile industrialists should keep an eye open for this readily usable or saleable waste.

Garment trimmings, also known as tailors' cuttings or new rags are the small strips and triangles discarded when a tailor cuts a pattern from a length of cloth. Cutting is often done using mechanical knives on thick stacks of cloth and the trimmings may occur in substantial quantities of the same kind of material, of known fibre and even the same colour. This can make them a most valuable material *if* a market exists.

Old rags such as used clothing, blankets, household linen etc. are often thrown away. They are inferior to new rags because different types of cloth and fibre may be mixed together, or combined with non-textiles (e.g. rubber coating to keep out rain) and the rags may have buttons, buckles, zip fasteners, and may be dirty. However, they occur in large volume in some countries and contain large pieces of cloth (Fig. 50).

Fig. 50   Roadside heap of tailor's trimmings, typical of countries where no reclaimed textile industry exists.

MARKETS FOR RAGS

Rags, new and old, can be sold to a variety of markets which are listed here in order of value in some ideal country where they all exist. In practice, the trader in a developing country will find that many of the markets do not exist and he will have to adjust his selling accordingly. This is why it is important to understand the industry, not just to know the techniques of reclamation. The skill of trading in rags is to sell each rag into the market that can pay the best price for it.

Knitted garments sometimes known as 'knits' or 'berlins' or 'comforters' are the most valuable type of rag. They are sold to an industry that opens or pulls (tears) them back to the fibres from which they were originally spun, known as shoddy or regenerated fibres. Shoddy can be spun into new yarn, either on its own or mixed with virgin fibre. If the garment was originally made of pure wool, the shoddy will have the characteristics of new wool and be cheaper. To spin, weave and tailor a

137

garment from it can be a profitable business. If it contains synthetic fibres, often used to strengthen pure wool or cotton, and if the exact nature of those fibres is unknown, there may be problems in manufacture or the qualities of the finished garment may be different. Thus it is pure, natural fibres that are most widely sought and fetch the best price.

White knits are more valuable than coloured because the shoddy can be dyed any colour.

Coloured woollen knitted garments are next in value. They must be sorted into different shades of each colour as they will be purchased with the colour of the end product in mind to save dyeing costs. There may be as many as twenty or thirty different shades of each colour.

White wipers (wiping cloths). Next in value come cloths woven from absorbent natural fibre (usually cotton, occasionally linen) that can be used as wipers in industry. The white ones are again the most valuable because they can be used in food processing and other situations where hygiene is important.

Coloured (cotton) wipers can be sold to industries such as engineering or motor repair where it is most important that the wipers really do absorb oil and grease. A process to make absorbent wipers from synthetic fibre has been developed in Hungary but is still secret.

Wadding. Only knitted woollen garments make good shoddy. Woven garments, especially those made from worsted yarn, are so tightly spun and woven that the process of pulling damages fibres and makes them too short to spin. Such garments are pulled, but the resulting material is used to make wadding for filling furniture or mattresses, or 'needle-felt' for carpet underlay and other uses.

Knitted synthetics. Some synthetics look and behave very like wool; for example, acrylic. When pulled, these form the basis of low-cost fashion fabrics of brightly coloured designs which are difficult to dye uniformly as the various ingredients have different properties of dye absorption.

Synthetic wipers. The lowest quality of wipers are made from thin woven synthetics, and although not absorbent they can be used, for example, to wipe hands clean.

Roofing felt is a thin, flexible, 'bituminous' felt, sold in rolls to make waterproof roofs, or as a lining to tile roofs. A low-quality type can be made from paper as described in Chapter 1, but the best quality is made using shredded and compressed rags soaked in bitumen. The lowest grades of rags, unsuitable for any of the uses already described, are used for this. Normally, roofing rags fetch a very low price, and in many countries they cannot be sold at all.

Re-use of garments and material. Before leaving the consideration of markets for rags, it is important to record the fact that rags fetch the best price if they are sold for re-use as garments, and the next best price if the material can be re-used to make new garments. Sacks fetch a good price if repaired and resold, as do bales and tarpaulins.

Comparative values of rag markets

To indicate how much higher a price can be obtained for certain types of rags than for others, here is a list of prices obtained in 1979 by Oxfam Wastesaver. It must be stressed that these figures apply *only* to the U.K. at that time; they are an indication of what the value can be *if* the markets exist, *if* the quality of supplies exist and *if* the principles described above are followed:

White woollen knits	2100 $ US per tonne
Coloured woollen knits	1000 $ US per tonne
White wipers (mainly cotton)	600 $ US per tonne
Coloured wipers	250 $ US per tonne
Heavy woven cloth	250 $ US per tonne
Knitted synthetics	150 $ US per tonne
Synthetic wipers	100 $ US per tonne
Roofing rags	30 $ US per tonne

Location of the reclaimed textile industry

Because prices for the best grades of material are so high, it is sometimes economic to ship baled, sorted rags around the world. The following is a guide to the principal locations of activity for anyone considering import or export of rags.

The main sources of rags are the industrialized countries with high standards of living: Europe, Australia, North America and Japan. Pure cotton rags for the highest quality wipers are to be found in rich cotton areas such as the southern states of the U.S.A.

The pulling of knitted goods for shoddy is widely practised in the industrialized countries, particularly Italy (Prato) and Britain (Yorkshire). It also occurs in those developing countries that have had long contacts with the British textile

139

industry (where it all began 200 years ago) such as India and Egypt.

The market for wipers exists wherever there is industry, but it may need to be awakened to manufacturers who have not purchased them in bulk before.

In the past, supplies of rags have not existed in developing countries where the poor accept or collect every cast-off garment, regardless of its condition. In many countries this is still the case. In others, while serious poverty may still exist, it is interspersed with pockets of wealth and a 'Western' consumer style of life. From these areas increasing supplies of rags are beginning to come, but at present they lie around as litter or end up on refuse dumps, because little awareness of their value exists. The best conditions for a trade to start in a developing country are:

- pure cotton goods produced locally and widely available;
- a growing middle class with a Western lifestyle (i.e. throw-away habits!);
- a large number of poor people who earn their living by collecting wastes;
- a growing industry with a demand for wiping cloths.

COLLECTION AND SORTING OF TEXTILE WASTE

Collection

Attempts to collect used clothing will succeed only in prosperous, middle and upper class housing areas. Some form of persuasion is usually necessary before householders will give away such materials instead of using them as cleaning rags or passing them to servants. One system which is quite effective is charity giving. If the collecting group is working to help the poor, sick, disabled or under-privileged, then many people willingly give away old clothing (and other used items). This works in Third World cities as well as in richer countries.

The following are necessary for successful collection:

i) A leaflet or letter should be sent to householders explaining the charitable work and how the rag collection helps. This should be delivered two or three days before the collection so that housewives have time to sort out suitable items.

ii) If some sort of sack can be obtained cheaply (e.g. commercial misprints) then it will be useful to include this

140

with the letter.

iii) Collectors must look tidy and reasonably well dressed. If they are ragged, it might be assumed that they will keep the best clothing for themselves! A printed badge or certificate pinned to the collector's jacket lapel helps remove any doubts.

iv) Collectors need a suitable cart or vehicle and the information included in Chapters 1 and 13 applies here.

Before holding a house-to-house collection of this sort it may be prudent to inform the police of your intentions to avoid any misunderstandings. Of course, you run the risk that the police may forbid the collection!

Sorting, storage and baling

A dry area where collected materials can be stored is vital as

Fig. 51 Baling of rags in a hessian wool bale. Note the method of hanging to hold the bale open and the double hook used at each corner to avoid straining the seams. Oxfam Wastesaver, U.K.

damp rags rot quickly. The collection is then sorted into the different types of rag already described: white and coloured woollens, wipers etc. Clothing to be resold or given to the poor should be set aside. If it is to be sold direct to the public it may fetch a better price if it is first cleaned, pressed with an iron and repaired, if necessary.

If you have a press it is worthwhile baling rags to reduce transport and storage costs. If not, it may be possible to obtain hessian or polypropylene bales of the type in which raw fibre is carried to the spinning mills. These can be hung from ropes (Fig. 51) and clothing sorted directly into them. When full, the bale is trodden to compress the contents before it is sewn up or stapled.

Depending on the market to which you are planning to sell you may stop handling the material at this point. Alternatively you may wish to process, partly or entirely, the material yourself; if no processing industry exists you will not have any choice.

Re-use without processing

Textiles can be re-used without processing. The following hand operations may be carried out by people with no skill or capital:

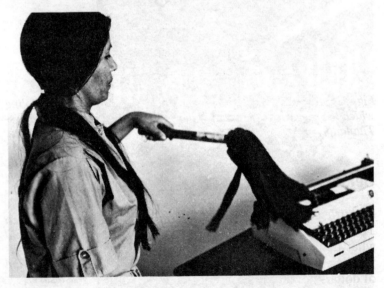

Fig. 52   Rag duster. Peru.

142

- manufacture of bags, rag dusters (Fig. 52) and similar objects;
- making cushions and stuffing with tiny pieces of plastic foam – flexible polyurethane;
- making dolls and stuffed toys: thoroughly wash material beforehand to safeguard children's health;
- sewing of clothing, patchwork etc;
- manufacture of rag rugs (Fig. 53); and
- making 'scarecrows'.

Fig. 53   Rag rug, the backing is a loose weave of canvas through which the rag strips are threaded in loops and then sheared off level. Thailand.

OPERATIONS INVOLVED IN RAG PROCESSING

Identification of textile fibres

To obtain best prices, the collector or sorter must know exactly what he is selling. A couple of acrylic sweaters in a bale of woollen knits will reduce the value of the woollens by hundreds of dollars per tonne. A number of tests to distinguish materials are possible and these will be described briefly. Several publications give a full and thorough explanation of these tests[1,2].

i) *Visual examination.* Some garments carry a label stating the material from which they are made. In general, natural fibres are softer to the touch than synthetics and their fibres do not have as brilliant a shine, although silk and mohair are exceptions, being famous for their lustre. Fibres longer than 20 cm are almost certainly synthetic. White wool is never the hard, bright 'starery' white of some synthetics.

Special wools can often be recognized by their natural colours: camel hair is usually fawn, mohair is a light golden yellow or white (but is frequently dyed), and alpaca may be white, grey or black, but brown is most common. Rabbit is sometimes spun into wool for children's knitted clothes and is very soft, smooth and usually in bright or light colours.

Knitted garments and coarse cloths for coats, cloaks, ponchos etc. are usually made from wool or its synthetic substitute, acrylic. Blankets are usually wool or cotton.

Thin cloth for shirts, summer or tropical dresses is either made of cotton, or the synthetic substitutes nylon, rayon, polyester, acetate etc. Very fine cloth is usually silk or nylon.

The variety of textiles is enormous and there will be many exceptions to all the above. A useful idea is to keep a stock of samples of known fibres, yarns and cloth with which to compare unknowns.

ii) *Burning* is the simplest test. Of the natural fibres animal yarns do not catch fire but shrivel with a smell like burnt horn. Linen and cotton burn easily, leaving an ash which turns to dust, and jute is similar. If they have been treated with resin, cellulose fibres burn more slowly. Pure silk burns slowly with a faint smell of cigars.

Of the synthetics, viscose burns quickly, smells like burning paper and burns away to dust. Acetates burn more slowly, giving off the smell of vinegar, and the fibres melt to small beads, which fall in drops when hot, and go hard when cold. Polyesters do not ignite but burn in the flame with a smoky yellow flame. 'Caseins' do not ignite and smell like burnt cheese. Polypropylene is difficult to ignite but, having done so, burns faint blue and melts. Nylon does not ignite, gives off no smell, but molten blobs fall away.

iii) *Microscope*. Even if you cannot hope to own a microscope yourself it may be possible to use one in a university laboratory, and to receive help with setting it up: many schools have microscopes, too. One cm and ½ cm objective lenses will be needed to examine individual fibres. The following descriptions should be read in conjunction with the diagrams in Fig. 54.

– Cotton is twisted as in (a).
– Wool has scales across the fibres and the edges stick out like a sawtooth (b).

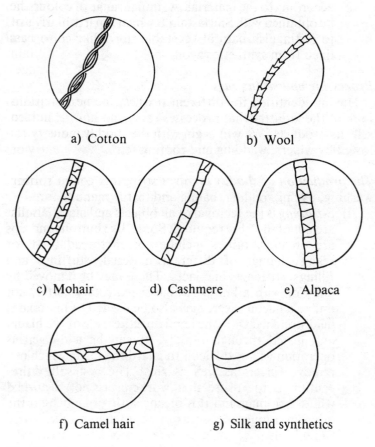

a) Cotton   b) Wool

c) Mohair   d) Cashmere   e) Alpaca

f) Camel hair   g) Silk and synthetics

Fig. 54   Textile fibres under a microscope.

- Mohair has scales but the edges are smooth (c).
- Cashmere, alpaca and camel hair are as in (d), (e) and (f).
- Silk is free from markings and looks like a flexible glass rod (g).
- Synthetic fibres are like silk, free from markings.

iv) *Staining tests*. Various types are available: one used in Britain is called Shirlastain. It can only be used effectively on white or bleached material which is first washed in water, then immersed and stirred in the stain for about a minute so that the dye penetrates, and lastly washed thoroughly in water again.

With Shirlastain A, different colours will appear according to the material. A similar range of colours can be obtained with Shirlastain B which is particularly used to distinguish natural vegetable fibres like cotton and linen from synthetic rayon.

Processing and selling rags

Having identified the different textiles, the next step is to look at the industry that processes rags, and how it, in turn, sells its products. We will begin with the shoddy industry followed by wipers, wadding and roofing felt.

The production of shoddy involves stripping, colour sorting, washing, dyeing, pulling, baling and textile manufacture.

i) *Stripping* is the removal of all objects and materials that are not of the fibre required. Some, like buttons and zips are obvious; others include cotton thread used for seams, linings of different material, stuffings and fillings, stiffeners and laces. These may be removed by hand or with a knife. A high-speed rotary cutter, not unlike a bacon slicer, may also be used. The material is held stretched with one hand on either side of the blade, and is fed through rapidly. It can be a dangerous operation as it is difficult to guard the blade which can remove fingers as well as zips! The best safety precaution is to ensure that workers are not disturbed whilst stripping and this means sitting one behind the other in a long line, so as to be unable to talk. There should also be regular rest periods to break the monotony.

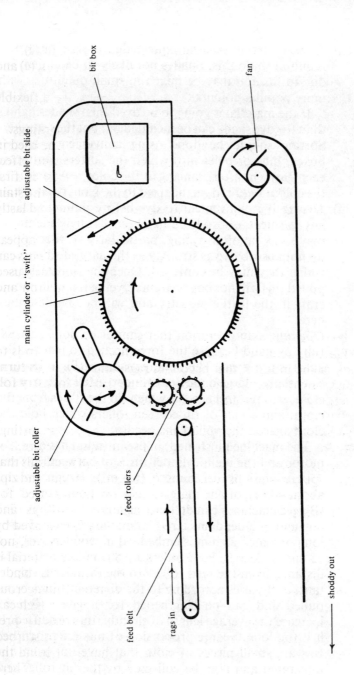

Labels on figure:
- bit box
- fan
- adjustable bit slide
- main cylinder or "swift"
- adjustable bit roller
- feed rollers
- feed belt
- rags in
- shoddy out

Fig. 55a   Diagrammatic view of rag pulling machine.

147

ii) *Colour sorting* A clear knowledge of the market is required to do this. Shades not likely to be in demand due to fashion may be mixed in small quantities with more popular colours.

If the material is going to be dyed then shades lighter than the dye shade can be included but not those darker. Sorting should be done using conveniently spaced boxes, bins or bales into which the sorters can throw each garment after glancing at the colour. A sample of the colour required can be fixed to the front of each bin.

iii) *Dyeing* It is convenient to dye before pulling because any garment whose fibre has been wrongly identified may show up after dyeing: particularly synthetics that do not absorb dye as strongly as the natural fibres with which they may be confused. Once the fibre has been pulled this will not be apparent. Dyeing is a well-known craft in the textile industry and will not be described here.

iv) *Opening* is an operation that cannot be done successfully by hand because the force needed to tear textiles apart is too great. The pulling machine (Figs. 55a-c) is essentially a large diameter cylinder fitted with rows of close, strong, steel needles which rip the fibres from the cloth, and a pair of fluted feed rollers which hold the cloth against the pull of the needles.

The machine illustrated, in use in India, has a 37 kW motor and the main cylinder turns at between 350 and 750 revolutions per minute (r.p.m.). It can process about 400 kg of any material in a 7½ hour work shift. (Bigger machines can do twice as much.) Width is 1055 mm and cylinder diameter 913 mm; the spikes are 50 mm long of which 25 mm is embedded in wooden slats and 25 mm sticks out. Feed rollers are 80 mm diameter. The distance from the feed rollers to the cylinder is important, as it varies according to the different fibres being pulled and can be lengthened for a given fibre to increase the average length of shoddy fibre produced. If it is too long, a large proportion of bits are produced. Bits are small pieces of cloth that have not been disintegrated and may be collected by the bit roller and dropped back on to the feed sheet to be fed again into the machine. Alternatively, they may be collected in the

Fig. 55b   The rag pulling machine is fed by loading rags on to the conveyor behind the man in the centre. Note that all moving parts are covered by guards. India.

Fig. 55c   View of the cylinder of the rag pulling machine, showing the input conveyor and upper feed roller. India.

bit box from where they are emptied from time to time.

The reduced material is sucked into a storage box by a fan, its quality is judged by the absence of bits, the length of the fibres, uniformity of texture, feel, appearance and freedom from foreign matter.

v) *Baling* is common practice for delivery to the customer and for storage. Cleanliness is important so the bale should be made with a cover of hessián or woven polypropylene sheeting. This is laid on the base of the baling press before loading begins and a second piece placed under the press platten before final pressure is applied. The two may be brought together tidily before wiring or tying the bale so that they are firmly wired in position.

vi) *Textile manufacture* Shoddy is an alternative to raw wool and therefore requires carding like any natural fibre before it is spun. It may be used alone or blended with virgin fibre in any proportions.

Production of wipers

This involves the operations of sorting, stripping, cutting, washing and drying, packing and marketing.

i) *Sorting.* If the wiper producer knows his customers and their business, he may be able to sell them a certain sort of wiper at a better price, or to persuade them to accept a grade that occurs in his supplies but for which there is no market elsewhere. This knowledge of customers will also decide the way in which he sorts: whether to separate light colours from dark, heavy cloth from light etc.

ii) *Stripping* of wipers is the same as for shoddy rags.

iii) *Cutting* may be done as part of the same operation as stripping. The stripped rag is cut into a number of rectangular pieces of convenient size – an area of 1000 square cm is a normal minimum with a width not less than 25 cm. For example, a shirt is stripped of buttons, collar and cuffs and cut into four or six pieces: each long sleeve is opened to make one wiper and, depending on shirt size, the back and front make one or two wipers each. Short sleeves are not big enough for a good grade of wiper but can form a lower grade.

iv) *Washing* is important in all countries, especially those with serious epidemic diseases as old clothing can serve as a disease carrier. To sterilize wipers, they should either be boiled, or washed in warm water containing detergent and dried in a steam drier at a temperature not less than 100°C.

v) *Packing* should be into bundles or bales of a size suited to the customer's business. A large car assembly plant will buy bales weighing 250 kilos but a small iron foundry will only want bags of, say, 25 kilos at a time. It is a good idea to have the package printed with your name and address, and a (truthful) slogan emphasizing the good quality and cleanliness of the product.

vi) *Marketing wipers*. Either send a letter to all factories in the district that might use wipers, or else visit them. Alternatively, sell through a company that already supplies some other industrial product like soap or roller towels, or cleaning fluids and solvents. They will do the selling work for you but remember that they will want a share of your profits!

Production of wadding

This involves stripping, washing, pulling, felting, needling, and rolling. The first two processes are the same as those used for wipers.

i) *Pulling* The machine for pulling must be far stronger than the shoddy-pulling machine as the 'feedstock' is woven and more tightly spun than woollen knits used for shoddy. However, the final product does not need to be as fine; bits that would have been rejected for shoddy are quite acceptable.

ii) *Felting* is spreading the pulled material on a flat bed and pressing it in uniform layers until the desired thickness is obtained. Machines may be used.

iii) *Needling* holds the felt together without thread and enables felts to be stacked without intermixing. Each layer is punctured with hundreds of saw-toothed needles, mounted on a board that moves up and down over the felt. Around 100–150 needles per cm width of felt are needed.

iv) *Rolling* is necessary to transport the felt to the user. It is a good idea to spread the felt on sheets of cheap, clean paper and roll it with the paper so as to prevent the layers of felt mixing. Pack the roll in polythene sheeting to

151

prevent dampness.
v) *Markets* include furniture makers, mattress makers, car seats, etc.

Manufacture of roofing felt

Roofing felt is manufactured from rags in a way very similar to that already described in Chapter 1 for manufacture from paper. The quality is superior, with a life of 20 or 30 years as compared to about five for asphalted paper roofing. However, the tendency in the industry is to use wood-pulp in preference to rags and, in view of the scarcity of rags in developing countries, it is unlikely that this will alter.

Manufacture of activated carbon

Activated carbon is used to absorb harmful gases, and for the purification of drinking water and other liquids. It is traditionally manufactured from coconut shells but can also be produced by carbonizing (burning in a limited supply of oxygen) textile wastes at temperatures of 200–250°C. The quality is slightly inferior to that made from coconut shells.

References

1. The annual handbook of the British trade journal, *Materials reclamation weekly*, P.O. Box 109, Davis House, 66 High Street, Croydon CR9 1QH, U.K.
2. *Identification of Textile Materials*, published by The Textile Institute, 10 Blackfriars Street, Manchester, M3 5DR, U.K.

Equipment suppliers

Pulling Machine
-   Alfred Briggs Sons & Co. Ltd., Caledonia Works, Gomersal, Cleck-heaton, W. Yorkshire, U.K.
-   Modella Woollens Ltd., 78 Veer Nariman Road, Bombay, 400 023, India.
-   Wilson Knowles and Sons, 6 Chapel Lane, Heckmondwike, W. Yorkshire, U.K.

Rag cutters
-   G.L. Murphy Ltd., Imperial Works, Menston, LS29 6AA, W. Yorkshire, U.K.
-   Eastman Machine Co. Ltd., 118 Curtain Road, London EC2A 3AP, U.K.

Shirlastain
-   The Shirley Institute, Didsbury, Manchester, U.K.

152

Chapter 7. Rubbers

In this chapter the reclamation and re-use of rubbers will be described. Although the former can be rather complicated technically, it is worth discussing because of the large amounts of rubber wasted in developing countries, especially in the form of old tyres. It is not widely practised for the reasons given below and also because some of the huge multi-national companies that dominate the world tyre-making industry also make big profits from their natural rubber plantations in West Africa and south east Asia. Rubber reclamation harms their commercial interest. The organization of a rubber reclamation project, perhaps at government level, could create many jobs.

The structure of rubbers
Rubbers may be either natural or synthetic. Natural rubber is made from the 'latex' (juice) of the rubber tree which grows in tropical countries. It is 'tapped' by cutting the bark through which the latex flows and is caught in a bowl: about 2½ kg per tree per year is obtained on average. The latex is dried and rolled: if dried in smoke, dark brown sheet rubber is produced; if air dried crepe rubber results, which has a lighter colour.

Raw rubber does not have the familiar elastic property of springing back to its original shape and size when stretched and released. This only happens if the rubber is 'vulcanized', a term which must be understood because of its effect on the possibilities of recycling. First, a simple explanation of the molecular structure of rubber.

A 'molecule' of raw rubber is so small that it can only be seen through the most powerful electronic microscope and yet is made up of about two thousand even smaller molecules connected together in a chain. These chains are very long and flexible, and there is nothing to resist them changing their shape. If, however, the long molecules of raw rubber are tied together or linked with molecules of another sort, in practice sulphur (or occasionally peroxide), the links resist flexing and the rubber tries to return to its original shape. This is vulcanization and it is done by mixing the raw rubber with sulphur and cooking it under pressure at about 150°C.

At the same time as sulphur, other substances are added, such as:
- carbon black to make it tough and resist rubbing away by rough or gritty surfaces;
- asbestos to help keep its friction properties at high temperature;
- oils to make it easier to work;
- paraffin to make it resistant to light;
- colourings;
- accelerators to speed up the vulcanization process; and
- chalk, silica, anti-oxidants, activators and a wide variety of substances (to improve particular characteristics).

Sponge rubber is made by foaming the liquid latex before vulcanizing it. Special hard rubbers are achieved by increasing the sulphur from the normal 1½-5% up to 15-30%. (The rubber molecules are more closely linked by adding more sulphur). Special shapes are moulded (such as shoe soles and heels, or motor tyres), or extruded (rubber pipes, hoses, window sealing strip) before vulcanization.

Synthetic rubbers are remarkably similar to natural rubber in their behaviour but they are made from chemicals, mostly obtained from petroleum. They can be mixed with additives and vulcanized in almost exactly the same way as natural rubber and, in addition, their properties can be varied by changing the way they are made. It is possible to mix natural and synthetic rubbers to combine the desirable properties of both.

Problems of reclaiming rubber

Once rubber is vulcanized, it is difficult to alter it chemically or physically. To reclaim used rubber products it is necessary to *'devulcanize'* them and *'revulcanize'* after a new product has been produced. The energy and equipment needed to achieve this are costly and this is one of the problems of rubber reclamation.

Secondly, we know that rubber goods are not all made from one substance, but from either natural or synthetic with widely varied mixtures of other things, each added to create some particular property (and, in the process, spoiling some other property). If, for example, rubber is hardened to make tough shoe soles this reduces its elasticity for use in elastic band manufacture. Reclamation involves using a variety of different rubbers, many of them from products that look almost identical, to produce a further product that may need quite different properties. This causes problems.

These are not too serious for the manufacture of low grade products treated gently in use, but it is characteristic of rubber products that they are harshly treated, like shoe soles and motor car tyres, and also that the consequences of their failure may be serious, like electric insulation or motor tyres again. Even if it does not cause serious failure, it will be annoying, be it a rubber band or water hose pipe! So, to use a rubber whose composition cannot be guaranteed is not popular with rubber goods manufacturers.

Reasons for reclaiming rubber

Why, then, reclaim rubber at all? There are a number of very good reasons:

  i) Its cost can be half that of natural or synthetic.
 ii) It has some properties that are better than those of virgin rubber; one tyre manufacturer uses up to 30% whole tyre reclaim in the side walls of certain motor tyres because it is better for coating the fabric with which the walls are reinforced.
iii) It requires less energy in the total production process than does virgin material.
 iv) It is an excellent way to dispose of used rubber objects which is often difficult. Burning rubber gives off clouds of black, polluting smoke and is forbidden in many countries. In a municipal refuse dump (or land-fill) rubber tyres cause problems because they do not rot, cannot be compressed and have a tendency to work their way to the surface if buried. On the surface they catch rain-water which cannot drain away and become breeding sites for mosquitoes. In mechanical refuse disposal plants, tyres resist baling, shredding or any other process. Also, tyres left lying around look ugly and spoil the environment.
  v) Finally, of course, reclaimed rubber conserves non-

renewable petroleum, which is used to make synthetic rubbers.

WHOLE TYRE RECLAIM

The reclaimator process – a high cost operation
Some half a dozen plants operate this process in various parts of the world. It differs from other processes in that it is entirely dry and only takes half an hour, compared with six hours for other methods. The operation is as follows:

i) *Examination*. Every incoming tyre is examined, and steel-reinforced, radial-ply tyres are discarded. Only tyres reinforced with textile are recovered. It is understood, however, that future developments will allow the acceptance of steel-reinforced tyres.

ii) *Cracking*. The tyres are broken into 1 cm pieces in a cracker, a powerful mill with thick, ribbed rolls. Any pieces over size are returned through the cracker, while small pieces fall through a 1 cm grid. Even the wire 'beads' at the rim are fragmented.

iii) *Separation*. Vibrating screens (trays of mesh of different sizes) separate the cracked material into:
   - small pieces of rubber which pass to the next stage.
   - pieces of rubber bonded to textile fibre which go to a mill that separates the fibre and returns the rubber to the next stage.
   - pieces of textile that are blown into a baling machine for separate disposal.

   The accepted rubber is further cleaned of textile fragments and passed under magnets to remove any bead wire.

iv) *Grinding*. The rubber pieces pass through corrugated grinders many times until they are reduced to 0.8 mm mesh (30 wires to the inch or 12 to the cm). They are then floated on blasts of air to separate any remaining metals, sand or stones, etc. that may have been stuck in the tyre treads.

v) *Reclaiming*. The rubber (now described as 'crumb') is mixed with special oils and heated, compressed and 'worked' for five minutes in the Reclaimator machine (Fig. 56). This is a screw extruder (rather like a large version of that described in Chapter 5) which devulca-

Fig. 56   Rubber reclaimator unit, illustrating the complexity of the process. Photo: courtesy United Reclaim Ltd. U.K.

nizes rubber at a temperature of about 200°C. The material emerges from the machine, is cooled by water sprays and mixed in a screw conveyor with minerals according to the customer's requirements. This is followed by further mixing in a hopper from which it is extruded through a die and cut into small pieces by a rotating knife.

vi) *Refining*. The pieces are passed through refining mills to ensure thorough blending, then extruded in thin sheets. These are cut, chalked on both sides and stacked for transport to the customer.

Advantages and disadvantages

It will be obvious from the description and photographs that this is a highly technical and expensive process needing equipment of great power, complexity and high capital cost. No organization without the necessary capital, a high degree of technical competence, and a core of well-trained technical staff would contemplate embarking on the process. However, the rubber companies themselves have these abilities and governments of Third World countries might well demand the use of a certain proportion of whole tyre reclaim in all tyres sold or made in the country.

Also, tyres used in developing countries need to be tough and sturdy to withstand poor roads and heavy loading, but may not undergo the long periods of high-speed motorway driving that makes such demands on tyres in rich countries. This opens up possibilities for a much-increased use of reclaimed rubber. It is unlikely that the rubber companies will allow this statement to go unchallenged and Governments will need their own advisers to ensure that standards of safety are maintained, but not used as reason for obstruction.

When considering the above, it should not be overlooked that small-scale shoemaking and repair may depend on the availability of used tyres. Rubber reclamation should not be allowed to absorb supplies needed for this essential purpose.

Reclaimator is not the only process available for reclaiming rubber from tyres or other sources; at least six different processes are in use.

An illustration of the possibilities of whole tyre reclamation in Third World countries is given by India, where twelve reclaiming units process about 24,000 tonnes of reclaim per annum. The largest has an output of 8,000 tonnes per annum. India produces 6½ million tyres per annum but, because of other uses for old tyres, there are not enough to reclaim, and attempts have been made to buy more from Europe, despite the very high shipping costs.

Uses of whole tyre reclaim

The following are typical: cycle tubes and tyres, automobile

158

tubes and tyres, battery containers, shoe soles and heels, extruded articles such as hoses. Dustbin lids use a specially cheap type of low quality reclaim with the textile left in. Up to 35% reclaim may be used in some applications with the same percentage of virgin rubber and a balance of other ingredients.

RETREADING TYRES AND USE OF TREAD CRUMB

This process is one of the most widely-applied reclamation (or, more correctly repair) operations in the world. The procedure is as follows:

i) The old tyre is carefully examined for damage to the sidewalls and the structure. In some countries more than half the tyres presented are rejected at this stage.

ii) The existing tread is removed by rasping. The tyre is mounted on a spindle and spun, while a rotating, rough-toothed cutter or rasp removes rubber to leave a flat (or slightly rounded) even surface, with a rough texture to which the new tread will bond securely. The dust or crumb produced by this operation is a valuable material; see below.

iii) New, uncured tread rubber, known as camelback, is then spirally wound on, and the tread markings cut. Alternatively, it is possible to lay a new, cut tread directly, in one layer, with a special bond at the joint.

iv) Finally, the completed tyre has to be revulcanized.

A serious problem is the large numbers of tyres that are rejected as unfit, due to holes in the fabric-reinforced substructure or weakness in the sidewall. Often, these are used by unscrupulous small retreaders, to produce tyres that appear sound but are a death trap to the buyer. The major retreading companies, anxious to preserve their reputation for quality, would perhaps co-operate in disposing of these damaged carcases, particularly if the process of refuse disposal was more efficient.

Often, the rubber companies provide machinery, know-how and publicity support in return for a contract to buy camelback from them. Because of the tough treatment it receives, and the difficulty of controlling the quality of retreading by semi-skilled small operators in widely dispersed workshops, with little technical supervision, camelback must have very good properties. It is carefully blended from 90% synthetic rubber, with 10% natural added to provide tack (the good 'adhesion' which is so important).

Tread crumb

The crumb that is rasped off the old tyre in the retreading process is a pure, 'homogeneous' rubber and therefore valuable. It can be used in the production of certain objects that do not require stiff quality standards. To demonstrate its use, the process of moulding rubber goods must be described:

i) *The 'formulation'*. The ingredients are blended according to the formulation, which is simply a list of materials and quantities, but is vitally important. Rubber producers supply a formulation to suit the needs of the rubber goods' manufacturer, devoting the high skills of rubber chemists and laboratory staff to get the best possible mixture. The manufacturer must make certain that the rubber company does not exploit this arrangement to increase sales of their product.

When selecting a formulation, the most important considerations for manufacturers of rubber moulded goods in Third World countries are:

a) Are all the ingredients obtainable in this country or nearby?

b) Can they only be obtained through one large rubber company, making us commercially dependent?

c) Does this formulation produce the quality of goods we require?

d) Can the overall cost be lowered further by:
- lowering the quality?
- using another company's material?
- using non-'proprietary' material?

ii) *Mixing* The ingredients have to be thoroughly mixed and this may be done on a large scale in a Banbury Mixer or with a smaller two roll mill. The material circulates round the mill for several minutes, with any lumps being broken down under the pressure of the rollers, and the ingredients are thoroughly mixed and devulcanized. Finally, they are discharged as a sheet of uniform thickness to suit the particular manufacturing process.

iii) *Manufacturing*. Rubber products can be made by the following processes:

Compression moulding. See below.

Transfer moulding, which is like compression moulding but the material is heated in a separate chamber and then forced down channels into the shaped moulds.

Injection moulding, which is a process similar to pressure die-casting, (described in Chapter 4).

Extrusion, which is similar to the extrusion of plastics, described in Chapter 5. The dies can be of various shapes to determine the cross-section of the product. As well as long, thin products such as hoses, sheets, sealing strips and mats, circular products such as solid cycle tyres and trolley wheels can be made from extruded material, with a single joint made with instant glue such as 'Loctite' and various cyano-acrylic adhesives.

Compression moulding is perhaps the simplest and can be used to make shoe soles and heels and a variety of saleable products, so will be described in some detail.

iv) *Compression moulding*. In this process the press has two functions: to apply pressure and to apply heat. Pressure is applied 'hydraulically', with a pump forcing oil into cylinders mounted between the press frame and the upper 'platten'. Rubber moulding presses usually have several plattens and a daylight gap between each (Fig. 57). Pairs of moulds, an upper and a lower, are inserted in each gap. The top platten is powered and the lower ones 'float' with each receiving pressure from the mould above it and passing it on to that below.

a) The pressure exerted by a rubber press may be as high as 200 tonnes, but for small operations on dense rubber, about 50 tonnes is sufficient. An hydraulic pump delivering oil pressure of about 100 kg. per sq. cm should be used on a 25 cm dia. press ram. For sponge rubber, much lower pressure is applied, and an hydraulic pressure of 28 kg per sq. cm should suffice. Heat is normally applied by steam. Each platten has steam pipes embedded in it and is connected to the single steam generator. The plattens are heated by the steam and the heat is conducted to the moulds. Electric heating is possible by an element buried in each platten: capital cost is less, running costs more.

b) The temperature required will be anything from

161

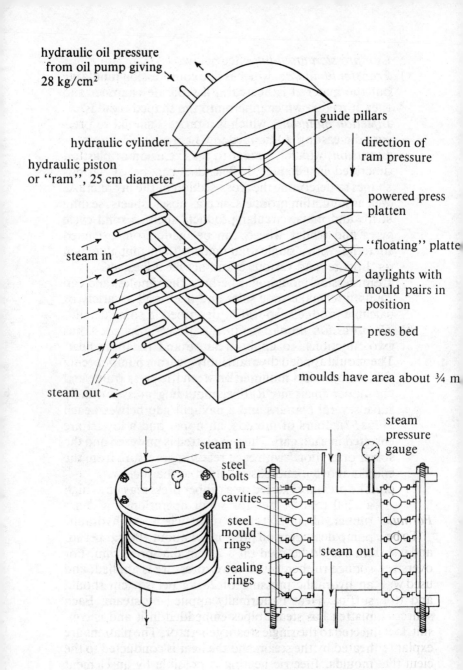

hydraulic oil pressure from oil pump giving 28 kg/cm²

guide pillars

hydraulic cylinder

direction of ram pressure

hydraulic piston or "ram", 25 cm diameter

powered press platten

steam in

"floating" platten

daylights with mould pairs in position

press bed

steam out

moulds have area about ¾ m

steam in

steam pressure gauge

steel bolts

cavities

steel mould rings

sealing rings

steam out

Fig. 57 Rubber presses.

162

100°C upwards and will depend on the formulation.

v) *The mould.* Each mould is in two halves, upper and lower. Each half has a flat side that fits against the platten and transmits heat and pressure uniformly, and a shaped side. The two shaped sides together form a mould cavity, the same shape as the object to be produced, but a little larger to allow for shrinkage as the rubber cools (about 0.016 cm per cm).

The material from which the moulds are made depends on the life required from the mould and the cost that is acceptable. Moulds made from hardened steel last almost indefinitely; those made from aluminium alloy are cheaper but wear more rapidly. White metal, (an alloy of 85% lead, 10% tin and 5% antimony) is soft and very easy to shape by hand, but can only be used for 250 mouldings, after which it must be melted and used to make fresh moulds.

vi) *The moulding operation.* The blended, mixed raw material is cut into a slab of about the same size as the mould. The mould is coated with a lubricant, such as soap, so that the moulded rubber will not stick to the mould, and the material is inserted. Pressure and heat are applied, for sufficient time for the rubber to vulcanize (often up to half an hour) and the doughy mass is converted into tough material. After removal of the pressed object, surplus rubber (flash) may remain at the edges and can be removed either by a hand-operated knife or in a press.

Formulation using tread crumb

To be useful for rubber moulding, crumb must be rather fine and it should be sieved in a sieve of about 0.8 mm mesh and the oversize material rejected. The amount of crumb that can be used will depend on the quality of product to be made. Tables 9 and 10 give a number of formulations supplied by different sources but it must be urged that formulations be adopted to suit locally-available materials. No attempt will be made to explain the tables or to change their technical data. It is sufficient that they illustrate that:

- different formulations are possible which produce similar products;
- many additional ingredients are included besides rubber;

163

- different formulations can give different physical properties;
- incorrect curing time can result in low properties;
- quite large proportions of tread crumb (over 50% in Table 10) can be used.

Equipment needed to mould shoe soles
- Two roll mixing mills. The smallest industrial size is 30 × 60 cm (the rolls are 30 cm dia. and 60 cm long) and of 26 kW (35 hp): it can roll a batch weighing 7–10 kg. The mill will need gearbox and motor etc.
- Hydraulic press with 4 daylights, platten size ½–¾ sq. m
- Suitable moulds. With 4 daylights at least 4 pairs of moulds will be needed. A ¾ sq. m platten will have room for about 24 cavities for adult shoes (12 pairs) so with 4 daylights, 96 cavities can operate at a time. If each sole weighs about 0.08 kg and the press can be charged, operated and discharged four times per hour, then 30 kg per hour of material will be needed. A press having 8 daylights would need double the supply.
- A boiler to generate the press heating steam; its size will be advised by the press supplier.
- Weighing scales – preferably one large machine for weighing out the rubber and a small one for the additives.
- Various small tools for extracting moulded items, trimming off flash, etc.

A smaller-scale operation
It should be possible to operate on a smaller scale using a single gap press of about a tonne acting on a platten of, say, ½ sq. m, electrically heated. Laboratory-size two-roll mills (15 × 30 cm) are made, but the author has not seen an operation as small as this anywhere. Small shoe manufacturers in most countries find it difficult to compete with the mass-produced output of big rubber companies and the same problem may exist with rubber moulding.

Use of 100% tread crumb
Although all authorities on rubber technology agree that it is impossible, the author has been advised that certain types of product can be made using 100% finely ground (0.8–1.2 mm mesh) tread crumb. Only if a hard, shiny surface finish is

164

Table 9 Various rubber formulations using tread crumb

	Parts	Parts	Parts
Cariflex S-1707	—	60	—
Cariflex S-1606	—	—	103
Cariflex S-1808	82	—	—
Whole tyre reclaim	60	40	40
Rubber tread crumb	40	80	200
Sulphur	2¼	2	2½
Zinc oxide	5	5	3
Stearic acid	1½	1½	1½
Coumarone resin	6	6	—
Antioxidant 'Nonox'	1	1	1
HAF black	—	50	—
Aluminium silicate	80	—	—
Clay	—	—	30
Whiting	30	80	20
Processing oil	3	5	—
Retarder	1	1	—
Other ingredients	2¼	2½	1¾
Total	350	370	424¾

Some properties

Best curing time (minutes)	3 @ 150°C	10 @150°C	10 @ 145°C
Tensile strength (kg/cm²)	65	85	85
Hardness (on the Shore A scale)	82/76	78/72	78/-
Density	1.36	1.33	1.30

Shell Co. Ltd. Manufacture of footwear soles and heels

Table 10 Non-commercial formulation for low grade black show soles

	Parts	Some properties		
Smoked sheet	25	Curing time @ 141°C	3 mins	6 mins
Whole tyre reclaim	100	Tensile strength		
30 mesh tread crumb	200	(kg/cm²)	26	51
Zinc oxide	3	Elasticity		
Whiting	50	(kg/cm²) 100%	12	16
Mineral oil	2	200%	20	30
Stearic acid	4	Hardness		
Sulphur	2½	(on the B.S.°. scale)	47	56
Vulcafor DHC	1	Density	1.27	1.27
Total	387½			

required are very small amounts of additives included. It is reported that this process has been operated successfully for forty years by one British company.

The crumb is heated to 35°C in the hopper and falls into the barrel of a ram extruder (an extruder in which the screw is replaced by a ram, or piston moving up and down the barrel) which has a very short stroke (4–5 cm). The ram forces the material into a long (40–50 cm) die where it is heated to 150°C and extruded very slowly – at only 7–8 cm per minute. Extrusions can be made up to about 5 cm dia., so the process is suitable for: channels, bicycle pedal rubbers, 'O' rings, solid tyres for carts, children's bicycles, baby carriages etc., rubber washers (but not oil-resistant washers), rubber hose, rubber bars for concrete paving on steep hill paths.

There is reported to be no obstacle to moulding products under the same conditions. Although the products do not have as good elasticity as those that contain some virgin rubber, wear resistance is reported to be as good. Waste that has a large oxidized surface is not suitable, so only fresh tread crumb, or solid objects ground to form crumb, should be used.

The process can be used for *very* small-scale production by using a steel mould held compressed by a nut and bolt, filling it with crumb, compressing and heating in a household oven at 150°C.

Any organization that wishes to learn more about this process should contact the author.

Products from rubber containing tread crumb
Any of the following might be made:

Cycle pedals and handle grips	Solid wheels for trolleys, wheelbarrows
Tips for crutches and artificial limbs	Car battery cases
	Dustbin lids
Motor car fenders	Extrusions for tubing,
Moulded rubber mats	hoses, packings etc.

Re-use of tyres
In most countries tyres are re-used, both whole and split, as raw material.

i) *Fish reefs*. From the U.S.A. it is reported that tyres have been sunk in the ocean, and tied down to rocks to form artificial fish reefs. It is well known to underwater swimmers that fish are vastly more numerous around rocks and coral reefs, and the tyres create the same conditions. In certain areas they become coated with coral within a few years. There is world-wide concern about the over-fishing of the oceans, and steps to ensure more rapid breeding are to be welcomed.

ii) *Dock and boat fenders.* Tyres have been used for this purpose for many years.

iii) *Plant pots.* The tyre is turned inside out.

iv) *Children's toys and swings* (Fig. 58) cannot cause injury to small children.

Fig. 58 Tyres are used by children for many kinds of games. Peru.

v) *Lining of pig and goat pens.* These animals scratch the ground and erode the soil in any enclosed area. By burying car tyres level with the surface this can be prevented so that the soil is fit for cultivation when the animals have been moved to another area.

Uses of materials from tyres

Shoemaking. The soles, heels and straps of sandals can be made from tyre material. The tyre structure consists of layers of textile-reinforced rubber sheets, laid one on top of the other with the 'grain' running in alternate directions, and with solid rubber moulded on top. These sheets can be split one from another and are about 2 mm. thick, or even less. Thus, the tyre provides:

a) Split material of even thickness to cut into straps.
b) Material with solid rubber adhering to it that can be carved, or the tread markings used, to form grips on the sole.

Shoes may also be repaired using tyre rubber: shoemaking and repairing from tyre rubber are huge industries in the Third World and the shoes that result are extremely strong and hard-wearing (Fig. 59a & b).

Fig. 59a   Tyre tread is used for sole grip. Note the leather insole and slots for sandal straps. Such sandals will last five or ten times as long as a mass produced plastic one. Photo: courtesy of Oxfam.

Other objects made from tyre rubber include: cords for tethering animals; mats for cars; household doormats; pads for handling glass in the glass industry; kindling in the firing of brick kilns; hinges for gates; stool and chair seats (Fig. 60); and hoops (the rubber rim of the tyre, which is in contact with the

168

Fig. 59b The use of tyres for shoemaking and repair is a huge industry employing thousands of people. Peru.

car wheel, contains wire beading and is therefore cut off before the tyre is split. Children have found a use for this!)

Uses for other materials from tyres

Wire from tyre beads or from steel braced tyres is used for many things, such as the cutter on a brick making machine. The nylon cord also used in tyre reinforcement is sold in market places for all kinds of applications. It has recently

Fig. 60   Use of tyre rubber for a stool seat. Peru.

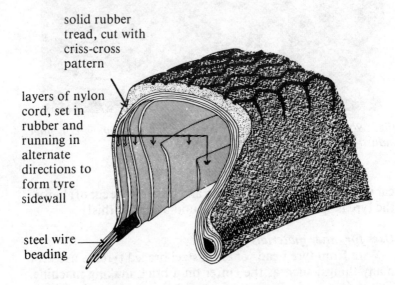

solid rubber
tread, cut with
criss-cross
pattern

layers of nylon
cord, set in
rubber and
running in
alternate
directions to
form tyre
sidewall

steel wire
beading

Fig. 61   Cross section of 'cross-ply' motor car tyre.

170

replaced the traditional cord of plaited reeds in the manufacture of reed fishing boats on Lake Titicaca between Peru and Bolivia.

Equipment suppliers

Rubber Reclaiming Machinery
- Rubber Reclaim Company of India Ltd., 62 Connaught Circus, New Delhi, India.
- Farrel Anand Machinery Manufacturing Co. Ltd., Mahalahshmi Chambers, Bhulabhai Desai Road, Bombay, India.

Two roll mill
- Francis Shaw & Co. (Manchester) Ltd., P.O. Box 12, Corbell Street, Manchester Mll 4BB, U.K.

Chapter 8. Glass

Waste glass can offer many forms of employment. First of all, the collection of cullet (broken glass) for use in glass-making, or sale to other industries. Used bottles can be collected and sold for re-use or made into saleable products. In areas where no glass manufacture exists, it may be profitable to set up a small glass workshop, and when experience has been gained, many items can be made. All these will be covered in this chapter, but it will begin with a brief description of how glass is made.

RAW MATERIALS USED IN GLASSMAKING

Glass is basically sand (silica or silicon oxide) which has been melted at a high temperature, and allowed to solidify in a certain way to give the familiar hard, clear, brittle, solid material. Because the temperature needed to melt sand is so high (about 1700°C) a 'flux' is added which reduces the melting temperature to only about 800°C. The common flux is sodium oxide which would need to be about 16% of the mixture by weight. A cheaper and more easily-obtainable material is soda ash (sodium carbonate) which is reduced to sodium oxide in the furnace and is added by about 21% by weight. The resulting material, however, is soluble in water and is known as water-glass. It can be made insoluble by adding a stabilizer such as limestone (calcium carbonate) about 16% by weight, which reduces in the furnace to lime (calcium oxide) about 9% by weight.

These three materials, mixed together in the proportion described, are known as the 'batch', and the resulting glass is called soda-lime-silica glass. Other batch materials may be used depending on the type of glass required; for example potash (potassium carbonate) and lead oxide are used to make the very clear lead crystal glass. Various other substances added to the batch include:

172

- 1½% aluminium oxide to reduce expansion of the glass when heated and therefore prevent cracking;
- ½% borax to assist and speed up melting;
- decolourizing agents: normally glass is slightly green, the result of iron in the sand. This may be removed by adding a decolourizing agent;
- colourizing agents are added if coloured glass is required: the beautiful blue colour of some ornamental glass is given by cobalt oxide.
- refining agents which help remove the small gas bubbles given off during the glass-making process, by releasing quantities of large gas bubbles, which rise rapidly and sweep the small bubbles out of the way. The most common refining agent is arsenious oxide with sodium nitrate. Pieces of potato, which give off water vapour, are commonly used in small-scale glass-making;
- cullet, often from the workshop's own production, which may be added to the batch. Cullet acts as a flux, reduces damage to the glass furnace from the corrosive, high temperature materials and reduces the cost of raw materials.

Manufacture of glass

This is a simple process. The batch materials are mixed dry and charged into the furnace which needs to be at about 1500°C to melt them into a treacly, amber-coloured liquid. This can be shaped in a number of ways, but as the liquid cools it becomes stiffer until, at a much lower temperature, it becomes too stiff to work. These temperatures may vary widely depending on the materials used to make the glass, but the principle is the same. If necessary, the object being made may be reheated to soften it for further working. Once finished, before it cools, it has to be 'annealed' to prevent cracking as it cools. The processes will be described in more detail later in the chapter.

CULLET

Proportions. In good quality glass-making, it is rare to use more than 40% cullet of which at least a third usually comes from the same factory. However, many small workshops in Third World countries use 80% or even 100% cullet. The problem with using high percentages is the small bubbles of dissolved gases that stay in the glass to produce 'seediness' (Fig. 62). If batch materials are used, the chemical reaction between them gives off quantities of large bubbles (and refining may be unnecessary) but with a high percentage of cullet this does not happen. Use of a refining agent can create some improvement and skilful manufacturers achieve a surprisingly high standard of glass. Besides spoiling the appearance, seediness also weakens the product, especially serious in bottles made to contain carbonated (fizzy) drinks under pressure.

Fig. 62   This jar is very 'seedy' due to the use of nearly 100% cullet in its manufacture.

Colour. If cullet is used, it must not discolour the glass product. To manufacture clear (flint) glass, only clear cullet can be used. For green glass, both clear and green can be used, and to make amber glass, clear, green and amber cullet may be used, though less of the green, strongly coloured glass should be used (Fig. 63a).
Purity and cleanness. These are most important. The best-

Fig. 63a   Sorting cullet into colours is a much easier task before the glass is broken.

known fact about glass is that it is transparent and any impurities will affect this. Metals in the batch or cullet may damage the furnace in which the glass is melted. Organic materials like wood or straw will burn off but may leave ash which will discolour the glass or give off bubbles of gas. Inert materials like stone or brick will also spoil the purity of the glass. Cullet is easy to wash with water; it may be hosed down in a heap or washed in a specially manufactured washing plant.

Types of cullet

Any glass object may be broken into cullet but not all will produce material free from impurities that can be used for glass-making. Suitable cullet includes:
- breakages from a glass-making workshop or factory;
- breakages from a bottling plant, provided they are free of bottle tops. Paper labels burn off in the furnace and do not matter;
- used bottles and food jars minus metal tops;
- glass crockery and household ware such as vases.

The following should be included only after discussion with the glass-maker who is going to use it:

175

- broken window glass;
- off-cuts from a glass-cutting workshop;
- lenses from motor car headlights.

The following should never be included:
- windows and windscreens from motor cars, lorries etc.
- lenses from motor car tail and winker lights;
- electric light bulbs;
- strongly coloured glass objects;
- wired glass.

Collecting cullet

This is not always a very profitable activity as the price for which it is sold will need to be lower than the price of batch materials, in order for the buyer to accept the problems of dirt and impurities that occur with cullet. If you decide to collect cullet you will need:

Transport. It is easy to collect paper in bundles but cullet needs at the very least a sack. As it is very heavy, a cart with a solid base and solid sides, that can be tipped for emptying is preferable.

Storage. A large quantity will fetch a better price than a few sackfuls. Store the colours separately. Cullet need not be stored under cover as long as it is safe from children, but must be kept away from motor vehicles, or else you will be asked to pay for punctured tyres.

Protective clothing. Gloves, face masks or visors, boots and possibly leather aprons and leggings should be worn. Try to provide a wash-basin near the workplace where people are sorting glass so that cuts can be quickly washed. Also, keep a bottle of 'disinfectant' handy and apply it to any cut, even if it is small or appears clean. Dirty cuts can go 'septic' and give great pain or even lead to loss of a limb!

Waste bin for all the material that is not glass and cannot be sold or used.

Broom or brush to sweep away broken glass from time to time to keep the working area clean and safe.

Containers are absolutely essential for cullet sorting and storage. If you sort into a container it will only take ten seconds to load that container on to a lorry; if you sort on to the ground it will take twenty times as long to shovel the material on to a lorry. Alternatively, build bunkers (with their base at the same

176

level as the lorry back to make loading easier) to keep the colours separate.

The collection of cullet is best done from:
   i) Glass-making factories and workshops, although most will re-use their own cullet.
  ii) Factories that bottle drinks or food such as jams, baby food, pickles etc. These always suffer a percentage of breakages on the production line and the broken glass is usually thrown away. If you provide a regular supply of containers, of a size and shape convenient for the workmen, they will usually be pleased to keep the glass separate from other wastes to save them the cost or trouble of throwing it away. A 200 litre (45 gallon) oil drum is too big and will need cutting down to half size to make it lighter to handle.
 iii) Breweries, dairies and soft-drink factories.
  iv) Hotels, restaurants, cafes, shops and factory or office canteens. It may be worthwhile to supply them with a container.
   v) Households.
  vi) Refuse dumps.
 vii) Bottle banks have been introduced in richer countries where bottles are often used only once, then thrown away. A bottle bank is a steel skip with a metal cover and openings through which the bottles are placed: these are sometimes colour separated. They are put in public places, such as car parks of big food and drink stores, so that customers can dispose of their old bottles on the same journey as they buy new. At present, there is too much demand for bottles, old or new, in Third World countries for such an arrangement to have any use, but in the rich suburbs of growing cities, in countries of rapid expansion and a developing wealthy middle class, such an arrangement may become fruitful in a few years time.

Markets for cullet and used bottles
These are mainly factories that make bottles and jars to contain food. However, there are many other products made from glass in which a high proportion of cullet is used, namely:
- bangles, beads, spun glass ornaments and handicrafts;

- crockery and vases;
- lamps, light bulbs, car parts etc;
- tiles for decorative floors and walls;
- school and laboratory glassware;
- fibreglass (fine fibres of glass in thick matting, used for insulation and to make lightweight structures such as boats, water tanks etc);
- window glass;
- balottini (fine balls of glass to make reflective paints for road signs, etc)

Factories making any of these may be willing to buy cullet (Chapter 21 describes the ways in which to find out their names and addresses). There may be among these a cullet merchant who will buy from you and sell to a number of different factories, or there may be a general waste merchant who buys many materials of which cullet is only one. As with the other materials, if you sell to these middle men, you will get a lower price than if you sell direct to a factory.

RE-USING BOTTLES

Bottles fetch a better price when sold to be re-used than when broken and sold as cullet (Fig. 63b). Many bottles have a deposit: you pay for the bottle when you buy the drink and get this money back when you return the bottle. Keep a special look-out for these; they are worth more than other bottles. Large drink-bottling plants often only use their own special bottles with a distinctive shape (such as Coca-Cola). Smaller plants, housewives or people who brew beer or liquor may be willing to use any bottle of the right size. Bottles cannot, however, be sold for re-use if they are cracked or chipped; very dirty; badly scuffed (worn by rubbing so that the glass is no longer clear); known to have been on a refuse tip; or known to have contained poisonous liquids. In any of these cases the bottles can be broken up and sold as cullet.

Sorting and washing bottles

You can often arrange with a brewery or soft drinks factory to borrow bottle 'crates' into which bottles can be sorted ready for a lorry to collect them. Otherwise it may be necessary to obtain cardboard boxes or 200 litre drums into which to sort the bottles for transportation. Organize the workplace so that you can stack all the bottles of one type together.

Fig. 63b   The little collection of bottles for re-sale probably provides this woman's only income.

If you intend to sell bottles to factories, visit them first and discuss what types they will buy, how they want them sorted and, of course, the price. Work out which method of sorting gives you the best return for your effort: will some factories take a mixture or do they all want you to select particular bottles? If so, how will you dispose of the remainder? Sell them to market women? Set up a stall yourself?

Some factories pay more for washed bottles; others, who have their own washing plant, do not. Often, bottle washing can be 'sub-contracted' to people who work at home. If you do this, check that they are using a clean water supply.

It is vitally important that bottles to be used as drink containers should be washed thoroughly, and also sterilized to kill bacteria, by soaking them in steam for a certain period of time. Usually, the Ministry of Health will control the drink bottling process to ensure this. If not, you may be blamed if people become ill after drinking from bottles you are supposed to have washed.

Objects made from bottles

Even if the main markets for cullet and bottles are not to be found in your district, it is still possible to cut bottles and jars to make new objects, using an electric wire or glass cutter. Candlesticks, funnels, drinking tumblers and ash trays (Fig. 64a) are among the products that can be made.

Fig. 64a   Objects that can be made by cutting bottles with electric wire. Peru.

1. Cutting with an electric wire

The item to be cut must be perfectly clean. A nichrome wire may be obtained by unwinding the broken element of an electric water heater, kettle or iron. You will also need a small electric transformer to reduce the 230 or 240 volts electric mains to about 15 volts. Do not touch any live metal parts on the 230 volt side or you could receive a fatal electric shock. The 15 volt side is quite safe. Connect the nichrome wire to the 15 volts transformer output and carefully wrap it around the bottle or jar exactly where you want the cut (Fig. 64b). Make sure the two ends of the wire do not touch where they cross or else you will get a 'short circuit' but if they are more than a tiny distance apart you will get a 'step' in the cut. Two people are needed, one to hold the wires in position and the other to

180

switch on the electric current. Allow the current to flow for one minute; the wires will glow red hot so do not touch them! At the end of the minute, dip the bottle in a bucket of cold water, and in a few seconds it will crack exactly along the line of the wire.

2. *Cutting with a glass cutter*

It is possible to cut bottles with an ordinary glass cutter. Groove the path of the cut with the cutter, making sure the groove is not interrupted. Heat along the line of the groove with a small spirit lamp, then dip the bottle rapidly in water and again it will crack at the groove. If it does not crack at first, give it a tap. Special cutters are made for cutting bottles but they are usually less effective than the methods described here. *Rounding off* the sharp edge left where the glass has cracked is the main problem with these processes. It may best be done with a 'carborundum' stone of the type used for sharpening tools. It is important not only to remove the sharp cutting edge, but also to fully round the whole edge, to make glass more pleasant to drink from.

MAKING SIMPLE GLASS OBJECTS

If no factories exist nearby, the other alternative is to set up a small glass workshop. It must be clearly understood, however, that this is not a simple exercise; a substantial sum of money will be required for the capital costs and the skills needed may take many months or even years of experience to develop. However, it is possible to begin on a simple basis, perhaps making just one style of glass tumbler or glass beads. From these it is not too difficult to progress to bottles and jars. Let us consider what is needed for a very simple workshop making glass bowls.

Source of batch materials

The proportions can be as given on page 172 or can be varied to suit local supplies. Soda ash may have to be imported.

1. *A pot furnace*

The pots that hold the glass are made separate from the heating furnace.

Pots. The pots are made of 1 part 'fireclay' and 3 parts of 'grog'. Many naturally-occuring clays can be used. Grog is crushed, burnt fireclay and is used to reduce the contraction of the pot, due to loss of water, when it is fired. The raw clay and grog are thoroughly mixed with water, left to stand for several months then thoroughly mixed again by treading. The pot base is then made as a circle, 7–15 cm thick, on a board. When this has dried it is removed from the board, with a wire if necessary, turned over (to give the pot a smooth interior bottom) and the sides built up, a few inches each day, using material in rolls, 10 cm long and 5 cm dia. Each layer is given a chance to dry slightly before the next is added, and the side walls are smoothed to press out all the air and holes. The pots are left to dry for several months before being fired in a furnace, called a pot arch, which is heated to red heat gradually, over about a week, and then, while still red hot, transferred to the glass melting furnace and heated to the melting temperature of 1400°C–1500°C. The end result should be pots of hard material with low 'porosity', able to resist the chemicals of glass-making. However, a pot in daily use will only last four or five months.

When pots are made in large numbers, as for the manufacture of optical glass for making lenses for spectacles, binoculars, cameras etc., they can be made by a much faster method called 'slip casting'. A mould and core are made of plaster of Paris, then the materials are mixed with water and an electrolyte and poured in. The water is absorbed by the plaster, and the core and mould are dismantled to remove the pot when it is nearly dry.

The furnace may be of any type or fuel with a large enough capacity to take and heat a number of pots. Fuel is fed in at the sides on to the fire grates and burnt with the 'primary air' to produce gas. This is burnt above the surface of the glass with the 'secondary air', which is taken into the 'combustion chamber' through pipes around the fire-boxes, so that it is heated before burning. The pots are placed on stands in the combustion chamber.

Alternatively, the furnace can use oil or gas, with the flame directed straight into the combustion chamber from nozzles and air jets set in the walls. An electric or diesel fan is needed and it is best if the air is pre-heated by piping it around the furnace before it enters.

The pot furnace is built of bricks and mortar of fire-clay as it has to stand up to very high temperatures. The size of the pot furnace depends on the weight of glass that will be produced each day. Each pot holds half a tonne of glass but is filled and drained on alternate days so a capacity of four pots is needed for each tonne of production per day. Extra pots will be needed if different colours of glass are to be made.

Melting the glass

The batch and cullet are mixed dry and the pot filled to the

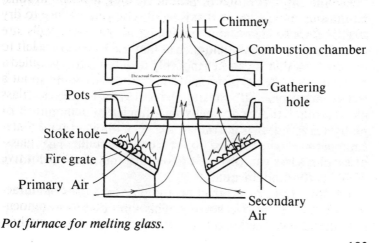

Pot furnace for melting glass.

183

top using a shovel. When melted, the materials slump down and the pot is topped up again, and then again as necessary. When the materials have all melted, the temperature is raised to refine the materials: the glass is made more liquid, and becomes less sticky, and gas bubbles are given the chance to escape. These changes may be helped by plunging a wet stick or a wet potato to the bottom of the pot. The molten glass is stirred to mix it, thoroughly but slowly, to avoid introducing air bubbles.

Material to be moulded must be stickier and the temperature is lowered to achieve this. When the right state has been reached, material is gathered on the end of a blowpipe. The pipe is about 1½ m in length with a hole about 7 mm in diameter through it. Its diameter at the nose (the end on which glass is taken) depends on the amount of glass needed for each moulding operation. The pipe is heated, entered into the pot at a shallow angle to the horizontal and rotated, just touching the surface of the molten glass, and removed when enough glass has been gathered. Care must be taken to avoid trapping air bubbles, and to get a symmetrical (same size and shape all round) 'gob' of glass. The pipe must be rotated all the time the glass is on it (Fig. 66). The gob may be cooled by pausing and may be made into a pear shape by rolling it on the edge of a smooth table or pad.

2. *Moulding equipment*

For the easy operation of producing a glass bowl, a simple mould and plunger are all that is required. Both can be made of steel and are solid, without moving parts. The plunger can be mounted on a vertical stand such as that used to mount an electric drill, so that it can be smoothly lowered into the mould. The gob of molten glass is placed in the heated mould and cut free from the pipe with shears. The plunger is lowered to force glass around the cavity between plunger and mould. The plunger is withdrawn and the shrinkage of the glass as it cools is enough to free the finished object from the mould. The 'flash' of surplus glass can then be broken off and smoothed down with a carborundum stone.

For high rates of production the plunger may need water cooling to prevent overheating. This kind of process, called pressing, can be used to make any object that does not have a

Fig. 66 Handblowing of glass. The girl is blowing the parison before final blowing in a mould. Thailand.

neck, narrower than its body, so that the plunger can be withdrawn after the object has been made. Such objects include dishes and bowls; wide necked jars; saucers; ash trays; car headlight glasses; and wide glass tumblers.

MORE ADVANCED GLASS-MAKING

When experience has been gained in simple glass-making, more technical operations may be done. There are many different processes, some using complicated equipment, others requiring skilful hand operations. Only three will be described: the use of a tank furnace, the hand-blowing of glass containers and the blow-moulding of glass containers. These are sufficient for the manufacture of jars and drinks bottles,

185

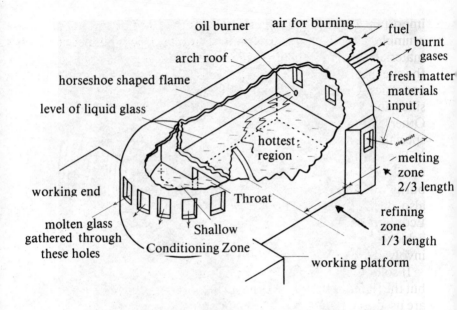

Fig. 67 Diagram of a small, oil-fired glass tank furnace.

the items with the widest sales in the greatest quantities.

Continuous tank furnaces
In the pot furnace, the glass remains in the same container and the temperature is raised to melt the glass, raised higher to refine it, then reduced for gathering. When all the glass has been used a new batch is melted from cold. A tank furnace does these operations continuously. It is made as in Fig. 66. Cold batch material is shovelled into the 'doghouse' at one end. It is melted in the melting zone, then flows slowly down to the refining zone which is kept at a higher temperature. It then flows through a narrow gap in the wall of the main furnace called the throat and into the working end, a shallow trough at a lower temperature where the glass is conditioned to the right viscosity (stickiness). The working end walls contain holes through which glass can be gathered, as many as are required by the number of people working. The furnace depth may be from 60 cm upwards. The tank roof is usually arched and it is

important that it be made of materials that do not soften or crumble. Usually, the tank is built of fire clay bricks but better materials, able to stand up to higher temperatures and to resist the chemical attacks of the molten glass, are available in many countries. One such material is Sillimanite, a material of 40% silica and 55% alumina that occurs naturally in Assam, India. Others are artificial. The selection of these is a matter for specialists.

The furnace may be fired by any hydrocarbon fuel: coal, gas or oil, or even wood if these are not available, although wood burns quickly and therefore needs continuous stoking. It is also difficult to obtain very high temperatures with wood. Economy of fuels, essential in large scale operations, may be achieved with special designs of furnace, but the methods involved are expensive and will not be discussed here.

If solid fuels are used they will be burnt underneath the tank but the flames will be above the surface of the glass. If gas or oil are used, the flames can sweep horizontally across the surface of the molten glass from fuel nozzles and separate air nozzles arranged around the furnace walls (Fig. 68).

Day tank furnaces

Continuous tank furnaces are most suitable for glass-making operations that are going to be carried on for twenty-four hours a day, seven days a week, often employing three or four shifts of workers. As the moulds, furnace and other machinery for even simple glass-making are comparatively expensive, this is usually the most economic way of working. However, in some communities it is not socially acceptable, or there is not sufficient demand for the products, or there may be other reasons why continuous working is not possible. Then, a day tank furnace may be preferred, a small tank that is heated up afresh every night, often taking about sixteen hours to melt the charge, and is gathered for moulding during the eight hours of daytime. A day tank is slightly simpler in construction than a continuous furnace, with just one simple circular tank containing holes arranged all around for both gathering and charging.

An example of oil consumption per tonne of glass for three/four ton furnaces:

Fig. 68 Glass furnace fired by oil. Previously fired by wood, this day tank has been converted very simply by fitting oil pipes and a burner. Note the raised platform and the sheets of corrugated iron used to reflect the heat. The electric fan is desirable in hot working conditions but care must be taken that newly made glass is not cracked by cold air currents. Thailand.

Day tank	– Peninsular type (inefficient)	100–125 galls/ton
	– Samanala (efficient)	83–100 galls/ton
Continuous	– Xavy glass (efficient)	75 galls/ton

Glass furnaces are usually raised up above the level of the surrounding workshop floor for any of the following reasons:

  i) To provide for circulation of cooling air on the tank bottom blocks to prolong their life.

 ii) Should the glass drill through the tank bottom it will be frozen by cooling air, thus extending furnace life.

iii) If heated from below by solid fuel, less excavation is needed and the fuel and ashes need less handling. However, it is worth constructing the furnace over a pit so that in the unlikely event of a failure in the furnace structure, the molten glass can be retained and injury avoided.

iv) The gathering pipes are long (to keep the gatherer away from the heat) and it is more convenient for the gatherer to transfer the gob to a mould that is below him (Fig. 69).

v) A glass factory is a busy, bustling place. Dangers of burns are less if only those people actually working the furnace are on its level.

Whatever the furnace level it is important that it is worked from a platform that allows access to the gathering holes at a convenient height.

Fig. 69 The raised platform helps the use of long gathering pipes. The girl at the bottom operates the mould for several blowers and cools it with water. Thailand.

189

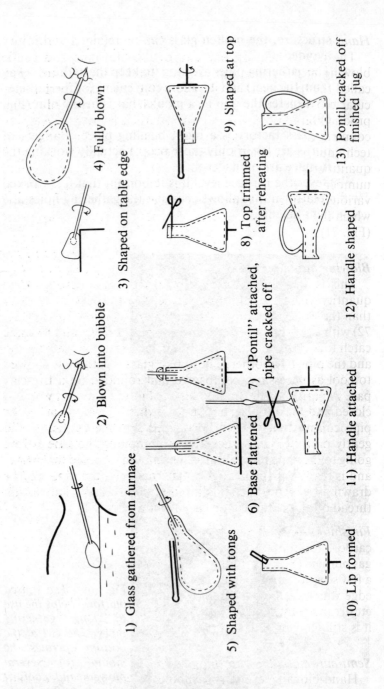

1) Glass gathered from furnace

2) Blown into bubble

3) Shaped on table edge

4) Fully blown

5) Shaped with tongs

6) Base flattened

7) "Pontil" attached, pipe cracked off

8) Top trimmed after reheating

9) Shaped at top

10) Lip formed

11) Handle attached

12) Handle shaped

13) Pontil cracked off finished jug

Fig. 70 Stages in hand blowing a jug.

190

Hand blowing of containers (Fig. 70)

The gob is held on one end of the blowpipe and gentle blowing at the other end causes a bubble of glass to form, called the 'parison'. The parison will only keep a perfect circular cross-section if the pipe is continuously rotated. Many products are still made, in both developed and developing countries, by highly skilled workers using this as their basic technique, particularly when the object is made in small quantities that do not justify the cost of a mould. A small number of hand tools are used, including tongs, scissors, various shaping tools and two parallel rails or chair arms along which the blowpipe may be rolled, plus a flat pad of fire-clay (Fig. 71).

Blowing into a mould

This is a logical next step for objects to be produced in quantity which cannot be pressed because the neck is narrower than the waist. The mould is made in two hinged halves (Fig. 72) with a short handle on each to open and close, and a simple catch to lock them shut. The mould is operated by one person and the pipe by another. The gob of glass is gathered, allowed to cool as necessary, compacted and rounded on a fire-clay pad. A parison is blown and inserted into the mould which is closed and locked. The container is then blown, rotating the pipe continually, the mould opened and the container laid gently on a bed and cracked off by tapping the pipe before going to the annealing furnace. The mould is cooled with water and is ready for the next gob. Alternatively, the pipe may be drawn away from the still closed mould to leave only a thin thread of glass that can be cut off with scissors.

Finishing the neck may be done by rubbing it on a stone of carborundum after annealing, but it is better to use a ring of gas burners (Fig. 73) in which the inverted container is spun for a few seconds until the jagged neck drops off, leaving a red hot edge which cools to a smooth, rounded rim. Handles, knobs etc are made by hand and stuck on to the container or lid while it is still glowing red: this requires some skill.

Semi-automatic blowing and pressing

Hand-blowing, even with a mould, requires a degree of skill, is tiring for the operator, rather slow and produces a product

191

Fig. 71 Hand shaping of glass. Note the long chair arm on which the pipe is rolled and the use of tongs for shaping. The scissors are for snipping off, later. The steel sheet protects the operator's feet from falling glass. India.

192

Fig. 72 Semi-automatic blowing of a screw neck jar. View of the second-stage mould used for blowing the full jar. Thailand.

which may vary in size by small amounts, sufficient to cause problems in a mechanical bottle filling operation.

For example, if the temperature of the container at the moment of blowing varies, then so will the size of the finished object, even though the same mould be used on each occasion. Semi-automatic blowing overcomes these problems. It is

Fig. 73   Hand blowing with a mould. The rim is rounded in a ring of gas burners. The glass spins while in the flames. Thailand.

usually a two-stage process, with the first involving pressing or blowing, and the second always employing blowing.

194

Sequence of operations in the manufacture of a screw-necked jar

First the neck is pressed, using a two-piece mould. The upper piece forms the screw on the outside of the neck and travels with the jar until moulding is complete. The plunger and the lower piece form a hollow, round-bottomed, cone-shaped parison. The parison is transferred, still red hot, on to the blowing mould, set on a turntable. A conical nozzle, connected to a compressed air hose, is inserted into the neck of the mould, air pressure is applied and the glass blown out to fill the mould. The nozzle is removed, the table swivelled and the mould opened by a second operator who uses tongs to transfer the still glowing jar to a standing table from where it is quickly moved to the annealing furnace.

For bottles, it is usual to blow both stages, the parison from the bottom and the bottle from the top.

Annealing

This is necessary for all moulded, blown or pressed glass-ware to prevent cracking. Cracking is caused by different parts of the object cooling and therefore shrinking at different rates. The annealing process has two stages: soaking for a period to allow all the stresses caused by the moulding process to be relaxed, followed by slow cooling to avoid further stresses. For normal containers made by the kind of processes that have been described, annealing may vary between soaking for 24 hours at 700°C followed by cooling over 24 hours, and soaking for three hours at 400°C followed by cooling over five hours. Normally, small glass producers anneal in a separate furnace which is held at the soaking temperature until it is full, at which time the temperature is controlled as described. Larger producers use a lehr, a continuous conveyor that passes through a tunnel furnace in which the temperature varies along its length: constant for the first part, slowly reducing along the second. Much more carefully controlled and therefore much faster annealing can be achieved. Lehrs can be made quite cheaply, with wire baskets or flat pans and can be made to form part of the furnace 'flue', so improving heat economy.

Marketing of glassware

It is no use mastering the methods of manufacturing glassware unless it can be sold, and a number of rules apply to choosing a product and the area in which it is to be made:

i) Find out what other glassware, if any, is manufactured in the country. Small-scale glassmaking cannot compete against largescale, industrialized manufacture unless the latter is done so far away that costs of packing and transport are high.

ii) Find out which small volume products are not made in the country at all, but have to be imported and are possibly subject to customs duties.

iii) Do not try to produce objects that need a very accurate shape or finish, such as beer bottles, for an automatic filling line, or optical glassware.

iv) Choose products where seediness resulting from the use of high percentages of cullet will not cause the customer to reject the home-made product in favour of imported goods of higher quality.

v) Try to position your glassmaking workshop near the areas of greatest demand. Glass is expensive to transport because:

  – it is bulky;
  – it needs bulky, expensive packing;
  – breakages occur in transport;
  – its own value is quite low while transport becomes dearer all the time.

OTHER PRODUCTS FROM WASTE GLASS

Manufacture of floor and wall tiles

Cullet, particularly from coloured bottles, can be used to make attractive and hard-wearing floor and wall tiles. The tile can be made of either:

– Waste glass in resin (polyester, epoxy or urea formaldehyde resins are all suitable);
– Waste glass in cement; or
– Waste glass in resin with a cement backing.

The waste glass should be:

– Colour sorted to enable attractive tile surfaces to be selected;
– Crushed;
– Graded into sizes: (i) coarse +6–19 mm; (ii) medium +1.5–6 mm; (iii) fine–1.5 mm, using sieves or screens with the above mesh sizes see p. 199;

- Surface treated if possible by washing in a solution of trimethoxy silane to make a stronger tile. If it is not possible to treat the surface, then the glass must be used soon after it is crushed;
- Coloured, if desired, with dye or pigment. Dyes that are not soluble in water are best.

The operation, as seen in Mexico, is as follows:

i) The glass is mixed thoroughly with the cement or resin. Cement should be 1 cement : 3 fine sand with no aggregate. Colouring can be added at this point.

ii) The mixture is then poured into a perfectly clean rectangular mould. The mould base can have a glossy, rough, or ribbed surface depending on the tile surface desired. A depth of between 14 and 20 mm is best.

iii) It is then covered with a layer of paper and pressed.

iv) In the case of wall tiles, a wire loop can be embedded in the back to assist fixing.

v) The tile remains in the mould until the cement or resin has gone off (set firm enough to handle gently). Cement tiles are 'cured' in a waterbath for twenty-four hours, followed by drying for three days.

vi) To make resin tiles on a cement backing, the backing (with wire loop) can be made first and placed on top of the resin glass mixture in the mould. With this process the finished tile can be removed from the mould sooner, so fewer moulds are needed.

vii) High gloss tiles can be obtained by polishing the surface with diamond or carborundum paste.

These tiles sell in Mexico for about $ US 5 per sq. m., but a higher price could almost certainly be obtained elsewhere. They are an expensive wall or floor covering and should be sold in upper and upper middle class districts. Normally they will sell best through builders' merchants and merchants who sell bathroom and kitchen equipment and enamelware.

Other methods of making tiles

Tiles that do not use expensive cement can be made with fly-ash from a (coal-burning) power station or other large industrial boiler furnace, with dried sewage sludge or cattle or pig manure, as filler. The filler is finely-powdered, mixed 50 : 50 with washed cullet and pressed in moulds as described above. The tile must then be fired in a furnace at about 900°C so that the glass melts and binds the particles of filler together.

Another type of tile can be made by mixing up to 70% crushed glass, 30% mixed china and broken porcelain (from basins, lavatory bowls etc). These have to be dry-pressed and fired.

Building materials from glass

Bricks can be made from a mixture of 30% clay and 70% waste glass (by weight) and these have a tough outer skin that will resist wind and rain. If the glass is powdered very finely it acts as a flux and reduces the temperature needed to fire the bricks by more than 50°C. About 30% more bricks can be made with the same amount of fuel. Another type of brick, very strong and resistant to water, is made from 31% crushed glass, 6% clay, 7% water and 56% crushed old bricks.

Strong, lightweight walls that economize on concrete or clay can be used by embedding complete bottles, in even layers, in the material.

Equipment suppliers

Glass Furnaces
- S.G. Blair and Co. Ltd., P.O. Box 3, Astmoor, Runcorn, Cheshire, WA7 1SL, U.K.

Glass Machinery
- Glassworks Equipment Ltd., Park Lane, Halesowen, W. Midlands, B63 2QS, U.K.
- Woodall Duckham Ltd., The Boulevard, Crawley, Sussex, RH10 1UX, U.K.
- King, Tauderin and Gregson Ltd., Grindlegate Works, 39 Scotland Road, Sheffield, S3 7BT, U.K.
- Shreno Ltd., Alembi Baroda Road, Baroda, Gujarat, India.

Trimethoxy silane
- Dow Corning, Cardiff Road, Barry, Glamorgan, U.K.

Chapter 9. Minerals, Chemicals and Oil

Minerals

SOURCES AND USES OF MINERAL WASTES

There is little difference between by-products and re-usable or re-cyclable wastes from industry. The coal and petroleum industries produce huge numbers of by-products, but they are a technology on their own and there is little opportunity outside these industries to develop uses for them. Many wastes from mining, quarrying and similar industries, however, can be used in building, agriculture and other activities. The uses of these wastes are listed below and in Table 11. It must be stressed that the list is far from complete as the subject is a vast one. Readers who wish to know more should read the report by the British Building Research Establishment[1]. The sizes given here are the sizes of square mesh through which the material (in mm) will pass (−) and will not pass (+):

Fill is any material used to fill holes or low-lying or marshy ground. It is also used to provide a stable or raised base for a road, building, sports area, etc.

Aggregate is inert material mixed with cement to make concrete. Fine aggregate is grit (size − 10 + 3), coarse aggregate is gravel and stones (size − 19 + 10).

Sand is the finest aggregate (size − 3 + 2, − 2 + 1, − 1 + 0 etc).

Railway ballast is inert material of even size, larger than coarse aggregate (size − 63 + 25) which is placed under the railway sleepers.

Roadstone, mixed with tar, is used to make the top layer of roads. Various sizes are used, all smaller than railway ballast (sizes − 40 + 25; − 25 + 19; − 19 + 11; − 11 + 6).

Sewage filters are beds of gravel over which sewage flows to expose it to the air. Size is as large as railway ballast but with finer material ($-$ 63 $+$ 10).

Gritblasting (or sandblasting) is a process used to clean the rust off steel or the dirt off stone structures: sharp-edged sand or grit (size $-$ 4 $+$ 2) is blown in a powerful jet of air or water.

Fillers are materials used in the moulding of rubbers and plastics to economize on expensive materials. Size depends on the product.

Plasters Many chemical processes produce calcium sulphate (gypsum) wastes. These wastes can be dried and calcined at a modest temperature to give Plaster of Paris, the most important plaster material. The other two common plasters are lime plaster and anhydrite plaster, which is also a possibility from by-product gypsum.

Mineral wool is a material made in slabs and boards of fibres. Drawn from molten minerals, it has excellent heat and sound insulation properties.

Blocks are wall building units, usually as large as six or twelve bricks, made of lightweight materials and often containing cavities used to improve insulation, ease handling and laying, and reduce weight.

Floorings are small chips used with resins or asphalt to produce smooth, often slightly flexible, interior floor surfaces (sizes $-$ 19 $+$ 11, $-$ 11 $+$ 6, $-$ 6 $+$ 3).

Foundry sands, soil conditioners are described elsewhere in the book and bricks and cement should need no explanation.

The main reason why mineral wastes are not used more extensively is the high cost of transport from the site where they occur to the location of their next use. It is often cheaper to pay the cost of quarrying new material, close to the point of use, than to transport waste from far-off locations.

No attempt will be made here to describe the millions of wastes and by-products that occur in the chemical and similar industries; their study is a matter for specialists in industrial chemistry. However, one material will be described as an example of the wide range of products that can be created from one apparently useless waste.

Blast furnace slag

In Chapter 2, it was explained how limestone and the other mineral impurities in iron ore, are melted to a slag by the intense heat of a blast furnace. This slag may be made into

Table 11—Major uses of mineral wastes

INDUSTRY	PRODUCT	WASTE	FILL	CONCRETE AGGREGATE	RAILWAY BALLAST	ROADSTONE	SEWAGE FILTERS	LIGHT AGGREGATE FOR BLOCKS	MINERAL WOOL	FLOORINGS	GRITBLASTING	BRICKMAKING	BUILDING SAND	FOUNDRY MOULDING SAND	INDUSTRIAL FILLERS	CEMENT	PLASTER	FERTILISER/SOIL CONDITIONER
Mining	Coal	Colliery spoil	√	P		√		√ P				√ P				P		
	Other	Tailings	√	√		√	√	√		√					√		√	√
Quarrying	Slate	Slate Waste	√			√		√										
	Granite	Granite Waste	√	√		√		√				√	√	P				
	China Clay	Sand & Rock	√					√				√	√					
	Stone	Small Stones																
Metals extraction	Iron & Steel	Blastfurnace slag	√	√	√	√	√	√								√		
	Copper	Slag		P			√				√	P						
	Lead & Zinc	Slag	√			√		P			√	P						
	Tin	Slag				P					√							
	Alumina	Red Mud																
Chemical industries	Phosphoric Acid	Calcium Sulphate						√							√	P	√	√
	"	Phosphogypsum														P	√	√
	Hydrofluoric Acid	Anhydrite	√							√								
Power stations	Coal Fired	Pulverised fuel ash	√					√							√	√		

√ = Common Use
P = Tests indicate possible use

201

different products, depending upon the conditions under which it solidifies. If it is broken up by high pressure water jets and cooled in a large volume of water it forms granules similar to cement 'clinker' which can easily be finely ground and mixed with Portland cement to make *slag cement*. Alternatively, it can be mixed with cement clinker and the two ground together, but their proportions must be adjusted to suit the percentage of limestone being used in the blast furnace, which depends on the quality of the iron ore. Slag for cement should contain less than 5% magnesium oxide, 2% manganese oxide, and 21% aluminium oxide. It is not a cement on its own but must be activated either by Portland cement or by calcium sulphate.

Finely ground slag with a small quantity of lime added may be used for mass concrete constructions like dams and aqueducts, and gives huge economies over the use of pure Portland cement. However, great care should be taken or expert advice sought before using anything but concrete to well-proven specification for these constructions.

Slag may be made into a foamed aggregate by dumping it into a pit containing a small amount of water. It is lightweight, economical and can be used with cement to make building blocks and other building products. It can also be poured directly into moulds to make bricks or paving stones of rather high density or may be processed to form a fibrous slag wool, used as a fireproof insulation and for sewage filters.

Ground slag has a high phosphorus content and is used as a fertilizer.

RECLAMATION OF OILS

Mineral oils, made from petroleum, become more expensive every year. They are widely used as a lubricating oil for motor vehicles and other machinery such as hydraulic pumps and motors, compressors and electrical transformers, and also for machining metals. In use they become dirty and contaminated with materials that make them useless or harmful: they then have to be drained off and replaced with fresh oil. There is no safe method of disposing of used oils: if they are tipped onto land they sterilize it so that no plants will grow there in the future; if poured down drains they cause them damage and can pollute sea or river water. Used oils can be reclaimed in three different ways:

i) Laundered (thoroughly cleaned) then re-used for the same purpose.
ii) Re-refined to make new oil.
iii) Burnt, in their dirty state, as fuel for certain types of small boilers or locomotives. This produces black smoke, however, if not properly managed.

By reclaiming used oils, it is possible to avoid a serious pollution problem, save the costs of expensive new oils, and create employment in the collection and reprocessing of the used oils.

There are, however, two problems:
i) The processes for refining, cleaning and using spent oils require expensive technical equipment (although a clever engineer could produce adequate equipment in the workshop far more cheaply).
ii) The spent oil is discarded by motorists, factories, air and shipping lines in many widely-spaced places, so transport and collection costs could be high.

COLLECTION OF USED OILS

In order to ensure collection, the oil user should be provided with a container into which spent oil can be poured. The size of container will depend on the amount of oil regularly thrown away at each place but two possible sizes are:
i) A tank, such as Fig. 74, for a transport garage, factory,

Fig. 74   Tank for collecting waste oil. Oxfam Wastesaver, U.K.

203

shipping quay or a large petrol filling station that sells motor lubricating oil. The tank (undamaged!) from a crashed road tanker would be suitable.

ii) A standard oil drum, with cover, fitted with a drainage tap for small petrol stations, garages or factories.

Very large dockyards or airports which use huge quantities of oil and have vast storage tanks will not be considered further except to note that it may be worthwhile checking whether they do reclaim their spent oils.

Transport and equipment

A tanker is needed to visit the various storage tanks, suck out the oil and transport it to the processing plant. The tanker may be animal drawn (Fig. 75) or mounted on a vehicle. It will need a suction pump (hand or motor-operated), a long, wide hose in case the vehicle cannot get close enough to the tank, a number of different sized pipe ends to the hose (to get inside small holes on small tanks), a dipstick to check how much oil is inside and a tap at the bottom to discharge.

An alternative enterprise

A group of young people who have neither a tanker nor an

Fig. 75   Animal-drawn oil collection tanker. Note the hand pump at the back and the long hose to reach storage tanks well away from the road. Egypt.

oil reclamation plant may obtain employment by persuading the owner of a petrol filling station to allow them to set up a tank in his yard, and offer a free oil change to customers who buy engine oil. They would receive the used oil free, store it in the tank, and sell it to an oil reclaimer. Everyone benefits with this scheme as:
- the customer gets a free oil change;
- the petrol station sells more oil;
- the reclaimer receives more used oil to reclaim; and
- the young people are usefully employed.

Used oil prices vary greatly around the world, but figures of between $ US 2.50–5.00 per 100 litres are typical. As a motor car commonly holds about 2½–5 litres of oil, the value of spent oil taken will be around 12–25 cents for every vehicle.

PROCESSING OF USED OILS

The following descriptions are intended to indicate the kind of equipment and activity needed, rather than as a detailed instruction in oil reclamation. Re-refining is done by refineries which are specially equipped to deal with the high level of dirt in used oil. The process is complex and will not be described here.

Laundering may be carried out by half a dozen different processes, of which two in particular will be described:

1. *The acid-clay process*

The oil is sieved to remove solid objects and placed in storage tanks. It is pumped (through a steam heater to reduce its stickiness) to a 'flash dehydrator' which removes any water at a temperature of about 150°C. The oil is cooled for two days then pumped into tanks to be mixed with 92% concentrated sulphuric acid at about 40°C. This precipitates oxide impurities which form an acid sludge at the bottom of the tank: these must be drained off from time to time. The oil is then mixed with a special clay and heated to about 300°C for twelve hours. Volatile impurities are given off, together with any remaining water. The oil is again cooled, filtered to remove the clay and stored for canning. Any 'additives' have to be replaced but, correctly treated, the oil should be good enough to perform its original function. Expert opinions differ as to whether the oil is degraded during use, and loses both viscosity and lubricating power. The problem with the acid-clay process is that the special clay must be bought and the acid sludge and spent clay are difficult to dispose of safely.

2. *The in-house reclaimer*

A compact plant suitable for installation in a factory or large garage is sold commercially for about $ US 22,000. Its operation is as follows:

Incoming oil passes through a heat exchanger where it is warmed by the outgoing oil; it then passes through an electric heater to bring it to a high enough temperature to reduce its stickiness. It is sucked through a filter of either activated clay (Fullers earth) or paper discs to absorb oxides and remove all solid particles greater than half a micron.*

The filtered oil enters an evaporator where it is heated electrically to vapourize any water or volatile gases. The clean oil flows to the collecting tank through the heat exchanger where it heats the incoming material. If paper discs are used for filtering, the additives are not removed and do not need replacement.

It is estimated that the cost of reclaiming is less than 1 US cent per litre of oil.

Use as a fuel oil

This is only possible with furnaces or locomotives that can use such a thick, dirty, sticky fuel. Normally, this will be restricted to those types whose fuel circuit contains a pre-heater that heats the fuel as it comes out of the storage tank before entering the burner pump, and reduces its stickiness.

Marketing used oils

As with all wastes, sell to a final user if possible. This means a refinery that re-refines used oils, a company that cleans oils or one that operates furnaces or locomotives that can run on this heavy, impure material. If none of these can be found it may be unavoidable to sell to a middle man.

References

1. *A survey of the Locations, Disposal and Prospective Uses of the Major Industrial By-Products and Waste Materials.* A Report by the British Building Research Establishment, Watford, England.

One micron equals one thousandth of a millimetre.

Chapter 10. Human and Household Wastes

The broad subject of agricultural wastes has been left out of this volume for reasons of space and will be included in another book. There are, however, a variety of organic wastes which arise in towns and may be treated in ways that are agricultural or that are normally used for farm wastes. This chapter will therefore discuss food waste, sewage and town refuse but before doing so it is necessary to outline three ways in which organic wastes can be used, namely to improve soil, to feed animals and to produce energy by the production of biogas.

1. SOIL

In order to provide good crop yields, year after year, soil must contain the following:

    i) *Nitrates* – to give nitrogen. Normally this is provided by decaying leaves and vegetable matter or by animal droppings. If these do not arise naturally, it may be provided instead by:

- Artificial or chemical fertilizers such as sodium nitrate or ammonium sulphate (ammonia is a chemical containing nitrogen).
- Growing legume crops such as beans, peas or clover. These contain bacteria (minute living creatures) in their roots that convert nitrogen from the air into more nitrates than the plants themselves need. This is called green manuring.
- Manures: of animal dung (droppings), rotting vegetable matter called compost, or of mixtures of these. These are regarded as wastes, quite wrongly because they are very important to the success of agriculture! An important matter is how quickly they release their nitrogen to the soil. Chemical fertilizers do so very

quickly (sometimes too quickly so that the rain washes all the value away). Legumes need a growing cycle (a season). Manures depend on how well they are rotted before being put on the soil, and on their make up, and these are expressed conveniently as their carbon to nitrogen (or C/N) ratio. A low C/N ratio means there is plenty of nitrogen to nourish crops.

Among the best manures are animal and human excreta. They have low C/N ratios (between 5 and 20) but tend to lose nitrogen due to ammonia "volatilizing" (being given off as a gas) with the familiar sharp smell and sting to the eyes.

ii) *Other nutrients* As well as nitrogen, plants need other 'nutrients' to feed them and help their growth. Of these, the most important are "phosphorus" and "potassium". Like nitrogen, they may be put into the soil either by rotating certain types of crops, by adding chemical fertilizers or by adding manures. However, the amount of these substances in some manures is small and chemicals are then needed in addition.

iii) *Soil structure* is important so that the roots of growing plants can take in air, water and the nutrients already mentioned. The water needs to be able to drain away so that the soil is not waterlogged and important nutrients are not washed away with surface drainage. The soil needs to be easy to plough. The presence of rotted fibrous matter helps provide this good structure which cannot be improved by chemical fertilizers, only by manures.

This ability, to improve and maintain good soil structure, is one of the most important qualities of manures, more so than the provision of plant nutrients in which they often need to be helped by chemical fertilizers or by crop rotation. For this reason some manures, such as town compost, should be regarded not as a fertilizer but as a soil conditioner.

Manures also have the effects of buffering the soil against excesses of mineral salts and providing microbiological activity. These are complicated and need not be discussed here, except to say that chemical fertilizers have neither of these properties.

2. ANIMAL FEEDS

These need to provide animals with:

  i) Carbohydrates to give energy to keep the animal alive and to increase weight:
 ii) Protein to provide energy and amino acids necessary for survival and growth.
iii) Vitamins and similar nutrients, essential for survival and health.
 iv) Minerals, essential for the health of blood, bones, teeth, glands and other parts of the body.
  v) Fibre or roughage to assist the animal's digestion.
 vi) Fats to provide energy and increase weight.
vii) Water which may also be provided separately.

Free ranging animals obtain these elements by instinct or, if they cannot, they become sickly and may die. Penned animals must be fed with a diet that has been blended to include all the ingredients necessary. Often, the diet is in the form of a natural bulk material such as grass, hay or oats with a supplement feed to provide the elements that may not be present in the bulk feed.

Generally, wastes are able to provide some or all of the bulk feed elements but often they cannot substitute for the supplement. Where farmers are poor and cannot afford to buy feed supplements it becomes important to try and find wastes that can provide everything in the diet. Some animals such as ruminants have very simple feed requirements and can eat material that is mainly cellulose, such as straw. Others, like pigs, have a simple digestive system that cannot manage straws or low quality fodder but have powerful appetites and eat almost any food wastes.

An important feature of animal feeds is that they should contain no harmful or poisonous substances. Industrial wastes must be critically examined for these.

3. PRODUCTION OF BIOGAS ENERGY

No process for using wastes has received so much recent attention as the production of methane gas or biogas from animal dung and vegetable wastes. In India and China huge programmes have been carried out to introduce biogas 'digesters' to the rural people and encourage their construction to provide cheap, renewable energy for cooking. A thorough

209

list of books on the subject can be obtained from Intermediate Technology Publications Ltd. No more will be attempted here than to describe the fundamental principles of digestion, the basic shape of a digester and the necessary character of materials to be used in feeding it.

Principles

It was earlier explained that, in the presence of air, organic materials rot so as to produce heat and give off carbon dioxide and nitrogen, provided the C/N ratio is low enough. The rotting is caused by minute creatures called bacteria and the kind of bacteria that need plenty of air are called 'aerobic'. If only limited quantities of air are present, a different, 'anaerobic' bacteria digest the material, if the temperature is high enough (above 28°C) and if the C/N ratio is not too high (preferably between 10 and 30 and never more than 35). Under these conditions, the rotting process gives off a mixture of about 35% carbon dioxide, a small amount of carbon monoxide (a poisonous, inflammable gas) and 60–65% methane, a non-poisonous inflammable gas with the familiar smell of rotting vegetation. This mixture is called biogas and is a safe and useful fuel for cooking, heating and lighting the home.

Human and animal dung (faeces or excreta) diluted with water in a ratio 1:1 or 1:2 have a low C/N ratio and their availability determines whether a digester will be economic to operate. If a substantial quantity of dung is available, vegetable waste can be added but ligno-cellulosic materials such as straws and wood wastes, are not satisfactory. Any materials used should not be strongly acidic or basic (approximately means alkaline). If so, they must be 'neutralised' by other materials to give a 'pH' between 6.0 and 8.0. At the start a biogas plant must be seeded with bacteria, either from fresh dung from a ruminant (e.g. a cow) or a sample of slurry from a working digester.

Design of a biogas digestor

The following are needed for a digester:

   i) A trough in which the materials can be mixed so that, even if they are disposed of at different times, the high C/N matter will enter the digester mixed with the low C/N matter.

   ii) A digester tank, to hold the materials in a slurry of

210

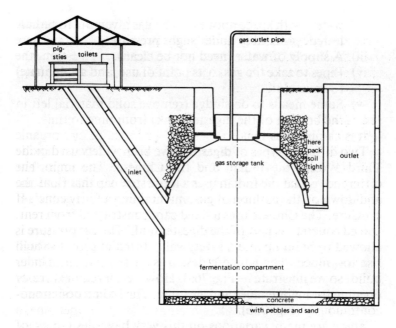

Fig. 76a   Diagram of Chinese biogas digester.

gas outlet pipe

pig-
sties   toilets

gas storage tank

here
pack
soil
tight

outlet

inlet

fermentation compartment

concrete
with pebbles and sand

*Fig. 76b   Digester of the Indian type with a floating steel gas holder.
Note the mixing trough to the left.*

water, with space above for the gas given off to be collected, preferably under slight pressure.

iii) A supply of water (need not be clean).

iv) Pipes to take the gas to its point of use, and a valve (tap) to control it.

v) Some means to de-sludge (remove solid material left in the bottom of the digester tank) from time to time.

It is as simple as that!

Two different types of digester have been widely used in the Third World; the Indian and the Chinese. The important difference is that the Indian uses a loose steel cap that floats up and down on the cushion of gas, maintaining a fairly constant pressure. The Chinese uses a fixed cap, constructed from reinforced concrete as part of the digester tank. The gas pressure is allowed to build up and a safety valve fitted in case it should rise too much. The Chinese design is quite a lot cheaper to build, so we illustrate it (Fig. 76a). However, it requires yearly opening for maintenance and cleaning. The Indian design runs continuously (Fig. 76b).

There are many variations on this very basic design: single and double stage, batch and continuous, heated and unheated, agitated and non-agitated – but they will not be studied here.

Table 12 lists some wastes suitable for methane generation and some that are not.

An important benefit from the production of biogas is that the sludge has a high fertiliser value but it is not clearly known whether, as a result of the action of the bacteria, all disease organisms are killed and it should not be applied to food crops, especially if human excreta have been used, without careful precautions. Animal feeding should not take place until a safe interval has elapsed. This will vary in different situations but as a guide, sludge that has been digested for three weeks should be on pasture for three weeks before cattle graze on it.

Some of the more common human and household wastes will now be examined:

FOOD WASTE

It is common practice to feed pigs and other animals on waste food from hotels, restaurants and houses. In some developing countries, pigs are fed on city refuse dumps and slaughtered for human food, a practice that poses grave dangers to health. Food waste that contains meat, or that has been in contact with

212

Table 12 Ability of wastes to generate methane

Waste material	C/N ratio	Gas yield (litres) per kg of material
Human excreta	6–10	—
Cow dung (up to 12 kg per day per cow, lower for poor animals or fodder)	18	90–300
Pig manure (up to 2½ kg per day per pig)	—	370–500
Chicken manure	7	300
Grass (hay)	12	Not suitable alone
Grass with chicken manure	—	350
Paper	—	Not suitable alone
Paper with chicken manure	—	400–500
Sewage sludge	—	600
Wheat straw	150	Not suitable alone
Bagasse (sugar cane waste)	150	Not suitable alone
Sawdust	200–500	Not suitable alone

A cooking gas burner needs 300–600 litres of gas per hour. Experience shows that peasant families use 4–5 cubic metres (4000–5000 litres) per person per month.

meat or any part of an animal carcass should be processed as follows:

   i) It must be batch sterilized for an hour by boiling in water at 100°C.

   ii) Different containers and vehicles must be used for delivering the sterile waste, from those used to collect the raw waste.

   iii) A wall must separate the input part of the processing shed from the output part. Entry to both must be through troughs of disinfectant.

   iv) Staff working in the two areas should be kept quite separate and should not move between the two jobs on the same day.

   v) A high standard of cleanliness should be applied to the whole operation.

   vi) As the operation is smelly it should be carried out away from houses etc.

SEWAGE

Sewage is the combined excreta and urine emitted from house-holds, which is often mixed with water. If piped sewage systems exist, then householders have no control over its treatment or disposal which is done by the municipality. It may be piped directly to the sea or to a river (both undesirable!) or it may be treated to separate and make harmless the solid matter, and discharge comparatively pure water. The study of sewage systems is a subject of enormous importance to health in the Third World and many books have been written on it; it is intended here to discuss only one element: disposal of the sludge, the dry matter that emerges from the treatment plant. If the home has no piped sewer then the householder may control how his 'nightsoil' is treated and may be able to use it in various ways.

All sewage has some value as fertilizer, biogas feedstock and animal feed, but whether it should be used is determined by the answers to the following questions.
- Is it safe or will diseases be spread?
- Is it economic?
- Is it pleasant or unpleasant, convenient or inconvenient?
- Is it permitted by law?

The value of sewage

Sewage contains nitrogen, potash and phosphate, in quite good ratios for growing cereal crops. When sludge is separated from the water, most of the potassium is lost and the sludge becomes mainly a source of nitrogen and phosphorus. In raw sludge, much of the nitrogen is not available to crops until the organic matter in the sludge decays. If the sludge is dewatered, much of the available nitrogen is lost with the water. With sludges that have been treated in a digester or in an activated sludge treatment process, the nitrogen is more rapidly available and 60–70% may be released to crops in the first growing season, compared with only about 20–30% from raw sludge.

Sludge contains between 1–5% phosphate: some of this is in the organic matter and is released as it decays. The rest is in inorganic chemicals but it is believed that about 60% of this is rapidly available. Fertilizer phosphates are expensive and of limited availability so, as crops need only about one-fifth as much phosphorus as they do nitrogen, it may be better to apply

214

only sufficient sludge to land to provide the phosphate needs and provide the additional nitrogen with a pure nitrogen fertilizer. Phosphates are held firmly in the soil for many years so yearly applications are not necessary. This has the further benefit of keeping the amount of sewage applied smaller, with less danger of poisonous elements getting into plant growth.

In sludge the ratio of nitrogen to potassium is in the range 7–12:1; plants require a ratio of between 2:1 and 2:3. Moreover, the potassium in sewage is soluble and most is lost in the water. It is, therefore, usually necessary to apply potassium to heavy crops of leafy material in the form of potash fertilizers. Grazing grass or fields that are regularly manured with animal dung only need this as starting applications where soil potash levels are low.

Sludge may contain magnesium which can be of value for grass growing.

Organic matter in sludge has the benefit of increasing the water-holding ability of the soil, making it more 'friable' and easy to work. It is especially good for sandy soils.

If more than 220 cu. m of liquid sludge are applied per hectare (20,000 gallons per acre), much may be lost as 'run off', especially if rain falls soon after, or if the soil is hard or dense. About 110 cu. m. per hectare (10,000 gals per acre) should be free from this, but not more than 60 cu. m per hectare should be applied to grassland.

If sewage contains material from industrial activities, these should be checked and, if doubt exists, chemically analyzed to ensure that poisonous minerals such as zinc, copper, nickel (at high levels) or cadmium, mercury, molybdenum, lead or arsenic are not present at dangerous levels. A report outlining the safe levels is available[1].

Safety rules for the use of nightsoil and sewage sludge
Depending on the development of the sewage service, material may become available for treatment:
- In the home, as raw nightsoil.
- In the home as treated sludge from a septic tank.
- At a municipal centre, as raw, untreated nightsoil.
- At a municipal treatment plant as raw sludge.
- At a municipal treatment plant as digested sludge.

Any of these materials may be safely used but the following general rules are essential to maintain public health.

215

i) Raw nightsoil must not be applied to crops, whether they are to be eaten by humans or animals. First, it should be either:
   a) Aerobically treated in a conventional sewage plant;
   b) Anaerobically digested to produce biogas and digested sludge; or
   c) Composted, usually with vegetable waste or municipal refuse, in such a way that it is maintained at a temperature of 55°C for a few days.
ii) Sludge that has been digested or otherwise treated can be used on crops provided certain precautions are taken, which will be described later.
iii) Neither nightsoil nor sludge should be fed to animals if they or their products are consumed by humans. This is one of the great dangers of refuse fed pigs. Where it is customary to feed fish on nightsoil, precautions must be taken as will be described.

N.B. Sludge that has only been separated from the liquid, e.g. in a settling tank, should be treated as if it were raw nightsoil as it still contains harmful bacteria. It is called raw sludge.

These processes will now be described in detail.

The use of municipal sewage

Raw sludge and municipal nightsoil. It cannot be too strongly urged that nightsoil and raw sludge be digested before disposal. If no treatment facilities exist they can only be used as a fertilizer on crops that will not be directly eaten either by animals or humans. Where there is any possibility of the sludge coming into contact with the edible portion, a safe interval must be allowed before eating. For example, six months should be allowed from the time the raw sludge is put on grassland, before cattle are grazed on it. Vegetables to be eaten raw should not be grown until twelve months after sludge or nightsoil is applied, but grain or other crops that are cooked before they are eaten may be grown in the season following application. No nightsoil or sludge of any type should be put on land close to ditches, rivers or other source of water supply, nor in parks or places where small children may crawl or play. Sludges from leather processing may contain long-living bacteria and should not be used for crops at all.

Digested sludge which has been recovered from a biogas or

other anaerobic treatment plant after a period of several weeks of anaerobic digestion will be greatly reduced in harmful bacteria. It should be stored in the digester for not less than three weeks and left on grass for another three weeks before cattle are allowed to graze. This period should be increased to five weeks for cattle that give milk that is not pasteurized.

Sludge from cesspools and septic tanks should be treated as raw sludge.

Solid sludges can safely be used if they have been kept for a year in total.

Lagooned sludges need to be two years old before use.

Composting of sludges and nightsoil is one way of ensuring that they are applied to land with almost complete safety. Digested sludge, however, has its nitrogen more readily-available, often in the form of ammonia. This may be lost during composting, or may become locked up if other material in the compost pile has a high C/N ratio, so it may be preferred to put digested sludge directly on to the soil and observe the safe periods above.

Home composting of nightsoil

In some towns and in almost all rural areas of the Third World, there are no drains and no municipal collections of nightsoil. The rich may have septic tanks but most people either have no sanitary device at all or else they have a simple privy dug in the soil. Some people make use of their nightsoil for fertilizing a garden, vegetable patch or field and there are commercial compost privies available for this. Most are expensive but the one shown in Fig. 77 is very cheap. It comes in two parts – a simple privy and a separate composting bin.

The privy consists of:
 i) A compartment under the seat, enclosed except for the hole in the seat which has an airtight lid and is itself hinged.
 ii) A tub under the hole, fitted with handles and set on bricks for the best ventilation.
 iii) A door in the compartment through which it can be withdrawn for emptying.
 iv) A ventilating chimney to the compartment, passing through the privy roof to the air outside.
 v) A can for ashes or sawdust which is sprinkled generously

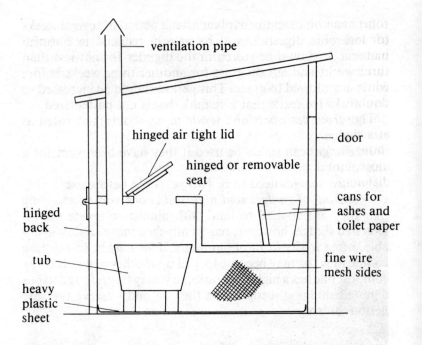

ventilation pipe

hinged air tight lid

hinged or removable
seat

door

cans for
ashes and
toilet paper

hinged
back

tub

fine wire
mesh sides

heavy
plastic
sheet

Fig. 77 Cheap two-part composting privy.

on the excreta each time the privy is used; the seat hinges
up for this.
vi) A can for used toilet paper.

Operation

The key to successful operation is that the excreta should be
dry in the waste tub; and urinating should be done elsewhere as
far as possible. The ashes or sawdust further soak up moisture;
this allows air to reach the excreta and permits aerobic bacteria
to operate, just as in composting.

The compost bin may consist of four sections. Material
from the privy is mixed with household organic waste such as
vegetable and fruit peelings and is put in one section only.
When that is full the material is emptied into the next section
and so on. When all sections are full the material from the

fourth can be spread on the soil, having had one or two years (or less with frequent turning) to compost into rich, black material free from smell. Air will get to the matter during turning but some people may prefer to add a pipe through which air can pass to the centre of the section, although it is doubtful whether this gives much advantage.

Those who can afford it can buy a composting privy with bin attached such as the Swedish "Clivus Multrum" version as shown in the photo (Fig. 78). It will require far less work and is more convenient but the quality of fertilizer will not be any different.

Fig. 78 *Commercial composting privies are expensive: Clivus Multrum. Note the door on the right for shovelling out the compost. Sweden.*

It is reported from China, that the peasant empties the contents of his chamber pot or latrine bucket into a large jar, placed beside the field on arrival in the fields each day. When the pot is full of this nightsoil it is sealed tightly for two to four weeks before spreading on the crops. This process is said to prevent the spread of *bilharzia* disease in the paddy fields. Anyone considering such a project should study Chinese methods.

219

Nightsoil or sludge as fish feed

In South-East Asia, both nightsoil and digested sludge are fed to fish and the privy may be built at the edge of the fish pond. In many places, however, this is not acceptable to the people. There is a risk of infection. This can best be reduced by treating the nightsoil in an oxidation pond for 15 to 20 days before it reaches the fish. The fish should be kept in a pond free from nightsoil and fed on other materials for two weeks or more before they are eaten.

Alternatively, 'algae' may be grown on oxidation ponds and harvested and fed to the fish in a separate pond. *Chlorella Vulgaris* is an algae that can be used for this but the fish will need other feed in addition.

As has been mentioned elsewhere, fish flourish on animal manure. Mud from fish ponds is a fertile manure for vegetables and other crops. In South-East Asia the paddy fields are constructed so that the water can be pumped from one to the other; each field can be used first as a fish pond, then as a paddy field and the two can even be done at the same time if the fish species does not eat green plants.

RECYCLING OF TOWN REFUSE

Chapter 13 described the routes by which household, trade and industrial refuse may be collected, recycled and disposed of. It did not describe the many kinds of disposal methods that exist which will be listed here. They will not be described in detail because many books have been written about them and their main concern is the safe disposal of the waste rather than the provision of employment by reclaiming it. The processes are:
- *Crude landfill* without covering.
- *Dumping* in rivers or the sea.
- *Sanitary landfill* where the refuse is covered with a layer of soil each day.
- *Baling*, followed by landfill.
- *Pulverizing* followed by landfill.
- *Incineration* (burning), with only the residue landfilled.
- *Composting*, with only the inorganic residue landfilled.
- *Resource recovery*, the systematic extraction of recyclables by hand or by machine, with a small residue landfilled.

Of the above techniques it may in general be said that:
Crude landfill and *dumping in water* create many pollution

220

and health dangers. *Baling, pulverizing* and *burning* are too expensive for most Third World countries although local circumstances may make them necessary. *Resource recovery* by machine is a process still in the development stage. *Sanitary landfill, resource recovery* by hand and *composting* are the most appropriate methods of refuse disposal currently available to Third World countries. The first is not a reclamation process and the best guide to its operation is to be found in a book by Frank Flintoff. It will not be discussed further. The second has been thoroughly covered in this book, but something must be said about the people who do it, sometimes called 'scavengers'. The third, composting, is thoroughly covered by Flintoff but some points, which need emphasizing are made here (see **Further Reading** for details of the book).

SCAVENGERS ON REFUSE DUMPS

The condition of scavengers

The presence of scavengers living and working on refuse dumps is common to all developing countries even though many municipalities make occasional and usually fruitless attempts to drive them away. Dump managements find it difficult to maintain a good standard of sanitary landfill as a result of scavenging activity. Most officials recognize the economic benefits of their activities, and the fact that scavenging provides their only livelihood, but are concerned at the serious health risks run by such communities.

Scavengers work with considerable energy but vaguely and inefficiently and with little awareness of the health risks they incur. Many of them and their families, often totalling several hundred people, live around the dump. They pick up bottles, ferrous and non-ferrous metals, cartons, tissue paper, wood and a variety of re-usable objects. They often keep animals which feed directly off the tip and they sometimes burn charcoal, using an earth kiln, adjacent to the tip. They often give the impression of a vigorous and sociable community who are on good terms with the junior officials who are in charge of the dump (Fig. 79).

These appearances, however, conceal the serious problems that seem common to scavengers the world over of which the most outstanding are:

i) *Poverty* Most scavengers earn far below the legal

221

Fig. 79   Scavengers working on a refuse dump. Note the dogs and pigs. The health risks of scavengers are very great but their money income may be larger than that of the poor in other occupations.

minimum wage set by the Government.

ii) *Ignorance* Scavengers often have few contacts with the world outside the dump, especially if they live on it, and know little of the rules of health, hygiene, reading or writing and less of business or social behaviour.

iii) *Illiteracy* is often common to 80, 90 or 100% of a community of scavengers.

iv) *Health* Scavengers often live and work in extremely dangerous conditions.

v) *Housing* rarely exists. Most scavengers live in a shanty built from waste materials from the dump which is often only accessible through a morass of rubbish.

vi) *Lack of services* such as medical, social or educational care, or public works like drinking water, sanitation or electricity.

vii) *Employment of children* is one of the worst features of scavenging communities because the children have no chance of education and are condemned to the same work for the rest of their lives.

viii) *Exploitation by buyers* Because scavengers tend to be ignorant, they are often ruthlessly exploited by those who buy their materials.

ix) *Inability to organize* themselves so that it is very difficult to help them.

x) *Lack of concern* by the public and the authorities, so that nothing is done to help improve their condition, and any general development of their country simply passes them by.

Little experience exists anywhere in the world of successfully helping scavengers break out of the trap in which they are caught. The following proposals are therefore totally theoretical, but might prove a method whereby determined agencies or other bodies could help the development of scavenger communities, by a two-stage programme.

Stage 1: Commercial and technical assistance

Some of the reclamation opportunities described in this book could be used by scavengers if various sorts of assistance were forthcoming. Opportunities might include the recovery of car shells; tin cans, possibly with a small de-tinning plant; paper and board, perhaps with the provision of a baler; improved charcoal burning using a steel kiln; improved animal husbandry through penning and other developments which might arise from the visits of a veterinary extensionist.

Further economic benefits could be achieved if the scavengers formed a marketing co-operative, appointed the best-qualified member as full-time salesman, organized co-operative transport of materials to customers and dispensed with middlemen. The mechanical installations mentioned above might be combined into a small, informal factory with concrete sorting pad and storage bunkers, covered working and storage areas where necessary, an accurate pair of weighing scales and a public telephone.

To achieve all this, a programme of discussions and training sessions arising from regular visits of a competent social worker, who understood the technicalities entailed, would be necessary.

Stage 2: Health and social development

The above programme might take some years to mature, depending on the skill and commitment of the social worker, the resources available, support from the authorities and the response from the people themselves. However, once the people start to increase their income, money becomes available

223

to create change and the process may accelerate. Unlike many communities of poor people, scavengers often have an abundance of space, labour, raw material inputs, animal feed-stuffs, combustible fuels, etc.

At some stage in the programme a confidence and rapport will be established between the people and the social worker which will be the basis for the second stage. The people will strengthen their existing community structure and leadership by forming a marketing co-operative and will begin to develop a sense of power to change their lives; the greatest need for any community to develop.

This is the stage at which the social worker suggests to them, or even better encourages their own suggestions of, such changes as:

    i) Enlarging the co-operative to cover purchase of house-building materials, food and clothing, and perhaps a taxi service.

    ii) Co-operative building of community facilities such as a meeting hall, latrine block, paths and roadways between houses, washing facilities adjacent to the dump, etc.

    iii) Putting pressure on the authorities to provide roads, lighting, drainage, clinics, schooling and other town services.

    iv) Development of a credit union within the co-operative so that the sums of cash which will arise from improved recycling activities may be used productively, rather than leading to increased drinking or other problems of successful scavengers.

    v) Training of children in other work so that they can make a living without scavenging.

    vi) A health programme involving the use of protective clothing, vaccination against tetanus, polio, infectious hepatitis; education in the causes of diarrhoea, dysentery and other diseases which are endemic among scavengers and cause terrible rates of infant mortality. The municipality could support this with an intensification of control measures against vermin and disease vectors.

    vii) At this stage in such a programme the scavengers would be aware of the health reasons for a high standard of sanitary landfill and would co-operate with the management of the dump. Often, any restraint on the spreading of refuse as soon as it has been tipped from the vehicle, a practice quite against good landfill technique, is met with threats of violence. City health officials who view with concern any of these proposals, which would develop or intensify scavenging activities, may perhaps feel that this would justify such a programme.

COMPOSTING OF TOWN REFUSE

The process is, in principle, similar to the composting of agricultural wastes, which is described in a book due to be published in the future. If the material is not too moist and is turned frequently to allow air to reach it then organic materials in the refuse will be attacked by aerobic bacteria. The bacterial action raises the temperature with the result that many harmful bacteria are killed, but it is important to make sure that all parts of the material reach this temperature. The final material is a rich, dark, free-flowing solid, free from smell and flies *provided* the treatment has been correct (Fig. 80).

The main difference from agricultural composting is that it is necessary to sort out a much wider variety of non-compostable, non-organic materials. This is usually done before the composting process begins but in some systems it is done after. Fortunately, the materials that are not compostable are also the recyclable materials that have been described in earlier chapters of this book. The only ones that really are not recyclable are inert materials such as brick, stone, rubble and dust, and these can be used as filler in marshy areas, under waterside shanty housing, in road construction etc.

Employment

The process of sorting non-compostables provides a substantial amount of employment, particularly for people who have low skills and, of course, for scavengers. In Monterrey, Mexico, when a new composting plant replaced the old refuse tip, the jobs went to former scavengers, a most enlightened and humane piece of municipal policy. There have been some problems, for people used to a free and independent life have had to change to work within a factory situation, but there have also been great benefits to health and security of employment.

Composting technology

The reputation of municipal composting has been rather

Fig. 80 *Composted refuse is a rich, dark, free-flowing solid if mad correctly. India.*

poor over the last few years for two reasons; poor marketing and inappropriate technology. The problem with the latter is that the theoretical attraction of the system has been exploited by a number of industrial companies from certain rich countries as an opportunity to sell large, complex composting systems. Unfortunately these have not been sufficiently proven in operation and demand a standard of technical management far higher than that normally available to Third World municipalities. Some attempts to devise more appropriate technology have been made in India during recent years but none has so far achieved unqualified success. Any municipality that is thinking of installing an industrialized refuse composting plant should first study the numerous failures, that may be seen around the Third World, with great care. The author will be pleased to assist with further information.

Marketing of compost

Some municipalities have been given the idea that municipal compost is a substitute for chemical fertilizers that will be eagerly bought by local farmers at a price to give the seller a handsome profit: this is far from the truth. Compost is not a substitute for fertilizers. However, it is an excellent soil conditioner with some fertilizer value, but its weight and bulk make it expensive to transport and to spread on the fields. Farmers will only use it if it is available, at low cost, close to their fields. It is therefore extremely important for any municipality that considers setting up a plant, to first research local markets for compost before equipment is considered.

Sometimes, the municipal parks and gardens can use enough compost to absorb the whole production and there will be no need to sell it to farmers. In this situation, it must be clearly realized that the cost of producing good quality compost is much higher than the cost of other methods of waste disposal, such as sanitary landfill, and certainly higher than the cost of crude tipping. If no income is to be received from farmers or the public then the municipality must be prepared to meet these extra costs as the price for having good soil in their parks and a reduced need for space for refuse landfill. Where a city has a booming tourist trade or is seriously short of landfill sites within the city boundaries, these may be acceptable. This is particularly the case where the cost of transporting refuse over bad roads to landfill sites twenty or thirty kilometres outside the city, will be greatly reduced. In other situations, it is not likely that any city will continue to fund an expensive operation for an indefinite time in the future just to get better roses and lawns in the parks.

The future of municipal composting

Provided these two matters are examined with the most careful attention, there can be nothing but good reasons for using composting as a means of refuse disposal. Perhaps the most important argument in its favour, and it is a pity it is not easier to put a financial value to it, is that the quality of soil is one of the most important assets any country can have. Municipal composting, once the problems of technology and marketing have been overcome, offers the best possible prospect of long term improvements and the education of the people in the enormous long term value of returning organic wastes to the soil.

References

1. *'The Disposal of Sewage Sludge to the Land'. Published by and available from Her Majesty's Stationery Office, U.K.*

Part II
How to start a Waste Business

Chapter 11. Which Waste?

Part 1 of this book has described dozens of different waste materials. The reader for whom the book has been written, however, is not interested in just knowing about wastes; he wants to create work, for him or herself or for others; collecting, processing, selling or doing all these to one or more materials. Part II is intended to help the small 'businessman' by explaining, stage-by-stage, how to go about creating work. It is illustrated by two case studies and summarized in thirty-two short, simple rules which are repeated at the back so that they can be constantly checked.

Few people will gain maximum benefit from reading Part II straight through. It is much better read *in relation to an actual business*. One way to do this is for a group of people, some of whom are running or considering a waste business, to meet together. The group may include an outsider: a local priest or social worker perhaps. One person who can read and write is needed. Each time they meet, after reading all or part of a chapter (or having it read out aloud), they will go through it, item by item, question by question and try to see how it relates to their own town or their own business. At first they will discover that they do not know the answers to some of the questions that are asked. Some research (that just means finding out) will be needed. Write down whether it can be done and the name of the person in the group who is going to do it, (just as do the characters in case study 1 and 2). Ask the person to agree to a day by which it will have been done and write that too. The notes will look a little like Fig. 81.

Some chapters, especially Chapter 18 on costing, may seem difficult. In fact they are only unfamiliar. Try to think of them as they apply to your own business; perhaps leave them for a while and come back to them when they seem more important for your business; in a few months the difficulty will disappear.

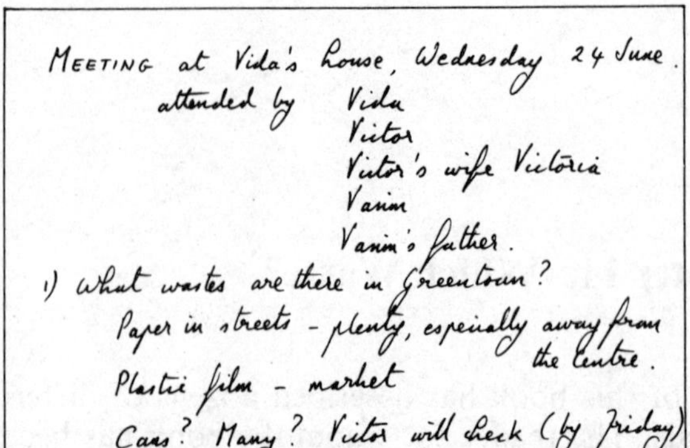

MEETING at Vida's house, Wednesday 24 June.
        attended by   Vida
                      Victor
                      Victor's wife Victoria
                      Vanim
                      Vanim's father.

1) What wastes are there in Greentown?
    Paper in streets - plenty, especially away from
                              the centre.
    Plastic film - market
    Cans? Many? Victor will check (by Friday)
    Tailors trimmings? Ask Smith - Vida tomorrow
    Vegetables - houses - how many?
               market
                  restaurants
2) What happens now? Who collects? ⎫ Vanim to
    Where does it go?   ⎬ Town Hall
                                ⎭ tomorrow.
3) What Markets?
    Paper mill? Vanim check Yellow pages today
    Can plastic be recycled - Vida, Tech College.
    Does the foundry by the railway station
    Victor to visit this week. buy cans?

NEXT MEETING - Sunday, same time & place.

Fig. 81   Notes from a meeting to find work from waste.

Most of the important decisions discussed in Chapters 13 to 18 depend on which waste is to be handled and it will save time and money if this is determined at an early stage. However, it is not an obvious decision and must be taken with great care, so this and the next chapter will tackle it. They will begin by asking two very important questions:

"What wastes occur in this district that are not being used?"

"What uses or markets exist for them?"

Both must be answered if jobs are to be created. You cannot have a marriage without a bride *and* a bridegroom and likewise you cannot sell wastes without a supply and a market.

232

1. WHAT WASTES OCCUR IN THIS DISTRICT THAT ARE NOT BEING USED?

To answer this, it is necessary to understand how and where wastes arise. Fig. 82 will help you. Consider the places shown in the diagram. Do you know where to find them in your district? You may suddenly realize that there are areas that you have never been to and that you only know a quarter of the factories in the town. What about the wastes that can be found at these places? You probably always noticed wastes lying around in the streets, but never looked closely at what they were.

If this chapter is being used as the subject of a meeting, perhaps the meeting could break off at this point while everyone walks around the town for an hour to look at the different wastes that occur. It may take longer if you intend to visit the backs of shops and factories. At this stage a glance through the wire of a factory yard should tell enough. Do *not* be so thorough that you are arrested as thieves!

Visit the town refuse dump at some point, too. Even if it is twenty miles away it will be worth the trouble. Someone who can write should go along with paper and pencil to list the items being dumped and important facts about them. There may be an army of people already working on the dump who may not welcome you if they know you are hoping to collect wastes. On the other hand, they may be able to help you: if they are working alone or in small numbers they may volunteer to join your group. Do you scorn this idea because they are dirty and ragged? They may have information and skills you need and you may have the ability to work as a group that they lack.

At the dump or in the streets you can find tell-tale information to tell you from where a particular type of waste has come, such as labels on cans or drums, letters or boxes with a trade name printed on them. It may be worth visiting the factory or office that discards these. Some waste will come. from households.

When you have a list of the materials that occur as waste, with as much information as possible about where they come from, try next to estimate the quantity of each material. It may not be possible to do more than describe it as 'a lot' or 'a little' but even this will help.

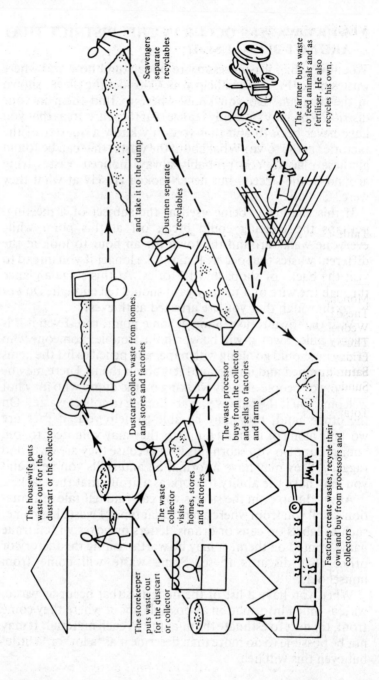

The housewife puts waste out for the dustcart or the collector

The storekeeper puts waste out for the dustcart or collector

The waste collector visits homes, stores and factories

Dustcarts collect waste from homes, and stores and factories

Dustmen separate recyclables

and take it to the dump

Scavengers separate recyclables

The farmer buys waste to feed animals and as fertiliser. He also recycles his own.

The waste processor buys from the collector and sells to factories and farms

Factories create wastes, recycle their own and buy from processors and collectors

Fig. 82   Showing how waste is moved around the community.

234

VEGETABLE WASTE CASE STUDY 1

Victor, Vida and Vasim live in Bluetown. They hold a meeting to discuss ways in which to find work. They walk round the streets looking at the waste which is lying in heaps waiting for the disposal carts to collect it. Most of it is vegetable peelings left by housewives. They decide to work out how much there is.

Vida and Vasim's wife agree to put each day's peelings into separate, labelled bags. At the end of a week they each take their seven bags to the market, borrow a scale from one of the stalls and list the weights (Table 13).

Table 13 Weights of waste per household in grammes

	Vida's family of eight people	Vasim's family of ten people
Monday	420	510
Tuesday	640	620
Wednesday	200	250
Thursday	610	700
Friday	520	540
Saturday	400	360
Sunday	780	800
Total	3570	3780

They calculate that the average is just over half-a-kilo per family per day.

Victor, meanwhile, has been to the mayor's office at the Town Hall to find out how many people and how many families live in Bluetown. He is told by the clerk that there are about 20,000 people, but the number of families is unknown because they keep splitting up and changing. There are probably about seven people in each family, which makes around 2,850 families.

Back at Vasim's house they calculate that half-a-kilo of peelings per day from each of 2,850 families, makes 1,425 kilos a day, which is about 10,000 kilos (1,425 × 7) a week or 10 tonnes.

"What can we do with 10 tonnes a week of vegetable peelings?" "Is anyone else collecting vegetable peelings?'' "Would we be allowed to?'' "Would we have to pay for it?''

Eventually Victor says: "First we must find out what we can do with it. If it can be sold, why has no one done so before?''

Victor, Vasim and Vida's process of working out the quantity of waste available can be called *supply research*. It needs to be done for any waste you may consider collecting and using or processing and selling and must answer these questions:

i) What waste is available? Vegetable peelings.

ii) Where does it come from? Households.

iii) How much is there? About 10 tonnes a week – but spread around 20,000 people in nearly 3,000 households.

iv) What will it cost? Nothing; it is thrown away at present.

v) Of what quality is it? That is a question to leave until later. It is much easier to answer if we know first what quality is *wanted*. To decide that, it is necessary to know the market into which it can be sold.

Rule 1
Find out what wastes occur in the district that are not being used.

Rule 2
Find out the quantity if possible.

2. WHAT USES OR MARKETS EXIST FOR THEM?

The way to answer this question is simple – ask people. It may be helpful to look in books as well, but asking people is the first step. The next case study shows how Victor, Vida and Vasim went about it.

236

VEGETABLE WASTE CASE STUDY 2

"Everyone knows" says Victor "that vegetable wastes make good compost to fertilize the fields and vegetable gardens. All we have to do is make compost and sell it to farmers and vegetable growers."

"The farmers round here are too poor to buy compost" says Vasim.

"I think the people who grow vegetables to sell in the market would buy it" says Vida. "They make plenty of money by charging high prices."

"Let us go and ask them" says Victor.

They go to the local vegetable market and talk to the vegetable sellers. Then they go to the local farmers store in which they hope to find out who buys fertilizers. The manager refuses to tell them, so they wait outside the store and talk to people who go in and out. Next, they visit the local agricultural extension officer who tells them (as they are beginning to discover themselves) that very few people use compost these days. Those who can afford it buy chemical fertilizers; those who cannot do without, and of course could not afford to buy from them. They decide there is no market for compost made from waste vegetables.

Vida, Vasim and Victor have just completed a successful piece of *market research* which has saved them many hours of wasted time making and trying to sell compost to people who do not want to buy it. In Chapter 15 market research will be examined in detail. At this stage it is important simply to recognize that market research is essential before putting time or money into the collection or production of a waste product. But what do you do if you get a negative answer from your research?

Vida, Vasim and Victor have another meeting and decide that they can do one of three things:

    i) Give up the idea of collecting vegetable waste and collect something else.

    ii) Persuade people of the value of compost so they will buy it.

    iii) Find another market for vegetable waste.

They decide to try the last alternative. Then Vida suddenly has a bright idea:

237

"Vegetable wastes can be fed to pigs. Who keeps pigs? What do they feed them on now? Would they buy vegetable waste if we collected it?"

They go to the local agricultural store to find out who keeps pigs and buys special feeds. They do not say that they want to know this in order to sell such people a different feed and the store manager thinks they want to buy some pork! They ask the local veterinary officer too. At the council office they ask the inspector who checks on swine disease. They look in the Telephone Directory, in the classified section that lists goods and services in alphabetical order: ("Physiotherapists, Piano Tuners, Picture-frame makers, *Pig Farmers*"). They visit the pig farmers listed to ask if they would be interested in buying 10 tonnes of pig food per week.

After walking several weary miles they understand why nobody else is selling vegetable waste as pig food; pig farmers are scattered all around the district. Many of them receive food wastes from their neighbours for their pigs, but most must also buy extra grain from the farmers' store at a cost of around half-a-dollar per kilo. All say they would buy vegetable wastes if they were available and cheap, but:
- They would have to be fresh.
- They would have to be delivered in the mornings when the pigs are fed.

They also say that if cheap food was available, they could keep more piglets for fattening instead of selling them to the market.

Victor, Vida and Vasim now have a list of possible customers and an idea of how much vegetable waste each wants. They know something about the quality of the material needed, too: it must be fresh. But does fresh mean the same day? The next day? Less than two days old? They have not thought to ask that. They wish they had planned their questions better.

At their next meeting they discuss the results of their second piece of market research. Victor sums up:

"We have a list of ten pig breeders scattered around the town who would like to buy vegetable waste providing it is cheap and fresh, and another five who get theirs from neighbours. Of the ten, four have forty animals and the other six have only twenty. Each animal on average will eat two kilos per day, so the total requirement will be 280 animals or 560 kilos per day – about four tonnes per week. This is much less than the supply available, but enough to start a business. Besides, there are other pig breeders we have not visited and some who currently buy from their neighbours but might come to us if we persuade them. We can do this by selling our material at a cheaper price than that of grain.''

The group now have both a supply of waste and a market for it, so they are in business. Or are they? There are other matters they need to examine before they can be sure and these will be studied in the next chapter. Meanwhile these rules can be stated:

Rule 3
Find out what uses or markets exist before starting to collect waste material.

Rule 4
Find out the quantity and quality required, where the markets are and the price they might pay.

Chapter 12. Other Needs – Technology, Transport, Premises, Labour and Management

Chapter 11 discussed essentials for creating work by recycling wastes: i) A supply of waste material, in the right quantity and quality, and at the right place and price; ii) A market for the right quantity and quality in the right place at the right price.

This chapter examines some other necessities. The principles are illustrated by the vegetable wastes case study and also by examples of a group collecting a more difficult waste to deal in – plastics.

TECHNOLOGY

Technology is not something of which to be frightened. It is a useful word that covers things people can do to make their lives easier. If a man walks to work he is not using technology, but he is if he rides there on a bicycle. Less time is taken for the journey and he is not as tired on arrival. The technology he is using is a simple one consisting of pedals, gears and wheels. If he buys a car and drives to work, using no energy himself (except to steer and change gear), but obtaining it instead from petrol, he is using a more complicated technology. Technology does not only mean using machines. It also covers processes. If you cook food to make it less tough or to stop it going bad before you eat it, that also is technology. If wood is burned to form charcoal that is lighter and cleaner to cook with, a simple chemical technology is being used. Technology covers the nature and structure of materials, the processes that can change them and the equipment used in these processes.

Most of the wastes discussed in the first half of this book needed something done to them before use. They needed to be sorted or baled or melted or shredded or pulped or composted or fermented, washed or dried or something else. Technology is the means used to carry this out; the tools and equipment, the energy and skill used, the materials needed, the time or temperature or pressure or force required.

What technology is needed?
The technology must be chosen after asking the question: "What form is the waste in when collected, and in what form can it be sold for a better price, or with less spent on transport?"

PLASTICS WASTE CASE STUDY 1

In the vegetable wastes case study, the pigs eat the material in a state similar to that in which it is collected from households. It seems no technology is required. The plastics case study, follows a group of people – Penelope, Prida and Paulo – who have decided to collect and sell plastics waste. They discovered that a *supply* exists, from homes, shops and factories and that there is a *market* for waste plastic among the small factories that make cheap plastic buckets. They have checked that the *quantity* of the supply is more than enough to satisfy the market, that they can obtain plastic waste *free* by picking it up in the street, the rubbish dump, or houses and stores, and that there is a *market* – two factories in Bluetown a short distance from Greentown where they live.

However, when they came to study the *quality*, they found that:

i) The *supply* was made up of sacks, bags and sheets of plastic film, often dirty. These were sometimes made of low density polyethylene combined with other plastics in the one object.

ii) The *market* was only for *pure* low density polyethylene which had to be clean.

iii) If it was chopped up into small flakes, the price for which it could be sold was twice as high.

iv) If it was made into tiny round pellets, the price would be five times as high.

They realized that although they could collect *some* clean plastic, they needed a technology that would clean the rest and enable them to distinguish and separate low-density polyethylene from other plastics. They realized, too, that they would benefit, by higher prices, if they

241

could produce the material in flakes or, even better, in pellet form.

Rule 5
Decide what technology is needed to change the material from the form in which it occurs into the form in which it can be sold and whether any further technology is desirable.

How to find suitable technology
The types of technology needed to process various wastes for sale in the principal markets have already been described in Part 1. Later in the book, a list of books that specialize in certain materials and which may give more detailed information is included, and a list in the appendices includes organizations that can offer advice. However, the answer is often near at hand: the customer to whom you hope to supply can often tell you all that needs to be known, but remember that he has a commercial interest, so try to check his information elsewhere. Perhaps a local technical school can help, or a Government extension officer or Small Firms Advisory Service. Often, there will be a bookshop where textbooks can be bought, or a city, school or college library; the librarian may help you find the information. Finally, there are many trade associations that exist to help their members and they *may* be willing to help you. If all else fails, write to the author of this book at the publisher's address, giving full details of the problem and your full address for a reply.

Limitations of technology
Most wastes can be processed by a very few technologies, as we have seen in Part I. However, any of the following problems may be encountered:
  i) The technology may not exist at all, e.g. no process exists for recycling 'thermoset' plastics such as Melamine cups and saucers, or Formica table top laminates.
  ii) The technology may exist but could be too expensive or elaborate to use, e.g. for briquetting sawdust into fuel pellets that can be burnt for domestic cooking. Often, the problem is one of scale; a large sawmill can afford to use a huge briquetting press to provide all its fuel needs

242

from its own sawdust, but for a small-town sawmill this is not economic.

iii) The technology may be in existence and usable, but there could be social or other objections e.g. burning plastic coverings from copper cables makes poisonous black smoke, so is often illegal.

iv) The technology may simply not be known about, or not known in enough detail to be used. For example, coconut trunk is seldom cut into timber for building because the technology used is not widely known and it is difficult and troublesome to obtain suitable equipment on remote islands or plantations. It is hoped that this book will help to ease this situation a little.

v) The technology may be known about, but may require too much skill or knowledge for those involved; e.g. the sorting of different plastics is seldom done because of the difficulty of training sorters to do it accurately.

PLASTICS WASTE CASE STUDY 2

Having identified the technology they need to sell waste plastics to the factory that moulds plastic buckets, Penelope, Prida and Paulo meet to discuss how to find out what is available. From this book they learn how to sort low density polyethylene from other plastics by hand, using simple tests when they are in doubt. Soon they become so experienced, they no longer need to use tests. They also discover that, unless they compress the plastic sheets, transport will cost more than they will be paid for the material. The customer offers to hire them a granulating machine, but suggests they bale the material which he will granulate in his factory. At first they are rather confused by the word granulator, but they talk to the instructor in the town's technical college who explains that it is simply a machine to chop plastic into small pieces. They discover that the cost of hiring a granulator is more than their extra payment for the work, so they decide to start by baling the plastic in a simple box, as described in Chapter 1. When they have earned enough money they will buy a granulator which can be made at the local engineering workshop, and power it with an electric motor, bought second-hand. The instructor promises to help them install it in the shed behind Prida's house (the only house with a supply of electricity). Meanwhile, the local carpenter will make them up a baling box, but will need two steel hinges. Paulo finds these on the doors of a car that had crashed nearby some months before.

They decide that all material will be sorted to see whether it needs washing, and agree to save cooking and washing water in an old oil drum. Prida puts a channel made of split bamboo along his roof edge to catch rain water which will then spill into the drum. After the plastic has been washed in it, the water can still be used, as at present, to water the women's vegetable patch.

Paulo thinks they should try to pelletize the granulated plastic as described in Chapter 5, but Penelope and Prida say they cannot afford the machine and, in any case, they do not really understand the process. They agree to study this possibility again after they have become used to working with plastics and are confident they can make money from this work.

Rule 6
With simple, home-made technology you can often process material cheaply to increase its sales value and reduce transport costs.

Rule 7
Leave complicated technology until you are familiar with the product and the market and can find the money needed without endangering the business.

TRANSPORT
Transport plays a very important part in any waste recycling business. Wastes are usually bulky and low in value compared with virgin raw materials or finished goods. Transport costs depend on the bulk of the materials and the distance covered and are not reduced because the material's value is low. Wastes have to be collected from where they occur and taken to where they can be sold. Anyone deciding to deal in a waste must consider his transport requirements with great care, particularly at the present time when transport costs are increasing

faster than any other type of expense due to rising petroleum prices.

Usually, two quite different transport operations are involved; collection and delivery. Collection may require many visits to collect small amounts of material, from houses, factories or collection bins. Delivery may be to only one customer; for example, waste paper to a single huge paper mill, or to a small number, for example, scrap iron to several small foundries. Sometimes, as in the vegetable waste case study, there are several customers involved, but even then they are fewer than the number of sources of supply. The questions that must be asked about transport are:

i) How much material has to be collected from the source of supply, from how many different places and to where must it be taken?

ii) How much material has to be delivered to the customer and how often?

iii) What transport is available?

iv) What will it cost?

The last two questions should really be asked together because transport is always available (except in very remote districts) if you can pay enough for it. What interests the collector of wastes is transport whose cost is not more than a reasonable proportion of the price he is going to receive for his material. This need not only mean transport he owns himself; indeed this book will counsel small traders against trying to own motor vehicles, as will be discussed in Chapter 16.

Often, considerations of transport will decide what sources of waste supply will be collected and what markets supplied.

VEGETABLE WASTE CASE STUDY 3

Vida, Victor and Vasim have definitely decided to collect vegetable wastes from households and sell them to ten pig breeders around the town. Victor obtains a number of oil drums and they discover that, if they put the wastes in these, the cart can hold twice as much material. They examine the possibility of compressing the waste into the oil drums using a press. This increases the amount of material in each drum by half, and the weight of the full drums that can be put on the cart is as much as an animal can pull. Vida suggests that, if the drums are already filled when it arrives, and if the pig breeders are not expected to empty the drums immediately but can return the empty drum on the next day's delivery, it would only take two hours for a small lorry to deliver the material to all ten pig breeders. They would need a second man on board to help the driver lift the full drums off the back of the lorry. This makes it worth hiring a lorry and driver for two hours every day, even though it would not have been worth buying a vehicle themselves. A local builder has a lorry that is only half busy and asks a reasonable price. Two things worry them. What will they do if the lorry does not arrive due to mechanical breakdown? What will they do if sudden increases in diesel fuel put up the price of the lorry? Both problems are solved by ensuring that an animal-driven cart can be made available at short notice. However, they hope that customers who have been satisfied with their service for several months or longer would not go back to their old sources of feed, even if a price increase were necessary.

They learn that the local pineapple cannery throws away five tonnes of pineapple waste every week. This could be used to feed pigs, but the factory is out in the country, thirty kilometres away, near the pineapple plantations. They consider their transport needs and wonder if they should take advantage of the pineapple waste, even though they are not yet selling all the household waste.

They decide that the household wastes can be collected by people with sacks walking down each street, plus one person with a hand-cart doing a round trip, twice-a-day, receiving the full sack from each collector and providing him with an empty one. The same cart *could* deliver to the pig breeders, but because they are spaced out all around the town, this will take too long. A second cart, with a horse, or a small van or open pick-up vehicle will be necessary. They do not have enough money for a vehicle and none of them has learned to drive, so it will have to be an animal-drawn cart.

They consider asking a local lorry owner to collect the pineapple waste, but after finding out his charges, they decide they will make more profit from just the household collections. They also believe that, if they made this arrangement, the lorry driver might end up doing the work on his own behalf and the factory might start to charge for the pineapple waste or even deliver directly to the pig breeders. Being prudent, Victor, Vida and Vasim decide to wait until they can afford a vehicle of their own before trying to use this opportunity.

The following rules can be stated about transport of wastes:

Rule 8
Transport is one of the highest costs in a waste business. It may decide which sources of supply or markets are economic.

Rule 9
Transport costs can be reduced by:
- Making door-to-door visits on foot with a back-up vehicle;
- Using carts drawn by people or animals instead of motor vehicles;
- Hiring vehicles for part-time work;
- Compressing materials and organizing material handling to reduce the time the vehicle is required.

PREMISES AND STORAGE

Premises and storage are usually necessary for all but the smallest waste collections. The ideal arrangement is for material to be collected and taken direct to the customer, but usually this is not possible because:
  i) The quantity collected is either more or less than the quantity the customer wants to buy.
 ii) The material needs some processing or sorting before it can be delivered.
iii) The supplier and the customer must not learn about each other in case they start to deal direct.

When looking for premises for a waste operation, consider the following:
  i) It should be situated so that the travelling distance of the material is not greatly increased.
 ii) Its cost must not take too high a part of the income from sales.
iii) Loading and unloading must not take too much time and effort.

iv) There must be space to store material in the quantities necessary.

v) The business must run without trouble from thieves, neighbours who object to the smell, the smoke or the noise, and the police or local authority.

vi) There must be water supplies, electricity, drainage, a road, and any other essential service.

vii) Because waste is often dirty, attracts insects and rats, or may involve the use of dangerous machinery, it is better not to set up the business next to your home. Even a distance of two hundred metres will keep them separate and allow you to forget your business troubles when you finish work in the evening. If you are worried about thieves there is no better solution than a dog with its chain running on a long wire.

viii) Some operations need to be carried out in an enclosed building with a roof; for example, non-ferrous metals are valuable enough for a thief to think it worth killing the dog (or the owner if he is trying to do the dog's job), while paper rots if left outside in a wet climate. Ferrous scrap is always stored outside; so is waste glass ('cullet').

VEGETABLE WASTE CASE STUDY 4

Having decided on the transport arrangements needed, Vida, Victor and Vasim consider suitable premises. They must be away from houses as they expect the material to attract flies and rats, even though they intend to clean up every evening and not store any material for more than 24 hours. None of them wants the premises near *their* house which, while poor, is as clean as they can make it; nor would it be fair to their neighbours! However, it must be near the housing area so the collection cart will not have far to travel, and they do not want to pay bus fares to travel to work each day.

They decide that no person is likely to steal their waste material, but are worried about animals. They decide to keep a dog which can also deal with rats. They do not need an enclosed building, but a roof is necessary to keep sun and rain off the material. They need to be close to a good road, as the transport costs will be increased if carts or the lorry have to travel over rough ground. They do not vitally need water, electricity or drainage although electricity would be useful to give light for night work, and water and drainage would allow the installation of a wash basin and a lavatory. However, all these can wait until some profits appear.

The most important need is for a 'loading dock'. This is a concrete surface beside and higher than the level of the road on which carts and lorry stand, so that the heavy drums of waste can be trundled on and off without too much difficulty (Fig. 83). They use a natural slope in the site to move soil from the lower level to the higher and lay concrete thick enough to stand the scraping of the loaded drums of materials.

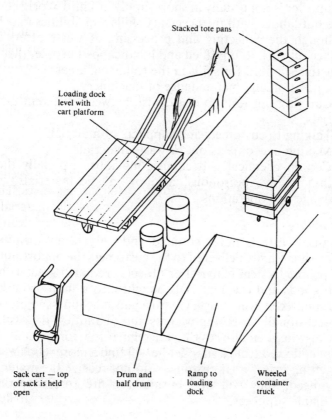

Stacked tote pans

Loading dock level with cart platform

Sack cart — top of sack is held open

Drum and half drum

Ramp to loading dock

Wheeled container truck

Fig. 83 Loading dock and some useful containers.

Because the material will rot, they do not need space to store more than twenty four hours' collection of materials, but they need space for empty oil drums. They save money by renting a small plot. It will be easy for them to move if they expand in the future.

Rule 10
Plan your workplace to minimise rent, transport costs, handling effort and outside interference. Decide which services and space you need now and which can be added later.

LABOUR

Skills
Manpower is not usually in short supply in Third World countries but labour with the necessary skills and abilities may be. Although the collecting and processing of waste offers the chance of work to unskilled and handicapped people, there is sometimes a need for skills in the following areas:
- Operation and maintenance of machinery.
- Carrying out tests to distinguish between different materials.
- Talking to customers and suppliers of material.
- Making new objects out of waste materials.
- Certain chemical and engineering jobs, especially those that involve poisonous, acid or caustic materials, and dangerous operations.

Reliability
Because waste is never counted and only rarely measured before it is finally delivered to the customer, the opportunities for people to steal material or objects are much greater than with goods and raw materials bought into a shop or factory and counted at every stage. Guard against dishonest employees by occasionally checking weights and quantities, if possible. You also need employees who are regular for work; if material is not collected from a supplier he will find a more reliable way of getting rid of it; if customers do not receive the materials they need, they will lose business so are forced to drop unreliable suppliers.

Strength
Much waste is heavy and bulky and has to be carried from

250

one place to another. Strong people, able to work hard all day, should be employed for this kind of activity, but even these need occasional rest and refreshment during working hours. No one can sustain heavy work without a meal in the middle of the day. Those who employ others will find it in their own interest to ensure they are paying their employees enough money to eat properly. The same is true of people working in the heat. If men labour in the sun they will lose strength and efficiency. An awning or roof over the work area, plus provision of clean drinking water at all times, is worth twenty per cent extra manpower.

Cleanliness
Waste is usually dirty, often smells unpleasant and may contain insects, vermin or other unpleasant impurities. Those who work with it need to wash their hands and faces before eating, and, preferably, their whole bodies at the end of the day. They need to come to work in decent clothing, change into working clothes and change back again at the day's end. They also need to wash their working clothes from time to time. On rubbish dumps all over the world, small shelters can be seen where scavengers change their clothes. Some of them, when they leave the dump, might be mistaken for office workers. People deserve encouragement and help in order to maintain their dignity and self-respect.

Those who are not employed full-time, but paid by the piece of work done, should be treated just the same as employees. In many developed countries people receive extra money for dirty work.

Rule 11
Although waste may be dirty, heavy, infested or of low value, the people who handle it should be treated with courtesy as valuable assistants and provided with reasonable pay, food, drink and wash places.

MANAGEMENT
Management is not something practised only in big factories or offices. Even in a one-man business collecting old newspapers in a sack, management plays an important part. The following are usual in the management of a waste operation:
-   Finding sources of material.

- Finding markets for the material.
- Arranging transport.
- Obtaining equipment, containers, storage space etc.
- Arranging processing of material.
- Paying for material or services bought.
- Collecting payment for material sold.
- Supervising other workers which means providing them with work, ensuring they have all they need to do it, making sure they do it and rewarding them afterwards.
- Discussions with customers, suppliers, the police or town authorities about the work.
- Making sure the business makes a profit, by budgeting and costing.

In some businesses, managers are quite distinct from actual workers. This often results in friction (or worse) between them, especially if the manager sits with his feet up while the workers sweat and carry heavy loads. In businesses where each person manages his own work, such as a partnership, it is easier to avoid the problems of personal relationships between a manager and a group of workers. These are also easier to avoid in small groups than in large ones. For this reason it is a good principle to employ as few people as possible without overworking the employees. This also keeps costs down and helps ensure that profits are made.

PLASTICS WASTE CASE STUDY 3

Penelope, Prida and Paulo have started to collect and process material and to sell it to the company in Bluetown and now meet to organize themselves. They agree to manage the business as equals but Prida, who has the best manner with other people, will take charge of collection and delivery to the customer. Paulo, who likes to deal with technical problems, will manage the baling and, later, the granulating of the plastic and Penelope, who is more thorough and careful than the two men, will be responsible for sorting and cleaning. Each will assist the others as work demands.

They decide that Prida will start collecting but, if more collectors are needed, he will not employ them by the hour but will buy a weighing scale and pay by the weight of material received.

They agree that Prida must discuss with the others any

changes in the selling of material; also that Penelope, who can read and write, will prepare an invoice (a note to the customer saying how much material is being sold, the type and price) for each load delivered. They will open an account at the bank if they start to earn more money than they expect to spend. Each week, on Friday evening, they will have a meeting to discuss how the business is progressing and take any big decisions, although minor matters will be sorted out between them as they occur.

They agree on the hours they will work and a list of services each will receive while working: purified, bottled drinking water, clothes washed once a week by the local washerwoman, soap and protective clothing, rubber gloves for Penelope and a spare pair for anyone else doing washing, safety goggles for Paulo when the granulator is bought and a raincoat for Prida in case it rains when he is out collecting.

Rule 12

Management is the most important activity but is done best by people closely involved in the running of the business. If all share in the management of a small business there will be greater sense of partnership but some do things better than others: only one person should be responsible for each activity and a procedure for taking big decisions is needed.

Chapter 13. How to Collect Waste

Chapter 11 explained that to create work from waste both a supply and a market were necessary. This chapter studies more closely the supply and its collection.

WHERE TO COLLECT FROM

Waste is found wherever humans live or work. Think about where it occurs and arrange methods of collection to suit these places. The following will be important:

i) *Homes* may produce small quantities of mixed waste including glass, paper, vegetable waste, a small amount of metals such as tin cans and plastics (in quantities that increase yearly as they are used more and more for packing). Usually, they are all mixed together and cannot easily be separated. In urban (town) areas, collection from homes means many small journeys made off a main route which will not itself be very long. Householders are not always in during the day.

ii) *Traders* include shops, stores and market stalls. They may be widely scattered as shops in a suburb, grouped together in a small market or group of town shops, or else exist in hundreds in a large market or city centre shopping area. Traders usually produce only certain kinds of waste. For example, a fish market will produce fish offal (heads, tails and insides) but little else; a group of suburban shops, on the other hand, may produce paper and cardboard and plastic packing, but little glass or metal. Waste is a problem to shopkeepers who want to keep their shops clear to display and sell their goods, and rarely have much space in which to store it.

iii) *Industry* includes all sorts of premises such as quarries, factories, mills, slaughterhouses, road depots, railway and power stations etc. They produce large quantities of a few, often specialized wastes and may be very well organized to dispose of it, with perhaps one manager responsible for disposal of all waste. If you visit a factory, try to find out who this is beforehand and ask for him by name. Industry is widely spaced and *may* be located long distances outside the town. Nowadays, however, factories are often located on new industrial estates, grouped together, an excellent situation for the waste collector because it cuts down on his travelling distance and time. Wastes from factories may occur in such large quantities and be so valuable as to be worth setting up special machinery or transport or employing people with the sole purpose of collecting and processing them. However, bear in mind that the factory management may discover their waste's value and either decide to process and sell it themselves, or else to increase the price. Secrecy in dealings is a wise precaution. Do not allow anybody in the factory (or any other place from which you collect) to learn where the waste will be sold. Teach lorry drivers and collectors to keep delivery notes or other information secret.

iv) *Institutions* include offices and big office blocks, hospitals, schools and colleges, town halls and government buildings and airport terminals. In general they all produce waste-paper, but some, for example, hospitals, may produce other specialized wastes, sometimes on a large scale. Often the waste paper contains 'confidential' information and has to be torn up or shredded on the premises under supervision. Institutions, unlike factories, are not planned for the movement of materials and it may be difficult to park a cart or van in the busy city street outside, to use passenger lifts or staircases or to find temporary storage space within. You will often have to deal with a chief porter or caretaker; be sure to treat him well and you may benefit!

v) *Farms* (and Forests) can be treated rather like factories except that the wastes may be scattered around large areas of land. Roads and tracks around farms are often bad, so it may take too long to collect farm wastes and therefore be uneconomic. However, wastes may well occur in huge quantities. For example, vast pineapple farms in Kenya use black polythene film for 'mulching' acres of land – a superb opportunity for plastics reclamation.

vi) *Hotels* are probably the waste collector's best source. They use large quantities of packaged foods and goods, discard them into a concentrated space and have good road access. However, they are less tolerant than any other management of dirt, noise, smell or irregularity on the part of the waste collector and may charge for the wastes. The cook or chief porter may have a private arrangement with his own family or a contractor who pays him personally. It is always worth taking the trouble to visit a hotel and find out; seek your information from the kitchen boy or maid and keep to the back stairs and away from the clients or you will not be popular with the management. If you are able to make an arrangement it will probably be with the housekeeper or manager, not with the staff who run the front office arrangements.

vii) *Streets, parks and public places* often contain huge quantities of litter consisting of paper mainly, but plastics, bottles and cans as well. It is dirty so less valuable than the same material collected direct from homes or offices. It occurs in small quantities, either scattered or in little bins. Usually, the Town Council is responsible for cleaning and employs street cleaners and park-keepers or gardeners to pick up litter. They are often among the poorest employees in the district and willing to earn a little money by selling the waste they separate out as they sweep (Fig. 84a). Sometimes municipal officials forbid this but the sweepers manage to do it all the same! It may help to provide them with a sack for certain materials.

viii) *Refuse vehicles* are also run by the municipality who are responsible for visiting every house in order to collect the refuse, although this responsibility is not always carried out. Refuse collectors usually separate certain recyclable materials as they travel round. However, because this slows the collection round and leaves litter in the streets, many municipalities forbid the practice, but not often successfully! It is common for waste merchants to set up warehouses by the road leading to the waste dump so that collection vehicles can stop on

Fig. 84a Recyclables collected from refuse at different stages: by the street cleaner. He is collecting tiny pieces of copper wire.

their way to and from the dump and unload recyclables in exchange for cash. In big cities, this arrangement may be controlled by powerful politicians with large sums of money involved. Be cautious of entering such a business!

ix) *The refuse dump* may be the official disposal site or a place used illegally because the municipality does not collect refuse, or only collects it irregularly and charges too much. In most Third World countries, the refuse dump is the workplace of 'pickers' or scavengers who separate the various recyclable materials (Fig. 84b) and sell them, often to merchants who visit the dump daily with a cart or vehicle. Material from dumps is very dirty and therefore fetches the lowest possible price, but this is balanced by the large quantities in which it occurs, the convenience of collecting it by hand without need for transport and (usually) the absence of interference from police or officials. Some municipalities try to keep scavengers off dumps for reasons of hygiene. They erect wire fences or send in the police, but the scavengers are

Fig. 84b   Recyclables collected from refuse at different stages: by waste collector from waste bin in the street.

frequently so poor that they will quickly return. The grave problems associated with scavenging on refuse dumps were discussed in Chapter 10.

HOW TO COLLECT

There are three ways of collecting from the various premises that we have considered:
1. Make separate collections, door to door.
2. Operate a depot and buy from other collectors.
3. Separate from refuse.

1. *Separate door-to-door collections*

The collector goes to where the waste arises, with transport or other means of carrying it away. There must be an arrangement with the occupier so the collector knows what he is allowed to take. The following arrangements may be used:

i) The *householder provides* a container, or else allocates a special place where the waste is left out. The collector empties the waste into his own cart, vehicle or container and returns the householder's container. Disadvantages are the time taken to transfer the waste, the second trip to the door to return the container and spillage of material.

ii) The collector provides the householder with a *sack* and collects it when full. If collections are frequent (daily or weekly) another sack is left. If not, as in the case of high value goods like textiles that are only collected every few months, the new sack is not left until a few days before the collection takes place. The disadvantage of this system is the cost of the sacks, many of which will not be returned but kept by the householder. It is only economic if the value of the goods or materials collected is high.

iii) The collector carries a container around with him and goes from house-to-house asking for the materials. The disadvantage is that the householder may be out or not prepared for the call and the collector may therefore waste time.

iv) The collector walks or drives down each street calling out or ringing a bell. Householders bring materials out to him. The disadvantage is that they often take the trouble to do this only if they think the collector will pay for the material, or when the material is a nuisance. This system is widely used for the collection of scrap steel as large pieces are of some value, and are a trouble to have in the house. However, their existence is not common enough to justify door-to-door calls.

v) The householder places the material in the street on a fixed day and time and the collector passes and puts them straight into his vehicle or cart. This is by far the quickest method for the collector to use, but has the disadvantages that:
- The wind may scatter the materials.
- Dogs and other animals might scavenge amongst them.
- "Pirate" collectors may get there first.
- If the collector is late or does not arrive, serious street litter results.
- Many housewives may not take the trouble to put material out.

All the above systems are used; choose the one best suited to the material you are collecting, the kind of houses, and the people who live in them.

VEGETABLE WASTE CASE STUDY 5

Vida, Victor and Vasim plan how they will collect vegetable waste from a middle-class district. Each house has a separate small garden and a path from the front gate to the front door. The back door leads on to a path too narrow for a cart to get through. They believe householders will be unwilling to carry kitchen waste through the house to the front door, so they will have to collect it from the back. The municipality collects refuse only once a week and vegetable waste forms more than half the total, so they believe that householders will be pleased to have this removed daily. They decide to build a light, two-wheeler trolley on which a sack can be placed with the mouth open. They will also use a horse-drawn cart, flat, with high sides and front and a low back. The horse and cart will stop at the path that runs behind the houses. The collector will take the sack trolley off the cart and wheel it down the path. He will take a woven basket or plastic bucket to each house, where the waste has been left in a bucket by the householder. He will tip the waste into his container, leave the householder's bucket to be refilled the next day, then tip from his basket into the open mouth of the sack before going on to the next house. When the sack is full he will wheel the trolley back to the horse and fling the full sack on to the cart, piling sacks against the high front and sides. Should he run out of sacks the contents of some will have to be emptied into the cart, but this should be avoided if possible. They must take great care not to drop waste on the ground in this district to avoid complaints and hostility from householders.

Note that four different containers are being used to facilitate handling of the waste: householder's bucket, collector's basket or bucket, collector's sack trolley and collector's horse driven cart. Even without a horse, the same arrangement could be made using a hand-cart, which might even be narrow enough to use on the path behind the houses. Note, too, that this collection arrangement is determined by the *social* habits or preferences of the householder *not* to have vegetable waste passed through the front door. If it had been a poorer district or lower class people, or if the waste had been paper, a different arrangement might have been possible.

Rule 13
House-to-house collections should be planned to keep the distance covered low, the handling of materials easy, and to gain the support of the householders by taking careful account of their social preferences.

Who owns waste?
This is a question you may need to answer on a door-to-door collection. For example, the time may come when someone will accuse you of stealing something left outside their house. Often, the Town Council objects because collectors go ahead of the municipal collection vehicles, picking recyclables from dustbins, sacks or piles put out for collection. In their haste to keep ahead of the dustmen, these unofficial collectors often leave a mess behind them; people complain and the municipality tries to stop them. They may try to stop you even if you try to be more careful and tidy. The easiest way to do this is to tell the police you have been stealing!

Before it is put out for collection, refuse belongs to the householder or the person occupying the building you are collecting from. After it has been collected by the municipality it belongs to them. The moment at which it actually changes ownership may decide whether you are guilty of stealing from the council or not, so it may be prudent to find out the law. The local library, the town clerk or a lawyer should be able to tell you, though you may find that no-one knows! One thing is certain: nothing belongs to you unless it is given to you by the previous owner. If, for instance, a maid accidentally gives you a valuable silver bracelet along with a pile of scrap metal, do not waste time arguing that it is yours. Return it as quickly (and quietly) as possible to avoid going to prison.

The dos and don'ts of effective collection

i) *Plan your route* and follow the same route on the same days of the week. The public, then, becomes used to seeing you on certain days and will save things for you.

ii) *For broken rounds* that do not cover all the buildings in a street, make a list of the names of the people or numbers of the houses that have to be visited so that none are missed. People who will willingly save material for you quickly stop if you do not visit regularly.

iii) *Paint the cart* a distinctive colour and put your name and address on the side. If possible wear clean overalls or a uniform to match the cart. It will make you feel better and the public are more likely to be responsive if you look clean and efficient.

iv) *Avoid* accepting materials you do not want. Reject them politely but do not leave them as litter. Carry a sack for unwanted material on your cart and empty into public bins or rubbish vehicles but not into the street or park!

v) *Advertise* your collection in a local newspaper or on local radio or have a handbill printed which can be put through letterboxes. Printing can be very cheap. Carry a card bearing your name, address and trade to give to people who show interest in your work or may be able to give you materials in future.

vi) *Improve your collection vehicle* using scrap materials where they are suitable but be willing to spend money to save time or effort. Figs 85a-f show a number of kinds of collection carts and vehicles.

vii) *Do not use a motor vehicle* for collections unless you are absolutely certain it will save or earn more than the large sums of money you will spend on fuel, tyres, repairs and maintenance, oil, tax or licences, insurance and, of course, the money you need to buy it. (See Chapter 16

Fig. 85a Light duty hand-carts suitable for collecting light wastes. May be fitted with mesh sides for paper, plastic, etc. India.

Fig. 85b Heavy duty hand-cart suitable for carrying bales, loaded sacks, etc. to the customer but not for door-to-door collections. India.

Fig. 85c Tricart, suitable for collecting wastes door-to-door. Peru.

263

Fig. 85d Animal drawn cart with pneumatic road tyres. Able to carry heavy loads of metal, baled paper for plastic, etc. Egypt.

Fig. 85e Light pick-up truck with mesh sides suitable for collecting wastes. Kenya.

Fig. 85f Motorized collection cart. The cart is built on the frame of a motor scooter with twin back wheels. Steering is with the scooter handlebars. Egypt.

264

for costing a vehicle). Motor vehicles are rarely suitable for door-to-door collections anyway because of the stopping and starting involved. A lorry may combine well with a team of collectors with sacks or hand carts who meet it at agreed transfer points or leave material piled at the roadside for it. This may only require a few hours a day and it is cheaper to hire than to have your own lorry standing idle for much of the day.

viii) *Keep wastes separate* during collection as this will save considerable time in sorting out. Label the sacks, boxes or drums containing the wastes in bright colours to avoid mistaking them. Make sure your careful work is not spoilt by mixing them up when the cart is unloaded.

PLASTICS WASTE CASE STUDY 4

Prida is planning the way in which he will collect waste plastics. He has walked round the town to see where most plastics come from and has chatted to the crew of the municipal collection truck. He decides that not enough plastics will come from households or offices to make visits to these worthwhile, but that certain factories and stores and the local hotel receive goods in plastic sacks, bags and wrappers which they then discard. He knows that plastic takes up plenty of space and hopes that, if he can make an arrangement that is easy for the suppliers, they will give him their plastic free.

His other main problem is to compress the plastic film and sheet on his cart to avoid frequent returns to the yard to unload. He considers three ways of doing this:

1. A wire cage over the top of his handcart: This will be expensive.
2. Carrying a baling box on top of the cart to bale the material as he goes along. This will take too much time.
3. Stuffing the material into sacks as he goes along.

He approaches the manager of the factory that is going to buy the material, who promises to let him have imperfect sacks from the factory production line when these occur. He arranges with Penelope that, when sorting the plastics, she will put aside any sacks they receive. He then visits each place that he is hoping will supply him and gives them enough sacks to hold a week's

265

waste. When he returns to collect he finds that most of them have hung his sack on a hook and filled or half-filled it. It is easy for him to squash one half-full sack inside another to compress the material as much as possible. The cook at the hotel, his best source of supply, asks him to pay for the waste. Instead he promises to provide the cook with 'misprinted' plastic food bags that the factory will sell him cheaply. The cook is satisfied. Later, when the business is making money, he has a wire cage made for the top of the cart and this increases the capacity of the cart by 50%.

Rule 14
Compact materials during collection, using waste containers or other simple means.

Collection depots
Door-to-door collection of waste involves much work and cost. It is even more expensive if collectors are employed and paid by time unless they are carefully supervised. Collectors work better if they are self-employed and paid by the weight they bring to a depot or warehouse. The advantage of this system is that it eliminates the need to supervise collectors; all that is needed is a pair of scales. In addition, the warehouse manager knows for certain what a material will cost to obtain and can plan his operation. Finally, the system gives opportunities for the poor, the old and the young, who have not the ability to organize processing and sale of materials themselves.

The danger of this system is that frequently the warehouse manager exploits the collectors, by paying unfair low prices, if they have no alternative customer. The arrangement robs the collector of the normal security or benefits of employment; if he is sick or cannot work he earns nothing and, at the end of his working life when he is too old to work, his earnings cease. It should be remembered that many kinds of formal employment in Third World countries have little better conditions: it is mainly in the rich industrialized countries that such luxuries as pensions, sickness benefits or maternity leave are provided to the employee by law.

There is an urgent need for responsible agencies, with concern for the thousands of people with no other livelihood,

266

to operate warehouses that pay fair prices and force other depots to do the same. Another disadvantage is that a depot is at the mercy of anyone who organizes a house-to-house collection and gets the material at source. Nor, if the market expands, can it increase the volume of material collected except by paying better prices. If the market becomes smaller and will not buy as much as is being collected, then the collectors suffer; the warehouse simply refuses to buy.

The collection depot may be a specialist warehouse handling only one material or may handle every kind. The former are often set up by paper or steel mills to secure their raw materials. They are only economic in big towns or cities where a large volume of material arises.

Unmanned units

In rich or upper-class districts people give away unwanted materials more freely and an unmanned collection point might be possible. However, although these have had some success in richer countries, it is doubtful whether they would work well in the Third World. Fig. 86 shows an example.

Fig. 86 Waste collection point. Hinged flaps allow material to be put inside when no attendant is present. Containers stand under the holes. The unit was made from a disused rail freight container and stood in the grocery supermarket. It was not highly successful. U.K.

267

Collection with refuse

This is a cheap way of collecting recyclable wastes. No extra call has to be paid. Unless some means is arranged to keep recyclable material separate from refuse it becomes dirty and loses value. The cost of labour to sort one from the other will be quite high and presents difficulty. This will need the full co-operation of the Town Council and of the refuse collectors themselves; both can best be obtained by sharing with them the profit from sale of materials.

Open vehicles If a cart, lorry or tractor trailer is used it is not difficult to have one or more separate compartments for the different recyclables.

Compactor vehicles These compress the waste to reduce its volume. Arrangements that have been tried to keep recyclables separate include the following:

- A trailer for waste paper and cartons is a favourable solution but creates problems when turning in narrow streets. If the compactor vehicle loads from the rear there is danger that the loaders will be hit by the trailer if the vehicle moves off unexpectedly.
- Roof racks can carry a limited amount but are hard to load and material can fall off.
- Sacks hanging from the sides and rear of the vehicle are the most widely-used solutions.

There is an urgent need for the manufacture of a twin chamber compactor vehicle, with one compartment for recyclables and the other chamber for refuse.

Chapter 14. Processing and Storage of Waste Materials

In the last chapter, different methods of collecting wastes were described. This chapter explains ways of dealing with the collected wastes. It covers a number of different activities, in particular: sorting, grading, shredding and milling, baling, washing and drying, storage.

To carry out any of these activities a depot is needed. It may be very simple – just a space on the edge of the refuse dump – or it may be a proper building in town with a yard, office and other aids. Whichever it is, certain rules can be followed to make it easier to work in and help produce a better quality product.

THE DEPOT
The following features are needed:

Space
Wastes take up a lot of space because they rarely arrive neatly packed in boxes or crates that can be stacked, one on top of the other, like warehouse goods. Often, it is not possible to sell material immediately because the price is too low, or because transport is not available, so it has to be stored. An extra sorting operation is often necessary to get the best price for a material, and this takes up extra space, too. Try to plan how much space will be needed, but do not allow too much, especially if you have to pay for it. Idle space has to be kept clean and secure, and increases the distance that things have to be moved.

Access
There must be a way in and a way out, wide enough for materials in bulky sacks or bales. It would be ideal if the depot

could be situated beside a road good enough for a cart or vehicle with a wide enough gateway for the vehicle to enter. If not, examine the ground between the proposed site and the road to see if it can be made passable for a vehicle. Can soft or marshy ground be filled in with rubble? Can concrete slabs be laid across a stream so it can be crossed? Can overhead wires be raised a little so as not to interfere with the top of a lorry?

Loading and unloading

A loading dock is a platform which the vehicle draws alongside or backs up to (Fig. 83). The dock may be either at the same level as the rest of the working area, with the vehicles running at a lower level, or else reached via a ramp of hardened mud, timber planks or concrete. The slope of a ramp should be shallow enough for loaded carts to be pushed up easily.

Flow

Materials should move into, through and out of the depot in an economical way. Goods being stored should be kept to one side of the 'flow path' so they need not be moved to allow other goods in or out. Materials must all move in the same direction so that people, carts or vehicles do not have to pass one another in narrow paths or gangways. Leave clear space around doors and gates so they can be opened without moving anything first. Plan enough space for vehicles or carts to turn if necessary.

Security

To process steel scrap, all you need is a barrier of scrap iron to show where your depot ends and your neighbour's begins. However, if you are dealing in valuable copper scrap, you will need a high wall with broken glass along the top and a building with lockable doors. Your security should be on a sensible scale; it is a pity to use hard-earned profits to erect an expensive fence around low-value materials or to employ a night-watchman to guard piles of low-grade waste paper. Fences and walls can often be erected using free waste materials such as:
- Timber from demolished buildings.
- Scrap sheet metal – but this may rust in rainy climates.
- Old car shells laid on their sides; very ugly but effective.
- Mud (or mud and wattle) with broken glass along the top.

Shelter

Workers will need shelter from the sun and rain if they are to work efficiently.

Office

This may be no more than a table and chair, but it is useful to have somewhere where papers can be kept and letters written. It is possible to run a waste business with no paperwork at all, but some desk work is helpful in order to get better prices, cheaper supplies and somewhere to keep the address of a possible future customer.

EQUIPMENT

Lifting tackle (Fig. 87)

If heavy materials such as cast iron are being handled, a

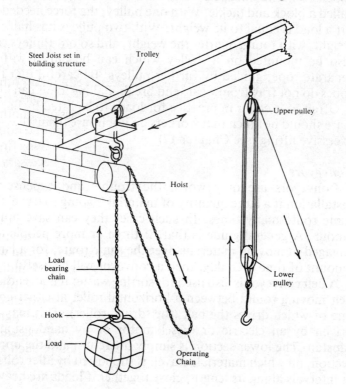

Fig. 87 Lifting gear — chain operated hoist and rope operated block and tackle.

271

small crane or hoist may be needed. A hoist is a box of gears with two chains. One chain is single, with a hook on one end for lifting the load. The other is a continuous loop which is pulled to raise or lower the hook. The gears are so arranged that less strength is needed to pull the loop chain than the weight of the load. The hoist can either be hung from a strong hook in the roof, or from a wheeled trolley that moves smoothly along a steel runway (called an I beam) so that the load can not only be raised and lowered, but also transported sideways. Whichever is used, it is *most* important that the building structure is strong enough to support the combined weight of hoist plus its load with a margin of safety. If in doubt get expert advice – otherwise you might pull the building down on yourself.

Hoists can be electrically powered, but these are more expensive. The cheapest form is a rope pulley, sometimes called a block and tackle. With one pulley, the force needed to lift a load is equal to its weight. With two pulleys it is half the weight, with four a quarter the weight, and so on. Pulleys can also be mounted on a trolley which can be pulled with a separate rope, guided by further pulleys. Be careful that the ropes do not fray from wear, and break. Falling loads can kill!

Often, it is easier in practice for loads to be lifted by hand. Care should be taken that workers do not injure themselves by excessive lifting (see Chapter 17).

Conveyors

Conveyors are only worth the trouble and expense of installation if a large quantity of material is going to travel the same route many times. In such cases they can save much labour. A general guide is that, if three or more people are engaged in moving materials over the same route, for a large amount of time each day, then a conveyor will be useful.

A belt conveyor is also used for sorting waste: It is an endless belt moving round between a horizontal roller at either end, one of which drives the belt (the 'drive' roller). This may be driven by an electric or diesel motor or by hand using a capstan. The lower section is simply the return and the upper section, on which materials travel, is supported by idler rollers at intervals along its length, close together if loads are heavy, spaced if they are light.

If sorting is to be done from a conveyor, then containers

*Fig. 88   Sorting off a conveyor with chutes. Note the ideal height of
the belt to avoid the need to bend. The sorters are former scavengers.
Mexico.*

must be arranged so that materials can be thrown into them
easily (Fig. 88). Also, the sorter must be able to get to and from
his or her workplace without having to climb or stumble over
containers or the conveyor.

Chutes

These are only used if one floor level of the depot is higher
than another. In such cases they provide a simple and efficient
way of moving material from a sorter or vehicle unloading
point without extra labour or machinery. Fig. 88 shows a well-
designed combination of chutes and conveyors for sorting
municipal refuse in Monterrey, Mexico.

Lifts and elevators

These are unavoidable if a building with more than one floor is used as a depot. However, they are usually expensive pieces of machinery, need expensive safety devices and can give much trouble in operation.

Containers

Containers are needed for moving material from one activity to another, for storage and for collection and transport. Material that is small such as broken glass, paper,

Fig. 89a Sorting into drums, carts and hanging bales. Note the ropes from which the bales are hung by the corners, the cardboard drums discarded by a chemical, plastic or wire factory and ideal for sorting and the correct position of lighting to avoid eye-strain for the sorters. Photo: courtesy of Oxfam. U.K.

274

rigid plastics, copper and aluminium, meat or fish wastes, needs to be stored in containers. Containers can be used that are themselves wastes, but for high value materials, such as textiles or non-ferrous metals, it may be worth buying special trucks, boxes, sacks etc. These are the main types of waste container used (Figs 83 and 89a):

- 200 litre (45 gallon) oil drums.
- Half oil drums (easier to lift).
- Corrugated cardboard cartons, but be careful that the bottom does not fall out.
- Bales (of jute or polypropylene sheeting) hung from ropes at the corners (Fig. 89a). Special bale hooks (Fig. 89b) can be bought or made.
- Sacks of plastic film, jute, hessian, woven polypropylene etc.
- Cardboard drums (from chemicals, plastics, raw materials etc).
- Large tinplate cans (from bulk foods such as jams, tinned fruit) as used by hotels.
- Woven baskets from straw, reed or other natural fibres.

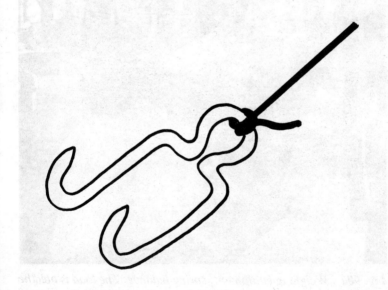

Fig. 89b   Bale hook — four needed per bale.

Containers not necessarily made from waste materials include:

- Carts with deep sides and wheels – or small castors – excellent for sorting paper, textiles etc.
- Tote boxes with handles that can stack on top of one another for storage.
- Sack carts that keep the sack mouth stretched open for filling and allow a full, heavy sack to be wheeled around easily.

Weighing scales

These are usually necessary as most waste materials are sold by weight. If you rely on other people's scales and other

Fig. 90a Weighing equipment: spring balance. The load is held on a hook from the balance and pulls the spring down. The balance is held from the ring at the top by the man on the left and steadied by the man in the white shirt who is reading it. The pointer which shows the weight is by his thumb. Kenya.

276

people's honesty you may lose a lot of money! The following types are used, in order of increasing cost:

i) *Spring balances* – The material is hung from the hook and stretches the spring. The weight is read directly from a vertical scale of figures (Fig. 90a).

ii) *Simple balances* – The material is hung from one side and a known set of weights from the other. The correct weight is reached when the beam is horizontal (Fig. 90b).

Fig. 90b   Weighing equipment: simple balance. The load is placed in one pan and the weights in the other. When the balance arm is horizontal the weights equal the load. India.

iii) *Lever balances* – The material is hung from one side and a weight moved along the lever arm until horizontal balance is obtained. The distance of the weight along the arm indicates the weight.

iv) *Platform scales* – The material is rested on a loose platform connected by levers to a weighing arm. The platform may be mounted on wheels or set into the floor. The weight may be indicated on a dial or by the distance of the balance weight along the lever arm (Fig. 90c).

Fig. 90c Weighing equipment: platform scale with lever balance. The weights are moved along the lever until the lever is quite horizontal, then the weight is read off a scale written along the lever. Note the wheels; the scale can be moved from place to place. Mexico.

v) *Weighbridges* for carts and vehicles. The vehicle is driven on to a large, flat, metal platform which is connected to a scale (sometimes in an office overlooking the platform). The vehicle is weighed when full, then when empty, and the empty (tare) weight is deducted from the full (gross) weight to give the nett weight of the load. Make sure that the driver is out of the vehicle on both weighings!

Sorting tables

Sorting should be possible without causing strain or back-ache, leading to tiredness and poor or slow work. The height of the tables depends on whether the sorter is going to sit or stand. They should be arranged so that the work flows across them, from a pile or container on one side, placed at a convenient height, to one or more piles or containers of sorted material on the other. There should be a container for contraries too. Often, six or eight grades are sorted and the layout of the sorting table and its surroundings is very important so that work may be done efficiently. Figs. 88, 89, and 91 show well-planned sorting arrangements.

Baling machinery

Fully described in Chapters 1 and 2, balers are the most important tools in the fight against transport costs and should be one of the first purchases when a business starts to make money.

Shredding and granulating machinery

Described in Chapter 5, there are many different types, ranging from tiny grinding mills to huge, powerful hammer mills that can reduce a car to small pieces in less than a minute. The latter are expensive, need electric or diesel power and create endless problems of maintenance: they will not be discussed further here. If it will increase your profits to shred, grind, mill, granulate or disintegrate your product, there is no difficulty in buying a machine if you have the money.

The same is true of flattening machinery, often used in industrialized countries for squashing cars so that several can be packed on to one lorry to be taken to a shredder. Chapter 2 describes how to flatten cans and similar small objects and larger equipment can always be obtained, at a price!

PLASTICS WASTE CASE STUDY 5

Penelope, Paulo and Prida have successfully collected

waste plastic film from stores, factories and the hotel, and sold it to the Bluetown Bucket Company. They began the work in the yard of Prida's house but, now they are confident that the work will be profitable for many years ahead, they decide to set up a small depot. They have a little cash and have talked to the local bank manager about a loan to pay for a granulating machine. The final layout of their depot is shown in Fig. 91.

They begin by making a list of all the operations needed to process plastic before it can be sold for a good price:

   i) Unload collection cart.
  ii) Sort different grades and remove impurities.
 iii) Wash dirty material (but not all).
 iv) Dry washed or wet material.
  v) Granulate.
 vi) Weigh before dispatch to the customer.
vii) Load on to delivery vehicle.

They note that they will need storage space at the following stages, as not all operations can be expected to move exactly at the same rate:

   i) After unloading.
  ii) Before granulating.
 iii) After weighing, awaiting the delivery lorry.

They also remember that they will have to remove a lot of bad material and rubbish and will need storage space for this, too.

Other necessary items are:
- A roof over the sorting area to shade it from the sun.
- A small shed to house the granulator and the scales so that they are not rusted by rain or stolen. A table and chair could be placed in one corner of the shed to serve as the office.

As well as the sheets and sacks of plastic film, they collect rigid plastic objects such as toys, broken buckets and bowls, plastic shoes and food containers. Many are too big to go into the granulator so they decide to have a bench with a hammer and saw where these can be reduced in size.

Finally, they give some thought to the future and their hope to buy an extruder and pelletizer. They decide that they cannot afford land or buildings for this now, but will seek a site with extra land to buy in the future.

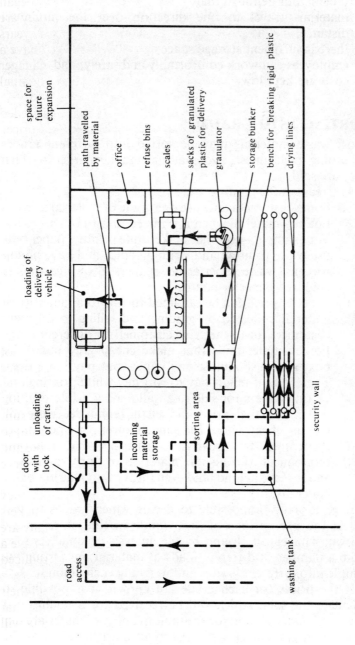

space for future expansion

path travelled by material

office

refuse bins

scales

sacks of granulated plastic for delivery

granulator

storage bunker

bench for breaking rigid plastic

drying lines

loading of delivery vehicle

unloading of carts

door with lock

incoming material storage

sorting area

road access

washing tank

security wall

Fig. 91 Layout of processing depot — plastics waste case study number five.

281

Rule 15

Is to plan your depot so that:

- materials travel in one direction over the minimum distance;
- there is sufficient storage space;
- employees can work comfortably and safely; and
- costs are kept low.

SORTING INTO GRADES

Most waste materials may be sorted into different grades according to cleanness, size, material and the market to which they are sold.

The reasons for grading are:

   i) Some customers only use one grade of material and will not buy material when it is mixed in with other grades. For example, mills that make white printing paper only use white printing and writing papers and have no use for such waste paper as newspapers, brown cartons or coloured paper or board.

  ii) A better price can be obtained for the total quantity of material collected by grading and selling to different customers (or to the same customer for different uses). For example, mills that make cheap grey board for boxes can use almost any paper, but pay low prices. Therefore, it might pay to sort any white printing and writing papers for sale to a mill making white printing paper, for a high price, and sell the remainder to the mill making cheap board for a much lower price per tonne.

 iii) Sometimes, transport is so expensive that it is only economical to transport materials of fairly high value and to leave behind (and even throw away) the low value materials.

It is normally impossible to decide which grades to sort unless the proportions of each grade in the materials are known. This can be found by the analysis of small samples from a number of different loads of material, by sorting the sample into different grades and weighing each amount.

If the prices for each grade are known, it is possible to calculate the total which will be received for a quantity of ungraded material, and for the same quantity of material after it has been graded. However, account must be taken of the

282

extra costs of grading, storing, sale and delivery of the graded material.

PLASTICS WASTE CASE STUDY 6

For six months, Penelope, Paulo and Prida have been selling low density polyethylene film and rigid pieces to Bluetown Bucket Company and think they are getting to know their business. They have been paid 50 dollars per tonne of material, provided it is fairly clean. One day Prida returns from delivering a load to say that he has been chatting with one of the workmen at the factory who has told him that theirs is the lowest grade of material that the factory uses. Other suppliers send a similar grade, but also send loads that contain only:

i) Transparent film which is used for making new transparent products.

ii) White 'opaque' film which is used for making white opaque products.

iii) Extra clean film that is used for making bags and sheeting of thin film which would tear or be spoilt by the presence of dirt or grit. This is either of transparent, white, or pure colours, or mixed colours for making black and dark green refuse sacks.

They discuss whether they should try to produce grades of this type, but cannot decide for lack of information. They arrange to find out how much of each grade could be obtained from the material they are collecting, and how much the factory will pay them.

Prida visits the factory manager, who is interested in the idea because he is paying high prices for pure colours, although he has no difficulty in obtaining mixed waste material.

He says he will pay them:

- 500 dollars a tonne for cleanest quality transparent material.
- 250 dollars a tonne for normal quality transparent material.
- 250 dollars a tonne for cleanest opaque white material.
- 150 dollars a tonne for normal quality opaque white material.

- 350 dollars a tonne for cleanest quality pure colours: red, blue and yellow.
- 200 dollars a tonne for normal quality pure colours: red, blue and yellow.
- 100 dollars a tonne for cleanest mixed colours.
- 50 dollars a tonne for normal quality mixed colours (as at present).

Penelope does an analysis of the material collected. She weighs out 250 kilogrammes of material every day for four days and sets it aside. She sorts it into the different grades, then weighs each.She draws up the result as a Table (14).

Table 14 Analysis of plastics waste

Colour	Quality	Weight in kg
Transparent	Cleanest	0
Transparent	Normal	400
Opaque white	Cleanest	0
Opaque white	Normal	100
Pure red, blue, yellow	Cleanest	0
Pure red, blue, yellow	Normal	200
Mixed Colours	Cleanest	0
Mixed Colours	Normal	300
	Total	1000

They consider the possibility of sorting the different colours and ask Penelope to present another table to show the amount of money they would get.

Table 14 Value of graded materials

Colour	Price per tonne in dollars	Price per 100 kg in dollars	Weight in kg (in 1 tonne total)	Value of that weight in dollars
Transparent	250	25	400	100
Opaque white	150	15	100	15
Pure colours	200	20	200	40
Mixed	50	5	300	15
			Total	170

When the material was not sorted they earned:

Colour	Price per tonne in dollars	Price per 100 kg in dollars	Weight in kg (in 1 tonne total)	Value of that weight in dollars
Mixed	100	10	1000	50

Obviously, they would get a much better price for the sorted material. Penelope thought it would take her a week to sort each tonne of material into colours so, if she was paid 35 dollars a week, it would cost 35 dollars per tonne. Paulo would need a little extra time to clean the granulator each time the colour changed. Delivery would cost no more because each colour would be put into separate labelled sacks. Penelope's only problem was – who would do the washing of the dirty material if she was spending so much time sorting? Neither of the others had time to spare, so they agreed they would employ Penelope's younger brother Peter to do the washing. As this was unskilled work, they would pay him 30 dollars a week.

Rule 16
By grading materials, their value is increased, often by much more than the cost of grading, and additional employment can be created.

CLEANNESS OF MATERIALS
Dirt is a severe problem in all countries, but particularly in the Third World where many roads and paths are unpaved; homes and even factories have dirt floors; soil is sandy and wind-blown; washing water is a luxury; and material may be used many times before it becomes waste. Dirt reduces the quality of goods made from waste, clogs and damages machinery and pollutes process water.

It is important that a processing depot, no matter how small, is organized to keep material as clean as possible. This may be done by:
- *Keeping dirty and clean materials separate* in collection, transport, and during processing.
- *Providing floors* for storage and processing areas whenever possible. These can be made of wood, matting or concrete. If these are too expensive, a thick polythene sheet is better than nothing.
- *Erecting walls or screens* to keep out wind-blown sand and dust and to keep material from being blown about and picking up dirt.
- *Training employees* to recognize the problem of dirt and keep materials clean in all possible ways.

- *Cleaning out carts*, lorries, containers and sacks before fresh materials are put in them.
- *Washing materials* where the increase in their value justifies it. Washing can often be done by outside people on a commission basis – they are paid so much per tonne of waste plastic or per thousand bottles washed.

Often, such washing is done in ponds and streams and may pollute water needed for washing clothes, or for people's personal washing and drinking. Care should be taken to avoid this and especially to ensure that containers such as sacks or drums that may have contained poisonous chemicals are not washed in such waters or in water that flows through open sewers or channels through districts where people live. If quantities are small, then municipal drains are the best disposal route for such water (but not for oils or pure chemical wastes). Filtering through sandy soil is also safe, provided that the water table (the level of underground water) is not too high. Where regular or large quantities of poisonous wastes are involved, the municipality should be consulted.

Contraries

These are objects or materials that are not wanted in a waste collection. Contraries can damage machinery and spoil the goods being produced and buyers of waste materials will seriously punish their presence in a load by reducing the price paid for it, or rejecting it altogether.

It is sometimes possible to remove ferrous metal contraries with a magnet placed over the conveyor carrying the material. The method is only successful if the material is evenly spread in a thin layer on the belt or if the magnet is positioned to catch the metal as the material falls off the end of the belt. The more powerful the magnet, the better the chance of success, but power costs money!

There is no better method of removing contraries than by hand sorting, and by training collectors and workers to recognize and remove them.

Another piece of equipment that helps remove dirt and contraries is a screen. This is a flat sheet of steel wire mesh with low sides. Material is placed on it and the screen vigorously vibrated from side to side, by hand or machine. Dirt, stones, broken glass, etc. will fall through the holes, leaving the larger pieces of waste paper, textiles or plastic on top. The size of wire mesh has to be carefully chosen according to the material you are collecting. An alternative use for a screen is to separate out pieces that are too big. For example, if glass cullet is being sorted, a screen may be used to separate stones, wood, straw, paper or unbroken glass that is too big for the mesh. Sometimes, several screens of different mesh are used, as in quarrying where stones and sands and grits for different uses are carefully graded by size, using different screen sizes (see Chapter 9).

The main objection to using screens for separating large, sheet materials like paper is that the sheets block the mesh and it takes a long time for the contraries to fall through. Screens are best used for materials that are no bigger than two or three mesh in any direction.

WASTE PLASTICS CASE STUDY 7

Penelope, Paulo and Prida were puzzled by the absence of any clean material in the analysis of plastics waste in Table 14. It was Paulo who discovered the reason. "All the material is dirty because the clean material is collected in the same sacks and on the same cart as dirty material, so it becomes dirty".

They discussed how to overcome this. It was not possible to wash all the material as their tank and drying spaces were too small, and in any case, even after washing the material was not clean enough for the factory to use it to manufacture thin film.

They asked Prida to make a list of the places from which he collected clean film. This was difficult because he could not write, but Penelope's brother Peter helped him: the hotel, three of the eight factories and five stores. Prida said that all were modern buildings with floors made of concrete or other dust-free material. It was agreed that, because the prices for clean material were so much higher than those for normal material, it was worth doing a special collection, one day a week, to visit these suppliers. The collection cart would be cleaned before starting and Penelope promised to sweep the unloading and sorting areas just before they returned. New sacks were bought to hold the clean material and the word CLEAN was painted on in large letters. Twelve cardboard drums were bought from the factory and thoroughly brushed out.

They had been collecting 2½ tonnes of material every week on average and found they could get ½ tonne of clean material, with a value about twice as high as it had been when it was contaminated by the dirty material from other sources.

Rule 17
Keep material clean and separate from dirty material to sell at highest prices.

Chapter 15. Marketing Wastes

Sales are of vital importance to the waste operator; without them trade cannot continue. This chapter describes not only how to sell wastes but also other ways in which to promote sales:
- studying the market for the product – sometimes called market research;
- developing the right product and the markets for it; and
- advertising and promoting the product – even one as unglamorous as waste!

These things combined are called marketing.

MARKET RESEARCH

What is the market for your waste material?

It is said that successful companies never make a product and *then* try to sell it. Instead, they discover a market, then develop a product that will satisfy it. This is certainly sound advice but it is difficult for the waste trader to follow. He does not have much choice about what he is able to produce, unlike the company that manufactures from raw materials, or which retails goods bought from a wholesaler. The waste collector can only sell those materials that other people do not want or cannot sell. So he has to be an expert salesman.

How is the market made up?

Is it big factories that will buy material in ten tonne lorry loads or individuals making handicrafts in their homes who will buy it in two kilo bags? Usually, factories make up the larger part of markets for wastes, but they differ greatly in size and kind, from huge buildings on a square kilometre site, often owned by foreign companies, to a little room behind a shop in a side street, worked by the owner's family.

You must know not only which factories use your kind of

material but also what other raw materials they use. Do they buy wastes from other suppliers? Are these local or imported? Do they have difficulty obtaining them? Will they have trouble getting them in the future, perhaps for political reasons? Are their prices likely to go up or down? Know, too, what items they produce, who buys them, whether their sales are likely to increase or drop.

How can this information be found? Companies are often very secretive but it is possible to:

i) *Read the newspapers.* They give news about local companies and their fortunes.

ii) *Consult libraries.* These usually belong to schools or colleges or government offices but sometimes there are public libraries, often set up by foreign governments or the United Nations.

iii) *Talk to local businessmen.* Word of what each company is doing gets around.

iv) *Talk to employees of the Company.* Outside the gate at finishing time, in the local bar, best of all when you are making a delivery of material because you will then be regarded as a person who is already helping the company and therefore are more likely to be trusted.

v) *Visit offices of trade or employers' associations.* They act on behalf of their members' interests but will probably feel that encouraging a supplier of waste is of benefit. They are likely to be better informed than many other sources.

vi) *Ask a friend* who has contacts Many agencies and individual people whose job or aim is to help the poor also know a great many important people. They may be able to get information more easily than you.

vii) *Ask the customer.* Do not be frightened to ask company managers directly about their business and their plans. They need raw materials. If you can supply wastes that are cheaper or less difficult to obtain than those they are using, they have a strong reason to help you. However, do not tell them too much about your situation; just enough to win confidence. Just as information about *their* business will help you to negotiate a better deal, so will information about *yours* strengthen their bargaining power.

290

When approaching any of these sources remember the important rule:

Rule 18
For an interview always wash thoroughly, be tidy and as smartly dressed as you can manage. Wear shirt and tie and behave with quiet confidence and good manners.

This rule will be repeated several times in this chapter but never too often. People will take you to be the sort of person you look like, sound and behave. If you look dirty, unreliable and as though you may steal the office typewriter, then not only will they be less willing to do business with you, but they would prefer not to have you in the office or factory at all! In the section on selling, this subject will be discussed further.

What companies are found in this district?
Which companies use, or might use, the materials you produce? As well as the sources of information just listed, you can find out much from the local telephone directory, especially if it has a classified section (that lists numbers for each type of business), sometimes printed on yellow paper and known as Yellow Pages. This is such a useful book it will be worthwhile to buy one from the telephone company, even if you have no telephone. Other directories can be found in a library or the manager of a local company might allow you to study his copy. Ask for help from a librarian or secretary if you have difficulty finding the information you need. Those who cannot read or write will need to go with someone who can or ask a secretary to write the information down. Some people are ashamed that they cannot read or write and might leave without the information they need rather than admit it. This is not necessary; those who have had an education are usually happy to help those who have been less fortunate.

What grade materials do those companies need?
This can only be discovered by asking them direct. It helps to understand a little about the work they do and the products they make. That is why Part I of this book not only described the uses for waste but also the uses for and manufacture of the products made from waste.

What kind of people are they?

You will form your own impressions of this by talking to employees, other suppliers and customers. It is of great value to know whether their business is going well, and if they have serious problems that might lead to them closing down or stopping production of the item for which you supply material. If you know this in advance, you will have time to look for another customer or to collect a different material. If you learn they are short of money, you can press to have your money paid quickly.

It is useful to know something about the personal character of the manager, the owner and the man who buys raw materials. Are they kind and likely to help someone who is poor or who has had bad luck, or are they ruthless and only interested in making bigger profits? Are they proud of the quality of their product (they might pay more if you can improve it) or only interested in keeping costs as low as possible (they might buy a lower grade material for which you had no market).

Once you start selling do not stop talking to your customer. Constantly ask what they think of your material. They will probably start by saying it is too expensive – you must judge whether this is a joke or whether they mean it. They will tell you frankly if your quality has got worse but may not tell you if it is much better than material they buy elsewhere (in which case you may decide to put up the price). Ask if they have any complaints about your delivery driver if you do not deliver yourself, or about any other matters.

VEGETABLE WASTE CASE STUDY 6

Vida, Victor and Vasim are now collecting more vegetable waste from households than they are able to sell to the dozen pig farmers in the town. They decide to study the market to see if they can find other 'outlets'. If not, they may have to turn to collecting something else.

Vida visits the local library and asks the librarian for help. They consult some directories, looking up not only farms that are listed as pig farms but also, general farms who may keep pigs although this is not their main activity; butchers who may keep their own animals as well as buying from farmers, and bacon factories. They discover a large bacon factory in the next town that keeps pigs on a large scale.

Victor visits the local extension officer from the Ministry of Agriculture who reminds him that not only pigs but goats and poultry also eat vegetable waste. Apparently there are two big poultry farms just outside the town, as well as many small ones. He also shows Victor an article in the daily newspaper saying that, for religious reasons, fewer people are eating pork meat, turning to poultry instead, and that this trend is expected to become more obvious the following year when there is an important religious festival. The article also says that many pig breeders have reduced their herds because of this while the price of chickens in the market-places has risen by half.

Vida and Victor telephone the bacon factory to ask if they may call on the manager to discuss selling him pig food. To their surprise he agrees to see them and, after careful washing and dressing, they go there by bus the next day. They take a list with them showing how much they have sold in each of the previous months, and a sample of the vegetable waste, neatly wrapped in a plastic bag. They are a little frightened of the factory which has barbed wire fencing and a policeman at the gate but when they say whom they have come to see they are allowed in without difficulty. The manager does not keep them waiting and is friendly. He asks about their business and tells them that he needs twenty tonnes a week of pig food but, by law, vegetable waste has to be sterilized before it is fed to the pigs. He has a sterilizing plant that can only do 10 tonnes a week so he can buy a limited amount of unsterilized waste. He takes them into a small laboratory where he shows them, under a microscope, the tiny 'parasites' that live on the sample of waste they have brought in, which can transmit diseases to the pigs.

Victor asks if the reduced market for pork that he read about in the paper also applies to bacon but is told it does not. Bacon is sold in big cities where people tend to take less notice of religious customs.

He tells them the prices he will pay for pig feed and they promise to telephone him as soon as they have discussed it among themselves.

Rule 19

Find out as much as possible about the markets into which you are selling, using sources of written information like libraries and talk to people, especially the managers of factories that use your products.

PLANNING THE PRODUCT AND THE MARKET

It is too easy, once a market for material has been found, to supply it and forget about other outlets. Later, one may wake up with a shock to find that the market no longer exists because the company has gone bankrupt, or because another supplier has taken the business from you, or the company is making a new product of higher quality for which waste materials cannot be used. The wise operator plans ahead the products that he is selling and the markets into which he sells them so that this need never occur. His planning should take the following forms:

i) *Forecasting*. This sounds like the action of a prophet rather than a waste collector and that is exactly what it is – an effort to set down on a piece of paper (or in your head) what will happen to the market in the future. You should consider such questions as:
   - Will the market grow or get smaller?
   - Will the materials needed change, if so how?
   - Will prices go up or down or remain steady?
   - Will the companies in the market change?

Also make a forecast about supplies of material and whether costs of collecting them will increase.

Having a forecast of this sort makes it easier to plan:
   - The type of new equipment, machinery or space that will be needed in the next two (or one or ten) years.
   - Whether more people are needed and, if so, should they start training immediately?
   - Whether new sources of supply should be developed?
   - If this type of waste continues to be profitable, should other kinds be dropped to concentrate on it; or will it become less profitable so that alternative products will be needed and, if so, when?

It is easy for forecasts to be wrong; unexpected events often occur, so a forecast should be reconsidered frequently, and a new one should be made if it is obviously proving wrong.

294

ii) *Varying the product* This need not mean collecting a completely different kind of material. It may mean grading differently, so as to separate out the high grade materials; more processing to improve the quality and increase the price; or less processing to reduce the cost so as to undercut (sell at a lower price than) competitors.

iii) *Developing new markets* Sometimes the collector learns that the market for his material is dying or moving, and he realizes he will be forced to drop collections in favour of something else. The sooner this is done the better, giving time perhaps to keep some income from the old while going through all the difficulties of developing the new. This may be done by:

- Persuading a company to buy from you instead of from another supplier as at present. (Only start a war if you are prepared for another supplier to do the same to you)
- Persuading firms that currently use your material to use more by offering them a lower price for a larger quantity (but check that you can afford to do so without making a loss) or offer them better quality or more frequent deliveries.
- Persuading firms that do not use waste to do so. Perhaps you can explain how your other customers (who may be their competitors) cut costs by using it, etc.
- Selling to companies further away (but check that the higher costs of transport will not lose you money).
- Selling to bigger or smaller companies than previously (but check again on costs).
- Selling to different kinds of companies: Make sure, though, that they will take the same quality, the same method of delivery, and will pay an adequate price and pay promptly.

iv) *Second outlets.* Even if your main outlet seems perfect in all respects, including price, it is as well to sell small, regular quantities to a second customer. Then, if something happens unexpectedly to the main customer's trade, it will be much easier to build up the volume of sales to the second outlet than to start from zero.

Having a second outlet puts the seller in a stronger position to 'negotiate' (that means bargain!) with the main customer. He will be less likely to cut your prices, or stop deliveries during his annual holiday or reject your loads because of poor quality, if he knows this will mean your supplies will go to his competitor. However, sometimes it may be more prudent not to let him know about the second outlet.

v) *Mix large and small customers*. It is easier to send a lorry-load once a week to a big firm that pays promptly, than to many small businesses all of whom have different needs and some of whom do not pay promptly. On the other hand remember that:
- Small firms grow big.
- If a big firm suddenly drops you, you will have a market to fall back on while you recover. Big firms often have seasonal ups and downs in their demands. They may make a product such as Christmas cards that requires large amounts of best white wastepaper for only three months of the year, or they may shut down for a month each year for maintenance during which time they will take no supplies at all. Supplies to the small firms can, by arrangement, be timed to compensate for these ups and downs so that your sales continue at an even rate.

vi) *Middlemen*. Merchants, traders, sharks, junk kings or dealers are found wherever waste is collected, bought and sold. They are sometimes processors or else keep warehouses; they rarely do much work on the material or collect it themselves. They usually seem to be richer than the people from whom they buy. They often control the market for one or more materials in an area and use their money to buy power over other traders (or to hire thugs!). The activities of middlemen are as much (often more) responsible for the poverty and hopelessness of small collectors and scavengers than the policies of the big companies that run factories that use waste.

Every waste collector should avoid selling to middlemen and plan ways in which to deal with any attempts that the middleman may make to force him to do so. It would be foolish to pretend that this is easy, or that there is much practical experience available of people who have been successful. However, the following suggestions may be of help.

a) *Avoid any dealings* that commit you to sell to a middleman (e.g. buying supplies or machinery, receiving credit and, above all, borrowing money from him).

b) *Sell direct to the final material user* whenever possible. If fewer people share the profit in a sale there will be a better deal both for the buyer and the seller.

c) *Try to avoid dealing in exactly the same market* or collecting exactly the same supplies as those in which the middleman trades. If you do not threaten his business he may leave you alone. If you do . . .!

d) *Deal honestly* and try to give your customers good value for money. Remember the final power lies with the big customers who are often managed by educated, more civilized people than the middlemen who have often fought their way to commercial success and power from being small collectors themselves. If the managers find you satisfactory to deal with they may give you information that can be used to persuade a hostile middleman to leave you in peace; take great care how you use such a method. Company managers will rarely give you any more solid help than this: they are interested in a quiet life and good profits; do not expect too much. Nor can you often expect the police to protect you from threats; merchants often use some of their profits to buy co-operation from the police and in very few countries are the police free of such corruption.

e) *Band together* with other small collectors and waste dealers. Without forming an elaborate co-operative or association you can agree to help each other in certain ways, but remember that not everyone will keep such agreement if threatened or frightened.

ADVERTISING AND PROMOTING WASTE SALES

The idea of advertising the sales of waste materials, which are not a glamorous product, may seem strange. Yet in Britain there is one weekly magazine which is almost entirely financed by such advertising. This kind of advertising is likely to be very different from the glossy colour pamphlets that advertise bath soap or hair shampoo, but this also means it will cost less.

Advertising

Advertising aims to bring the material you have to sell to the attention of someone who might buy it, and then persuade him to do so. Alternatively, it may be used to notify people that you are willing to buy something they have; for example, to advertise that you want to buy clean waste paper or plastic. To do this, the advertisement must be seen by as many people as possible and there are a number of different kinds of advertising you may consider:

- Local newspapers.
- Local radio stations (television is too expensive).
- Posters in the street or on buildings or along railway lines.
- Posters in or on buses and trains.
- Signs on your own cart, truck or lorry.
- Handbills to be distributed in the streets or placed through front doors.

An advertisement should be designed to do four things:
1. Gain attention.
2. Create interest.
3. Give information.
4. Lead to action.

Promotion

Advertising is aimed mainly at people who do not know or have forgotten your product or your needs. Promotion is to encourage those who already know about it to buy it. To promote your sales:

i) *Make your product look good.* Deliver it neatly packed, in tidy bales or bundles that do not fall apart when they are lifted off the vehicle.

ii) *Develop a symbol or name* to use on your product, on the side and back of your vehicles, on your notepaper or invoices and over the door of your depot. Give your employees badges.

iii) *Develop a slogan.* Decide on the strong points of your product and develop a slogan which is a saying that emphasizes them. Use it wherever possible so that people remember it.

iv) *Have a leaflet printed* to describe your product and list the good things about it. Perhaps a photograph can be included. Make sure the printing is neat, the information accurate and honest and leave out anything that will rapidly become out of date, such as the price. In particular remember to include your address and a telephone number where you can be contacted if you do not have your own. Leave it on the desk of any customer you visit so that, after you have gone, he still has information and a reminder of your product.

v) *Gifts to customers.* A favourite alternative among bigger firms is to send customers a gift, small in value but useful, that will stay in the office for a long time. Calendars, sent at New Year, are very popular, but check on the cost before you order hundreds! Be sure the subject is suitable: calendars bearing naked ladies are fine to send to the man who buys scrap metal from you (and will stay in his office for a whole year and not be taken home for the children) but it is not a suitable gift for ladies who buy scraps of cloth for rug-making!

PLASTICS WASTE CASE STUDY 8

Prida, Penelope and Paulo have been successfully selling granulated waste plastics to one of the two factories in the next town that mould plastics, but have decided that they are too dependent on one single market outlet. However, they cannot supply their one customer with all the material he wants, and Prida, who is regularly asked for more whenever he delivers, does not want to reduce deliveries by sending material elsewhere. They decide that Prida will talk to their customer, The Bluetown Bucket Company, to find out his needs during the next two years. Then they will consider ways in which to increase the amount of material they collect.

Penelope is to carry out a study of the market for plastics and try to make a forecast. Paulo is to examine the effect the purchase of a pelletizer will have on their ability to sell.

The results of these investigations are as follows:

i) Their customer has been unable or unwilling to give them any useful information and they are suspicious of his reasons for this. All he would do was to assure them that there was a need for their material *at the moment*.

ii) Prida considered how to increase the collections and decided that, instead of doing further collections themselves, they would buy from other small collectors.

The others objected because most of the small collectors only dealt with paper and metals and were not accustomed to collecting plastics. They agreed that it would be necessary to advertise for waste plastic and that, as many of the collectors live and work in the streets, street posters would be the best way of doing this. Posters were also a good idea as they could be made large with enough room for a picture as many street collectors cannot read. The picture would show a happy collector carrying a pile of plastic waste and receiving a pile of glittering money at the door of their depot. It would bear the words:

MONEY!

WE PAY TOP PRICES FOR CLEAN WASTE PLASTICS

VISIT OUR DEPOT AT 36 TOWN STREET

START COLLECTING NOW!

(Note how it does the four things described on page 298).

iii) Penelope had worked hard in the local library and talked to the secretary of the Chamber of Commerce. It was obvious that more and more goods were going to be made of plastic in the future, which was good news for them, but the Government had started building a huge plant to manufacture plastic raw material pellets instead of importing them as at present. The plant would be ready next year, and the pellets would cost one-fifth less than imported ones. Three new factories would be built to make products from the pellets and it was hoped that these would be exported.

iv) Paulo told them he had visited a company in the capital city that made extruders and pelletizers. The smallest complete plant would cost 10,000 dollars, new, but he might be able to buy a second-hand model for 6,000 dollars. Additional parts could be bought if they wanted to start moulding their own products. He suggested they ask the manager of the factory to whom they sold material for a loan of the money.

They decided that future supplies of raw pellets, at a lower price than imported ones, explained why the manager had been so unhelpful; he probably expected to stop buying waste from them then but did not want to say so, in case they sold their material elsewhere before the new material began to be available. It was obvious that they must find a second outlet for their material and they agreed to approach a factory in the next town. They also agreed that it was important to buy the extruder and make their own pellets, as the value of these would be such that they could afford to sell them much further afield than they did the present material. They agreed not to approach the factory manager for the money as that would tie them to selling to him. They would all think about other ways of raising the money.

Rule 20
Use the information you obtain to plan your marketing so you do not depend on a single outlet. Sell to final users not middle-men. Avoid being 'tied' to a customer.

SELLING
When a possible customer has been identified, the next task is selling to him. He *may* want your material so much that he will buy it at your asking price without argument but this does not happen very often! If it *does*, it might mean that the asking price is too low!
Selling can be split into three parts:
1. Contact
2. Negotiation
3. Follow-up

Contacting the customer
This can be done by telephone, personal visit or through a middle person.

In every case the principles are the same. A brief but courteous message has to be given to the right person indicating:

301

- Who you are.
- What you have to sell.
- Why they will benefit from buying it.
- How you propose to negotiate.

Who is the right person to contact?

It is the person who will in due course decide whether or not to buy your product. You can explain to him or her all the advantages of your product and ensure he understands and has the facts right. If you talk to his secretary, clerk or to a junior 'buyer', you can be sure that the facts will not be put to the right person in the way you would have wished.

Even more important is the matter of relationship. It has been said that "salesmen do not sell the product; they sell themselves". In practice, this means that buying and selling are acts that demand an interplay between two people – of understanding, trust, patience and tolerance – and that these develop far more easily if there is some mutual liking between them. This relationship cannot be built up through a third person, only through direct contact, even though this may have to be by letter or telephone and not face-to-face.

There are situations where this relationship between buyer and seller is obviously lacking and in this case it is better to conduct the business through a third person as the hostility could be damaging the chances of business. This often occurs when one person knows that the other is exploiting him, a common situation between small, poor waste collectors and middle merchants. It is made stronger if one is obviously rich and the other visibly starving. This kind of tense relationship can be seen all too often in the cities of the Third World.

To contact the right person, the seller may have to be both cunning and firm. He should make every effort to find out their name beforehand. If you ring up and say "May I speak to the person who buys waste paper" you may be put on to a junior. If you then argue that you want the managing director you will be told he is busy. On the other hand, if you ring up and say, with confidence, "May I speak to Mr Asif please" few secretaries or telephone operators will dare ask:

"Please tell me what it is about" and if they do it is easy to say:

"It is a confidential matter between Mr Asif and myself" or:
"I would prefer to explain that to him personally".

This kind of approach takes nerve and only becomes easier as experience is gained, but it can make a great difference to the final result. Even if you have aimed too high and Mr Asif puts you on to the junior buyer, you will have gained an advantage; the junior buyer will think of you as someone who has been introduced to him by Mr Asif and will take care to treat you accordingly.

A word of caution: do not be too arrogant or you may make enemies. Always be polite and gentle, even to the most junior staff; not only does this avoid unnecessary upset but may help you if you have to deal with them in the future.

Telephone calls

This is a difficult means of contact for those who are not used to it, as they cannot see the person who is at the other end, nor how they are reacting. It is probably better not to be too friendly until you know the other person or until you have gained confidence. Once these have been achieved it can be possible to have a satisfactory conversation, at short notice, with someone whom it might take you days to contact by letter, or to visit. Around the world, billions of dollars worth of trading is done on the telephone – but usually by people who either know each other or who are confident of being regarded as equals by the other person.

Here are some suggestions for making telephone contact:

i) *Avoid coin box calls.* To be interrupted by the money running out at the vital moment can spoil a deal. Pay a little more to use a phone belonging to a friend or at the telephone office. If there is no choice, make sure you have the right kind of money ready, and enough of it, and preferably put it in in advance to avoid interruptions.

ii) *Write down what you are going to say.* If you are a good talker just write notes. If you think you may become tongue-tied or dry up write down word-for-word, but make sure you do not sound as if you are reading it over the telephone.

iii) *Be persistent* if you do not get what you want. If he says "Very well Mr Chiwawa, I will let you know", then reply "I do think it would be best if you saw a sample; may I call on you tomorrow?" If he then replies: "No, I shall be busy tomorrow" then ask:

"Which day would be convenient to you?"

You have actually caught him out and established that you are going to visit, because he gave being busy tomorrow as an excuse instead of saying:

"No, I do not want to see a sample, so do not call on me".

If he really does not want to buy your material, then no number of visits will be any use, but the purpose of the visit is to change his mind if possible.

iv) *End the conversation* on a note that leaves him feeling good and that also leaves the way open for a future approach. Say "Thank you for having been so extremely patient; I look forward to meeting you soon", or even if things have gone badly:

"Well, I am sorry we cannot persuade you to do business but it has been very interesting talking to you and, if I may, I will contact you in a few months time to see if things have changed".

v) *Make notes* of what was said. It is surprising how quickly the details of a telephone call can be forgotten. Note the date of the call, too.

The letter

This is a much easier way of making contact. You can prepare what you want to say with great care and, if necessary, get someone else to write it. The big disadvantage is that you may never get a reply; unlike the telephone call or personal visit which *have* to be answered by someone. There are ways to overcome this problem, such as writing the letter in one of these ways:

"I propose to visit you next Thursday with full details of this material. Please would you let me know if, for any reason, this will not be convenient".

If they do *not* reply then you have established your right to visit them and you arrive at the door next Thursday saying:

"I have an appointment with Mr Asif", and if the reception-ist says:

"I am afraid he is out today" then you reply:

"He knew I was coming from my letter of the 23rd; perhaps he has arranged for me to see someone else".

The receptionist then *has* to get someone to see you or else it seems like bad manners on the part of Mr Asif or inefficiency on the part of the company.

A few pieces of advice on the letter:

i) *Use clean note paper*, never a piece of waste paper.

ii) *Pay someone to check it* for grammar and spelling mistakes, and *to type it*. This gives a good impression of your company even though you may be a person who scavenges from the refuse dump or collects from households with a cart.

iii) *Use a suitable name* "Riverton City Recycling" or "El Cortijo Waste Paper" sounds better, although it is only the name of the refuse dump from which you pick your living. Do not use a name that is dishonest like "The Riverton City Recycling Company Limited", when you are neither a company nor limited (a legal term meaning you personally will not pay the company's debts).

iv) *Use letterhead* (notepaper printed with your name and address) if you can afford it. It can be printed cheaply by a small jobbing printer but make sure it is done well with the letters all straight, level and properly spaced, with no smudging. Double check that the spelling and numbers are correct.

v) *Address and sign correctly*. If you know the name of the person you want to deal with, write: "Dear Mr Asif," and sign the letter "Yours sincerely".

If you do not know, address it to the title "The Managing Director" if it is a small company or "The Purchasing Manager" if it is a large one, and write: "Dear Sir", and sign it "Yours faithfully".

vi) *Remember to stamp the letter* as nothing spoils the chances of a deal more than the buyer receiving a letter and having to pay the postman!

The personal visit

This is the best way of selling anything. It makes it easy to form a good relationship, as explained earlier. It is easier to show your samples to the potential buyer and advantageous for you to see how the material is going to be used and what size of lorry can or cannot get through the door. Here are some hints:

i) *Prepare* what you are going to say beforehand and make

sure that you know all the facts and figures about your operation. You should be able to tell the buyer, without stumbling:

- how much material you can deliver;
- how often you can deliver it;
- when you can start;
- how you will deliver (lorry, railtruck, cart etc);
- what prices you are asking; and
- why the price should not be any less!

Take along any samples or photographs, as these will be a great help in making it plain that you really know what you are talking about.

ii) *Wash thoroughly* beforehand, all over! It is impossible to work with waste without handling smelly material and some of the smell will always remain. If the buyer cannot bear being near the seller, he will not make a deal that means he will have to be near him often in future! Clean your teeth and mouth for the same reason. If you have bad or rotting teeth try to have them treated for your own health and comfort. If this is not possible, find out if they smell. (The person you live with is the most likely person to give you an honest answer!). If so, use a fresh smelling toothpaste before the visit and try not to breathe into the other person's face!

iii) *Dress* as smartly as you can. Wash and press clothes and clean shoes even if they are not new or smart. Sew up any holes and take special care that the buttons or zip on the front of your trousers work properly. Wear a tie if that is customary among business and professional men. Wear a jacket unless it is hot enough to provide an excuse not to. The care with which you dress will be taken as a sign of your importance by junior staff and as a measure of respect by the person you are meeting. However, do not overdress. Loud, jazzy ties or handkerchiefs may suggest a loud and jazzy character when you want to be thought efficient and reliable!

iv) *Let the other person develop the meeting* once you have explained to him what you want. If he wants to chat about the conditions in the trade or even just about the weather, join in. If he wants to be brisk and get through the business in the minimum of time, do not delay him. Just make sure that you have the chance to say or show

all that you want and that you get the kind of answer you
need.
v) *Try and clinch the deal* (agree to sell and buy) there and
then, while you are together. It is much more difficult to
do so afterwards but he *may* have genuine reasons for
not doing so and you may irritate him if you are *too*
pressing. In this case, try to agree the next step clearly;
should you contact him again a little later, send samples
or a trial load.

The trial load is a useful way of advancing if the customer is
showing doubts about committing himself. It means that you
send in a load and he inspects and possibly uses it, to see if it is
the quality he needs or is paying for. If it fails he is free to send
it back without paying. If he uses it satisfactorily, he pays for
it. The price should be agreed beforehand to avoid argument.
The trial load gives the supplier the chance to take special care
to sort and process carefully, but beware of cheating. If future
loads are much less clean or pure or well-packed, the trial load
may be used as a standard for comparison and the price
reduced for loads that fall below it.

THE PRICE

Price is a subject which causes more argument than any other
matter. The price of your material may decide whether or not a
sale is made and, if it is, may cause the seller to lose or gain
heavily. There are three ways to decide the price at which you
want to sell:
1. Cost plus profit.
2. What others sell at.
3. What the buyer will pay.
All of them may be used in agreeing the final price.

1. *Cost price*

If you sell below what it costs you to produce the materials,
you lose money; if this happens too often, you go out of
business. Cost price is so important that most of Chapter 18
explains how to calculate it.

Profit is the money you keep for yourself, as a reward for the
risks and troubles of running the business. If you are a single

collector, it will be the money on which you depend for your living. If you are running a small company you may already pay yourself a salary, in which case profit is something extra, which you may decide to 'plough back' into the business to buy new equipment or to finance a new activity. If no profit is made, the main value of running the business is to create employment.

2. *What others sell at*

This is a good guide but remember, their situation may be different. They may be selling a different quality material or transporting it further or selling smaller quantities. It is such a useful guide that time is well spent asking others the prices they are receiving, from which buyers, and the quality, quantity and distances involved.

3. *What the buyer will pay*

This may be difficult to find out except by bargaining with him. The price he is paying to other people is a guide to the lower limit of what he will pay.

The price he will pay is affected by:
- How much he needs the material.
- Whether he can get it elsewhere and at what price.
- The price of virgin material.
- How much it costs him to transport, store and use.
- The price at which he is selling his product.

Timing. By knowing these facts the seller can judge whether to press for a higher price and at what time. It is better to ask for a higher price when the customer has just put his prices up because of a strong demand for his goods, than when he has just had to meet a big wage demand from his workers and is losing sales to another competitor.

Quantity. Prices are often higher for goods that are supplied in larger quantities. So it may pay to stockpile – keep goods in a store until you have a large quantity to send. However, you cannot do this if you need money quickly. What you can do in this case is to join with other collectors and sell jointly. This may also reduce the cost of transport to the customer.

Haggling. Generally, a deal is made when the price the

308

customer is willing to pay is the same as, or higher than, the cost to the producer plus the profit he wants. Sometimes, the producer is faced with accepting a lower profit or none at all, or else losing the sale. He will be influenced by whether:
- He has a chance of selling to someone else
- He needs to sell immediately or can wait
- He thinks the customer *will* actually pay more if it appears the price offered is not accepted. This is a matter of judgement, bluff and good information. Haggling over prices is a skill known to every market woman in the Third World. The methods are endless and fascinating but we shall make no attempt to explore them here!

Often, the poor or the small collector is faced with a price which is lower than his costs or which does not allow him enough money to live, let alone prosper or develop his business. Both choices available – to sell or not to sell – are disastrous. All that can be said is that it is hoped that this book will, probably through the help of a sympathetic friend or agency, help such people to avoid that situation happening.

TERMS OF PAYMENT

You may be paid when you deliver the material or later, by cash or by cheque or some other way.

Cash on delivery

Being paid in cash at the time of delivery is the safest payment for a small collector. The only reasons for agreeing to any other method would be because:
  i) It is safer. Robbers are likely to attack a person who has just collected cash.
 ii) It enables a sale to be made that would not otherwise have gone through. Beware of this, because if the customer is so short of cash that this matters to him, he may well be unable or unwilling to make the payment at the agreed time (or at all)!
iii) Other arrangements are customary in the trade. This is often an excuse by the buyer to avoid prompt payment and need not be accepted by the seller. Sometimes it is a sensible arrangement; for example, if delivery is made by a transport contractor then the seller is not present to be paid and must accept some delay.

Cash in advance

Sometimes a customer is willing to pay in advance, for instance to help a small collector to buy the cart he needs to get started. This kindness is usually a calculated action by the customer (often a merchant) to tie the collector to him so that the price is kept low, and the collector cannot go elsewhere because of his debt. Often, the loan has a condition that heavy interest be paid if materials are not delivered in the time and quantity stated. This starts the spiral of debt that causes worry, suffering and worse to many poor collectors who are trapped in this way.

The best way to avoid this kind of snare is never to borrow money from the person you trade with, but this advice is of little use to those who cannot trade without some money to start and cannot obtain that money anywhere else. However, there are agencies who will help poor people in this position, especially if they have plans to start a small business to improve their state in the future (see Appendices).

Debtors

What should a seller do if he has given the buyer 'credit' but cannot get his money? The first thing is to discover whether the buyer is a rogue who is making a fat living by such practices, or whether he is an honest man who has run into difficulties. In the former case, there are legal ways of making people pay their debts but they are usually slow, expensive and not always effective. They are better used as a threat than actually practised (unless you have a relative who is a lawyer or a policeman). Probably the most effective and cheap way is to visit the customer every day and (loudly) demand your money, refusing to leave until you get it. Your very presence will prove an embarrassment to him if he is still practising any sort of business and, if you follow him to his home, he may pay up to avoid loss of face among his neighbours. He will probably make promises of future payment and it is up to you to judge how trustworthy he is. Take care, however, as people turn nasty if hounded. If you have a big strong brother it may be a good thing if he is standing at the next corner!

If a customer is in genuine difficulties, tells you about them frankly and has clear plans of how to get out of them, it may be worth your while to avoid damaging his business reputation and to assist his chances of recovery. Do not, however, give him any further credit unless you are very rich or very loving!

In many towns there are debt collection agencies who will collect bad debts for a fee, but they do not always use legal methods. Sometimes they will buy the debt for a percentage of its value and make a fat profit if they recover it or a loss if they fail. Your chances of successfully recovering a debt by this or other means are much better if the debt is clearly shown on proper documents and these will be discussed shortly.

Keep a register of your customers if you have many, and record what they buy and when they pay. Look at it from time to time and, if a customer is a bad payer, decide what to do: stop selling to him, warn him, or ignore it because you cannot afford to upset him or lose his custom at present. In some countries it is possible to find out in advance whether a possible customer is reliable at paying; this information may be expensive and may not be true or up to date. Your own judgement and shrewdness is the best protection you have.

Some people think it does not matter *when* they are paid so long as it comes in the end. They are lucky. Think of it this way. If you sell 100 dollars worth of material every month and are always paid one month late it is the same as giving that customer a gift of 100 dollars, never to be returned. Few waste collectors in the Third World can afford to do that! If a collector is paying back 200 dollars a year on a loan of 500 dollars to buy a cart, at an interest rate of 25% (and few are fortunate to pay so low a rate), by collecting that 100 dollars and using it to pay back part of the loan he will actually *save himself over 250 dollars* (because of the laws of 'compound interest') and *repay the loan a year earlier*. It is well worthwhile ensuring prompt payment by your customers!

Agreements

These are written documents, signed by both buyer and seller, and state how much material one will sell the other and at what quality, quantity, price etc. Sometimes, they include a method of calculating changes in the price according to some agreed formula, which is often related to the price of the virgin raw material that is substituted by a waste material. For example, waste paper prices may be agreed as a certain percentage of the price of pure wood pulp.

An agreement is a valuable document for a small collector if it protects him from losing business when the market becomes

311

slack or from sudden price cuts if a competitor appears. However, it may well contain conditions that are too hard for him to meet, especially about the quality of the material, something he has great difficulty in controlling.

It may tie him to his customer for a long period after he has decided that the agreement is against his interest. A general rule is that small collectors should only sign an agreement with a large customer if:

i) They clearly understand every part of it and have thought carefully about how it will work in the future, possibly under very different trading conditions.

ii) They have taken advice from an expert, possibly a lawyer but, much better, someone with experience of the trade over a number of years.

iii) There is provision for price inflation (the situation where prices go up and money steadily loses its value).

iv) There is provision for the collector to break the agreement after giving a reasonable period of notice (three or six months would be suitable).

v) They are confident the customer will stick to the agreement (or give proper notice to end it) without need for legal action.

PLASTICS WASTE CASE STUDY 9

Penelope, Prida and Paulo, having decided to approach the second plastics factory, discuss their plans. They decide to write and ask for an interview.

No reply was received to this letter so Prida and Penelope left for Bluetown early on Tuesday morning, dressed in their best clothes. They had agreed that the best chance lay in selling transparent material as Bluetown Moulding Company made large numbers of transparent plastic bottles. They had worked out that this material cost them 300 dollars a tonne for cleanest and 200 dollars a tonne for normal quality. The prices for which they sold to their present customer, The Bluetown Bucket Co. (Case Study 6) were 500 and 250 dollars respectively, and they thought that Bluetown Moulding Co. would be able to pay more, as bottles use less plastic and sell for higher prices than buckets.

They agreed that, in order to establish a second outlet, they would agree to the following prices:

Greentown Recycling Company,
36 Town Street,
Greentown,
Colours District.

23rd April 1980

J.R. Asif Esq.,
Bluetown Moulding Co. Ltd.,
Industrial Estate,
Bluetown.

Dear Mr Asif,

This company is the largest collector and processor of secondary polyethylene in Colours Province with a growing annual production of clean, high quality material suitable for all types of moulding operations. We have supplied material to one of your competitors for the past year and are continuing to do so. However, the success of our operation has encouraged us to expand our collection and we are now in a position to offer you up to ten tonnes of material a month. A small sample is enclosed for your inspection.

Despite the high purity of this material, our prices continue to be very competitive and offer companies like yourselves large savings on the ever-increasing costs of virgin plastic raw materials.

I will call on you next Tuesday at 10 a.m. with samples of our whole range of production. Please let me know by return should that not be convenient.

Yours sincerely,

P. Palajiva
Sales Manager

350 and 230 dollars a tonne for a trial load.

400 and 240 dollars a tonne for any other quantity with an agreement to review the price after three months.

However, they decided to ask in the first instance for 600 and 300 dollars a tonne for deliveries of three tonnes or more and to allow themselves to be beaten down.

Mr Asif made it clear when he met them that he had only agreed to see them because he had been impressed by the small sample they had pinned to the letter. He wanted to see the other samples and said he did not believe they could provide such clean material in large quantities. They explained that they sold two different qualities of material: cleanest and normal; and he said he would be interested in buying the cleanest but would only buy the normal if they could improve its cleanness. He asked their prices and nearly fell off his chair when they told him! However, he soon agreed to pay 550 dollars a tonne for cleanest transparent but would not go over 225 dollars a tonne for normal. As they were plainly likely to have difficulties with him over the quality of the normal, they refused to accept this and he asked for 10 tonnes a month of cleanest. They explained that cleanest was only a small part of their collections and they could only supply two tonnes a month.

In the end he agreed to pay 250 dollars a tonne for five tonnes a month of normal, as well! Obviously, he had intended buying normal all along and had been surprised when he could not beat them down to 225 dollars a tonne. They agreed that the first load would be delivered in a week's time and asked for payment to be in cash to the delivery driver, a friend whom they could trust. Mr Asif said that normally they paid their suppliers of plastics by cheque at the end of the month. Prida pointed out that those were large companies that could afford to wait, while they were a small but growing concern. Mr Asif agreed to their request. He asked to keep the samples as a standard against which the quality could be checked and, somewhat reluctantly, they felt they had to agree. However, they left well pleased with the day's business and wondering how they could increase their collections of transparent material. They would need more donkey carts and more staff.

314

Rule 21
This is similar to Rule 18. Be professional in your salesmanship
– in telephone calls, letters and *especially* visits. Plan ahead, be
neat, clean and courteous.

Rule 22
Never negotiate a price without first finding out what price you
ought to get, what others get, your own costs, and how much
your customer needs your material. Work out the lowest price
you can accept and start by asking for more.

EXPORT MARKETS FOR WASTES

If there seems to be no market for a particular waste material in
one country, there is always the possibility of exporting it to
another. Many developing countries lack certain basic industries that may exist in the country next door; sometimes such a
market may be closer than if it were located in a far off capital
city.

Exporting is a rather fearsome process because of the
official paperwork involved, the customs duties and problems
of payment in other currencies. These deter all traders alike
and it may be that the enterprising seller, who is prepared to
risk or struggle with these problems will reap the rewards of a
market free from competition, where he can obtain much
higher prices. Many countries are part of a free trade area or
have customs agreements with their neighbours that may make
the problems of exporting much less troublesome.

The best idea is to forget about exporting while a business is
being built up, unless a particularly attractive market is known
about or some experience already exists. Pursue the idea once a
business is soundly based, when teething problems have been
overcome and the manager feels he is completely in control and
able to deal with any problems that may occur unexpectedly.

It is also possible to consider the import of waste materials
from neighbouring countries whose economies may be so
different that these are not recycled.

Mexicans who live near the US border cross over to collect
wastes and often cross it again to sell the same materials to US
firms who cannot afford to do their own collection. Textile
waste is a completely international commodity that is shipped
half way round the world from rich countries to markets both

315

in developing and industrialized countries.

Advice on how to export can usually be obtained from a shipping agent or from the Government Office for Trade. The embassies or trade delegations of foreign governments will usually provide information on the industries that exist in their countries and will help to make contact with them.

The costs of shipping are not connected with the distance from one country to another. They depend more on whether there is a regular trade route between the two ports in question, whether the cargo normally carried is similar to the waste being considered for export and what quantity of material is involved. A shipping agent can usually advise on the cost of shipment.

Chapter 16. Transport of Wastes

The transport of material from the collection depot to the customer is one of the most expensive operations, and everything possible needs to be done to reduce costs. Some suggestions have already been made in Chapter 12, Rule Number 9, and the subject is so important that it will now be discussed at length:

i) *Animal-drawn transport* may be cheaper than motor-driven vehicles in districts where fodder is cheap or fuel expensive. It is much slower and allowance must be made for the loss of time, but a separate driver can be employed. If distances are short this may not matter. It is very expensive to hire a motor vehicle for a short journey but even more expensive to buy one. Animal-drawn transport is more reliable than motor vehicles where competent mechanics are not widely available.

ii) *Location of the collecting depot* between the area of collection and the customer will reduce distances to the minimum.

iii) *Compacting* materials in a baling press allows the maximum load to be put on the vehicle. Road vehicles are rated by weight and it is unsafe to exceed the safe or recommended weight. The result of overloading could mean that: the load falls off when the vehicle turns; the vehicle overturns; the vehicle brakes do not work properly; or the police prosecute the driver, the vehicle owner or the person who owns the load!

iv) *Return loads* are those put on a vehicle that is returning from delivering another load. It has to make the return journey so the extra cost of carrying a load is less than the cost of a special journey. The skill is to find a vehicle or fleet of vehicles that make regular, empty, return journeys and to negotiate with the operator on this basis. He will always try to charge the full rate, as if he was doing the journey specially or even try to charge you for the outward journey too!

v) *The customer's vehicle* may be available and he may try to persuade you to use it. If you are considering this, first get a 'quotation' from an independent transport contractor. Beware of customers who offer to transport your material free or at a very low price. They must be paying you too little for material if they can afford to do this!

If you enter into this kind of agreement ask what will happen if you decide to transport by some other means in future. Will you lose your customer? And if you decide to change customer, will you lose your transport?

vi) *Quotations* are essential before sending a load by transport. The quotation is a statement made beforehand, by the transport contractor, of how much he will charge you per kilometre, per tonne weight or both. It is even better to get a firm price for a vehicle of a certain weight (that means load weight) from your depot to the customer's site. This should include all possible extras. If the vehicle has an accident, it should be the transport contractor's cost. Be clear whether he is also covering insurance on your load or whether you have to do this yourself. You might decide not to, to keep costs down. Waste is rarely damaged in a road accident: the main problem is sweeping it up and reloading the vehicle.

vii) *Rail, river and canal* transport is nearly always cheaper than road for large, heavy, bulky materials. It takes far longer, but this point is not as important as keeping the cost down (but you will have to wait for your money until the load has arrived). The important thing is that either you or the customer should have access to a depot beside the railway or dock. Loading and unloading with cranes or by hand may cost more than you save and short distance road transport at either end may be necessary, too. However, this possibility should always be investigated; if your customer has a factory on a rail siding or canal ask yourself if it is possible to move your business to a similar site; the savings may be huge.

viii) *Your own vehicle* will only save you money if it is used all the time. If it stands idle it will be losing money. As your business gets bigger you may save a lot of money by having your own transport. On the other hand, because your volume of work is larger, transport operators will quote you better prices. The operation of motor transport is an expert job and if you are a specialist in waste it is difficult to be one in transport as well.

ix) *Processing before transport* can reduce the weight or volume of material. Unwanted material may be removed by sorting, or else material may be made easier to handle by melting down or drying. This has the further advantage that it means more work for you, and less for your customer. You will charge a higher price per tonne and transport will become a lower percentage of your total costs.

x) *Trailers and tractors.* If you can load the materials on to a trailer and employ a tractor or lorry to tow it only when it is fully loaded, (leaving it at your customer's site for unloading) then you will not be charged for using the towing vehicle for so long. Do not despise tractors for hauling waste. The standard agricultural trailer has a huge capacity and can be tipped to unload. If you are in a farming district it may be possible to hire a tractor far more cheaply than a lorry, especially outside harvest time when trailers may not be fully used.

PAPERWORK

It is a good rule never to send material to a customer unless accompanied by the correct paperwork. By using carbon paper or self-carboning documents (careful, these are expensive!) it is possible to produce several copy documents for different purposes Fig. 92. The most common are:

i) *The advice note* This travels with the materials in the driver's cab. It *advises* the customer of what he is receiving and is kept by him for his own records.

ii) *The delivery note* is sometimes called the proof of delivery note, because that is what it does. It travels with the driver, is signed by the customer to say that he has received the material and is then returned to the seller and kept by him, with its vital signature, as proof of delivery.

iii) *The invoice* is the paper against which payment is made. It is sent to the customer through the post (or presented to him in person) and a cheque or cash is given in

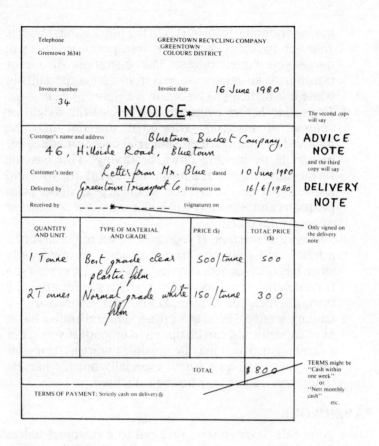

Fig. 92 An example of copy paperwork. The invoice, advice note and delivery note can all be written out together, using carbon paper.

exchange. If it does not agree in quantity, date etc. with the advice and delivery notes then something is wrong.

The advice and delivery notes do not always show the value of the goods (e.g. if the seller does not want the transport contractor to know this and charge more for his service). The invoice must always show the value.

iv) *The seller's copy* is a fourth piece of paper often kept by the seller, because the other three pieces leave his possession at various times and it is safer to have a complete record of every sale that has been made. These are usually filed in a book or drawer, either in date order or else under the names of the customer, so that it is possible to see, at a glance, how many loads a certain customer has received. This copy is usually marked when the customer has paid.

v) *Statements.* Where a customer does not pay immediately for material but pays, for example, nett monthly cash (payment at the end of the month following the delivery) it is usual to send him a monthly statement of account stating which invoices are still outstanding and their total value (Fig. 93).

Paperwork will serve the following purposes in addition to providing buyer and seller with accurate information about the sale:

i) It serves as proof that the load described on the paper was actually delivered, on what date and that its weight, description, quality etc. were as described. This is invaluable if there is any legal dispute about payment for the load.

ii) It may serve as a basis for paying the transport contractor.

iii) It helps you to keep accurate records of your production. These may be useful in the future when you are calculating your ability to take on extra work.

iv) It serves as a check on your own employees that all the materials are being delivered and that you are being correctly paid for them.

PLASTICS WASTE CASE STUDY 10

Penelope, Prida and Paulo have increased their sales of granulated plastic waste to 20 tonnes per month. They meet one Friday evening to consider how they can reduce the cost of transport from Greentown, where they collect and process, to Bluetown where their customer is based. They consider moving the whole business to Bluetown but decide against it as other collectors operate there, whereas they have Greentown to themselves. Prida presents a paper showing the possibilities open to them:

i) The present method is delivery by donkey cart. The cart holds, at most, sixty sacks weighing about 30

321

```
Telephone                          GREENTOWN RECYCLING COMPANY
                                              GREENTOWN
Greentown 36341                        COLOURS DISTRICT


                                   Statement date


                        STATEMENT

Customer's name and address      Bluetown Bucket Company
     46, Hillside Road, Bluetown


The following invoices are now due for payment:
```

INVOICE NUMBER	DATE	VALUE (S)
32	5th June 1980	650
34	16th June 1980	800
35	23rd June 1980	700
	TOTAL	2150

Fig. 93   An example of a statement.

kilos each, a total of 1.8 tonnes per load. The
journey is 25 km each way and takes a whole day
there and back. At present, he is making a trip
every other day (except Sundays when the factory
is shut) i.e. three times a week. It costs about 20

dollars a week to look after the donkey and cart.

ii) They could buy a small truck, second-hand, that would carry about one tonne but do the journey, there and back, in under half a day, allowing time for loading and unloading. It would cost about 10,000 dollars to buy and about 10 cents a kilometre to run.

iii) They could hire a lorry, with a 10 tonne carrying capacity, that would take about 230 sacks weighing around seven tonnes. They would need to buy more sacks. The cost would be 60 dollars a time for the round trip.

iv) They could arrange for the customer to collect the material on his own lorry, which comes to Bluetown once a week to deliver goods to the local stores. This will be done free of charge, but the price paid for the material will be reduced by 20 dollars a tonne.

They have some difficulty in deciding which of these is the cheapest and eventually call in Paulo's cousin, a schoolteacher, to help. He suggests they draw up a Table (16).

From this it is clear that their slow and inefficient donkey cart is the cheapest method of transport and that, if they wish to use something a little more modern and release Prida from frequent trips to Bluetown, the most economical method is to hire a lorry, when they need it. Even though they do not know the rate of interest that they would have to pay on a loan to buy their own truck, this is clearly an expensive method but not as dear as using their customer's 'free transport'.

Prida, who had been rather excited at the idea of driving a truck, suggests that they have been rather gloomy to assume that a truck would only last five years. The others remind him that:

- If it does 240 trips of 50 km per year, it will do nearly 300,000 kilometres in five years.
- It will have to be second-hand to begin with.
- None of them are skilled motor mechanics; indeed none of them have ever owned a vehicle before!
- The roads between Bluetown and Greentown are very rough and full of holes.

Table 16 Plastics waste case study 10: Yearly costs of transport

Method of transport	Weight of load per trip in tonnes	Number of trips per year	Type of cost	Cost unit	Cost per unit in dollars	Number of units per year	Cost per year in dollars
Donkey cart	1.8	about 150	Keeping donkey and cart	per week	20	52	1040
			Driver's wages (half time only)	per week	$17\frac{1}{2}$	52	910
							Total 1950
Own truck	1.0	240	Cost of buying truck if it lasts five years	per year	2000	1	2000
			Interest on loan to buy truck	per year	not known	1	not known
			Running costs	per trip of 50 Km.	5	240	1200
							Total 3200 plus interest on loan
Hired lorry	7	36	Cost of hire	per trip	60	36	2160
Customer's transport	—		Reduction in selling price	per tonne	20	240	4800

Prida agrees that the estimate is, in fact, rather optimistic!

Rule 23
Transport is one of the highest costs in waste handling but can be reduced in many ways. Use of your own lorry is one of the most expensive forms of transport.

Rule 24
All deliveries of material to a customer should be accompanied by suitable paperwork.

Chapter 17. Health and Safety in Handling Wastes

Some people are only interested in earning a great deal of money as quickly as possible and do not consider or even mind if they harm themselves or other people in the process. This chapter is for the other people who enjoy their lives, want to live for a long time, and care about their well-being and that of their employees. They think these things are more important than earning a little more money by working without safety precautions. For them, this is one of the most important chapters in this book.

There are three ways in which the person working in waste can keep good health, and help the people who work with him to do the same:

   i) By keeping simple rules about health.

   ii) By keeping simple rules about safety.

   iii) By avoiding certain well-known dangers.

HEALTH RULES

There are many books that explain why people do not stay healthy. Here, there is only space to list some of the important rules with a very brief explanation.

Drinking water

People become ill if they drink dirty or polluted water. If your water supply is not safe to drink, you should try to:

- buy bottled pure water;
- use a water filter;
- use chlorine or other disinfectant;
- boil water before drinking.

Sanitation

People become ill if they eat food that has been in contact

with excreta and other dirt either when it is grown, sold or prepared. This danger can be lessened by:
- washing food that will not be cooked, especially fruit and salads that are eaten without being peeled;
- using a latrine so that no excreta is lying around where people live and work. If nothing else is available, a pit latrine may be dug and the excreta covered with soil or sawdust on each occasion it is used.
- washing the hands with soap and water before eating, in case dirty material has been handled.

Cuts
Cuts and open injuries become poisoned if they get dirty. Clean them with soap and water as soon as they occur (with an antiseptic if possible), cover them with a clean dressing and protect the dressing with a glove, sock etc. See a doctor about serious cuts or minor cuts that do not heal.

Drinking and eating properly
People lose moisture when they work; they need regular drinks, and cover from direct sunshine if possible. People also need enough good food to give them the energy to work hard. It should be balanced, that is, contain the right mix of vitamins, proteins and calories to produce energy.

SAFETY RULES
The following simple rules give safety both to the worker and others around.

Tidiness
To keep the working area tidy, decide on a place for everything, mark it on the floor with paint, chalk or pegs and try to keep things in their correct places. Plan clear gangways down which materials can be moved, and then make a narrow passage from the nearest gangway to every person's workplace. Mark gangways on the floor with paint and insist that they (and passages) are kept clear all the time. Many injuries are caused by tripping over things when carrying a load.

Cleanliness
Mop up any spilt liquids, especially oil or grease, so that no

one slips. Keep wastes together in piles or, even better, in bunkers to avoid the risks of fire or falling. Make sure dirt does not get into sources of water or near places where food is prepared or eaten.

Dirty and strong smelling wastes attract flies, rats and other pests and they in turn carry diseases from excreta and other sources. Try to keep such wastes to the minimum, get rid of them quickly and clean thoroughly where they have been (Fig. 94).

Fig. 94   Dirty waste attracts flies. A heap of plastic objects beside this one had been washed and was quite free of flies. Flies carry diseases, especially on to food and are a serious health danger.

Protective clothing

Wear protective clothing where necessary and see that other people do too, particularly the young. The following items are especially important (Fig. 95):

328

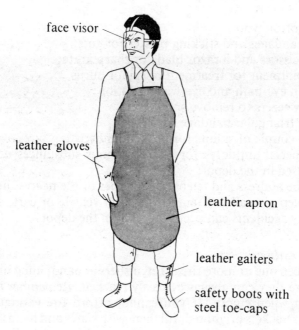

Fig. 95 *Protective clothing for working with hot metals.*

- safety boots with steel toe caps for people handling or working among heavy objects;
- leather or rubber gloves for people handling hot metal, acid or caustic liquids;
- overalls or separate working clothes for people working with dirty materials;
- leather aprons and gaiters for people working with hot metal, acids or caustic chemicals;
- face masks, eye goggles or visors for people working with hot metal, acids and any kind of chemicals, grinding or cutting tools etc.;
- caps for women or men with long hair who work with machinery.

First aid kit

Keep a first aid kit near, in a clean place. It should contain:
- soap and a clean towel;
- a clean dish;
- antiseptic ointment or liquid for wounds;

- cotton wool;
- bandages and sticking plaster for cuts;
- scissors and a razor blade or sharp knife;
- ointment for treatment of minor burns;
- an eye-bath and eye-wash solution;
- tweezers to remove splinters;
- a triangular bandage for arms;
- a couple of splints for broken limbs;
- special antidotes for any poisonous substances normally used in the depot;
- the address and telephone number of the nearest hospital.

Keep a small first aid kit on each vehicle or cart, as well; many accidents can occur away from the depot.

Fire extinguishers

Keep one or more fire extinguishers at hand, hung on a wall where they can always be easily reached. Remember to refill them when empty. If you cannot afford fire extinguishers, paint buckets bright red, fill them with water and hang them on a wall. Do not let them be used for anything else. Fill a bucket with sand for use on fires that involve electrical machinery, or buy a special fire extinguisher for electrical fires. Hang them near electrical machinery. Never use water or foam-type fire extinguishers on electrical fires.

Fire escape

If anyone works on an upper floor, a loft or roof, make sure there are *two* separate ways down – in case one is blocked by fire. If no stairs exist, hang a stout rope from a strong point above a window and put a notice up to indicate that it is there.

Fire drills

Once every three months carry out a fire drill. This should include:
- A noise signal to warn people of fire.
- Teaching people the safe route to leave the building.
- Assistance to any old or disabled staff, children etc.
- A roll-call at an outside assembly place to find out if anyone is left in the building.
- Knowing how to call the fire brigade (but do not do so except for a real fire).

Training

If you are the boss, train the people who work for you. Show them how to do their jobs, how *not* to do them and make sure they know the dangers and safety rules. Spend half an hour a week talking about work and various safety points as described above. Walk round the depot once a week looking for potential dangers. Half an hour a week spent discussing safety can save you many hours, days, weeks lost through sickness and injuries.

DANGERS TO AVOID

Drugs and alcohol

Working under the influence of drugs or alcohol can result in serious accidents due to falling, dropping things, misusing machinery or worse, getting tangled up with it.

Dangerous wastes

Beware of wastes that have serious health problems such as dead animals that may have had anthrax, poisonous liquids, lead which is a poisonous metal etc. Read the chapters of this book that cover specific materials and note any special dangers.

Inflammable liquids and gases

Any liquids or gases used to burn or heat, and many others as well, are inflammable. Make sure that they are stored in a cool place, away from heat, fire or naked flame, and that they are kept in closed containers, clearly marked and free from leaks. These should only be used by trained adults.

Children

Children in a workplace can be more dangerous than any machinery, both to themselves and other people. If they cannot be kept out, make sure they are watched all the time. If they are old enough, explain the dangers to them.

Lifting weights

Learn how to lift heavy weights properly and teach your employees, too (see over).

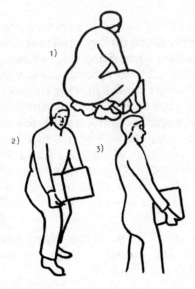

HOW TO LIFT HEAVY OBJECTS SAFELY

1) Stand close to the load, bend at the knees, keep the back straight, grasp the load with the full hand, keep the elbows in close to the body.
2) Straighten the knees. Let the thigh muscles do the work, not your back. Support the load on your knee half way up if necessary. Keep the back straight.
3) Carry or put down the same way. Keep the back straight.

Machinery

If anyone is working with machinery, make sure they know how to turn it off in case of accidents. Try to install an off-switch that is easy to reach and operate; a big mushroom shape that you punch off is the best. Paint it bright red and position it on a wall, by a clear gangway near the machine. Never let it be covered up. Anyone with long hair working machinery should tie it back. Long ends to clothing such as sari sleeves, scarves etc. are all dangerous.

Have a guard made to cover any part of machinery that moves, especially rotating parts. Only let this be removed for cleaning, but make absolutely sure it goes back before the machine is used again. Never allow a machine to be cleaned while in use.

Make sure every machine has a clear space round it so that no one can stumble or fall into the machine while it is moving. Machine operators should work alone so that they will not be distracted while working.

332

Power-operated presses, shears and guillotines are particularly dangerous. There are special safety devices made for them. When deciding whether you can afford a machine, take the cost of the safety device into the sum and do not buy the machine without it.

Electrical

Make sure all electrical equipment or wiring is safe and has a proper electrical earth. If in doubt, call in a qualified electrician. Check that wires and cables are fully insulated and that the insulation is not damaged or worn. Do not allow anyone to use electrical equipment if they are wet or standing on wet ground or floors. Put up a notice showing how to deal with cases of electric shock (an example is shown overleaf).

Ladders

If ladders are used, check that they are not damaged and make sure someone foots (stands on the bottom rung of) the ladder if someone is on it.

Stacking

Make sure materials, especially bales that are stacked up for storage or transport, are steady and cannot topple over.

Smoking

Do not allow anyone to smoke in a depot that handles waste paper or plastics, or any other inflammable material.

Buildings

Beware of hanging heavy gear from buildings, or mounting machinery on walls etc. Make certain the building is strong enough not only to stand the weight of, but also the 'vibration' of machinery. If in doubt, ask an architect or engineer to advise you.

If vehicles pass close by, make sure the building is protected by an extra wall or a guard rail, or that it is built so that the structure will not crumble if a vehicle hits it.

Rule 25

The safety of your business and its people can be ensured by learning and acting on a few simple rules – and in the long run these will increase your profits, too.

Treatment for electric shock

1) SWITCH OFF THE CURRENT OR PULL OUT THE PLUG.

2) IF YOU CANNOT SWITCH OFF – Stand on dry wood, cardboard or other non metal surface and pull victim away using dry cloth, rope or other non metal.

3) LIE VICTIM ON HIS BACK – With head a little higher than feet.

4) TILT VICTIM'S HEAD BACK – Lift his jaw.

5) CHECK VICTIM'S BREATHING
   Quickly
   – Can you hear it?
   – Can you see his chest move up and down?
   – Are his cheeks, ears, lips, nails a blue colour?
   This means breathing has stopped.

6) IF BREATHING AND AWAKE – Watch for breathing to stop. Keep warm.
   Do not give food or drink. Get medical attention.

7) IF BREATHING BUT ASLEEP – Turn on front with head on one side. Keep mouth clear of vomit. Keep warm till awake. Follow 6).

8) IF NOT BREATHING GIVE THE KISS OF LIFE: DO NOT LOSE TIME.

   A) PUT ONE HAND UNDER CHIN, ONE HAND ON HEAD, BEND HEAD WELL BACK.

   B) TAKE A DEEP BREATH, PINCH VICTIM'S NOSE CLOSED, OPEN HIS MOUTH, SEAL YOUR MOUTH OVER HIS, BLOW GENTLY INTO HIS MOUTH.

   C) TAKE ANOTHER BREATH, WATCH HIS CHEST RISE AND FALL, REPEAT EVERY 5 SECONDS OR WHENEVER CHEST HAS FALLEN.

   D) CONTINUE ON AND ON AND ON UNTIL BREATHING RETURNS. Then follow 7) above.

   E) SEND FOR MEDICAL HELP AS SOON AS POSSIBLE BUT DO NOT STOP KISS OF LIFE.

334

Chapter 18. Controlling Money – The Secret of Making a Profit

Few people are familiar with the world of money, the place of accountants, auditors, bankers, economists and businessmen. It has a language and life of its own which can appear secret and mysterious to the rest of us. For this reason people become afraid of money, forgetting how easy they find spending and handling it themselves. This chapter shows how a small waste recycling business can control its money, in order to increase profits and keep clear of disasters. There is nothing in this chapter that cannot be understood by a person who has completed primary school. The three activities described are budgeting, accounting and costing.

Budgeting means planning what you are going to spend before you spend it and what you expect to earn before you earn it. We all do it!

"If I get paid $3.00 tomorrow and spend 20 cents on bus fares and $2.00 on food for the family, will I have enough to buy a new knife for $1.05? No, I must not spend more than $1.75 on food if I am to buy the knife". That is a simple piece of budgeting such as a school child may do and budgeting a business is not much more difficult.

Accounting means recording what you receive and what you spend and checking that you have the right amount left at the end. Again, it is an everyday practice.

"I actually earned $3.20 and spent 20 cents on bus fares, 80 cents on bread, 40 cents on potatoes and 20 cents each on two bottles of milk, and have only $1.00 left to buy the knife. I ought to have 1 dollar 40 cents left. What have I done with the other 40 cents? Ah! They have slipped through a hole into the lining of my jacket."

Every housewife does such simple pieces of accounting. The important thing is that as a result of accounting, the 40 cents have been found and it is still possible to buy the knife. Without the accounting, the cash would have been counted, found to be only $1.00, the knife would not have been bought, and no attempt made to explore the linings of the pockets!

Costing means adding up all the money spent and earned in each way and comparing it with the budget to see whether any midway change in plan is needed or is possible. Two alternatives are:

1. "I planned to spend $1.75 on food and have spent 80 cents on bread, 40 cents on potatoes and 40 cents on milk. Can I afford to spend 30 cents on sugar? No, because I have spent $1.60 on food so far, so I have only 15 cents left."
2. "Although I have spent $1.60 out of my $1.75 food budget, I earned $3.20 instead of my budget of $3.00, so I can afford to spend another 20 cents which will be enough to buy the sugar."

Notice how in this last paragraph there is complete control over what money is available and how much is needed for food and yet no thought has to be given to the matter of bus fares and the knife. They are both on budget and can be ignored. Only the item that has varied from the budget (the amount earned) is examined to find out whether another variation (the extra spent on food) is possible. This is the value of costing; it allows you to devote your attention to the things that are changing, either going wrong or getting better, and not to waste time on things that are going to plan. It also helps you to plan better next time, as you have an accurate, easy-to-understand record of what happened before.

Businesses that do no budgeting, accounting or costing find life very difficult. They are constantly being surprised, usually unpleasantly, by their financial affairs. They are unable to plan new activities because they do not know if they can afford them, nor what results they may have. They continue to do the things that lose them money and fail to develop others that make a profit. If you want your business to be a success and yourself to be free of worries, read on!

Profit or cash?

In Chapter 15 the difference between credit and cash sales

was explained. In a cash sale, the sale is made (i.e. the material delivered) at the same time as the cash is received. In a credit sale the cash is received later. When compiling a budget it is necessary to decide whether to show the sale at the time it is made or at the time the cash is received.

The answer to this is to decide what the budget is meant to show.

i) If it is the profitability of the business then show the sale at the time the material is delivered, that is, the date on the invoice. Similarly, the costs can be averaged out equally over the period during which they were spent. For example, electricity costs can be shown as being spent only when the electricity is being used. The more electricity used during production, the more the cost.

ii) If the budget is intended to show how cash moves into and out of the business, then the sums of money will be the same but the *timing* will be quite different. The sales will only be shown when the cash is actually received from the customer. The electricity cost will not be shown when the electricity is being used but when the cash payment of the bill is actually made. If the bill comes every quarter-year and you manage to delay payment for two weeks after the bill is received, then you may *actually* pay cash about fourteen weeks late for some of the electricity. If you rent an electric meter, however, you may pay for it in advance.

Both types of budget are important. The profit budget will show whether an activity is profitable, whether another is more so, etc. The cash budget will show whether, despite being profitable, your business will, at some time, run out of cash to pay its wages and bills (when your customer is on holiday for example). Should the latter occur, you may need a loan to see you through for a month or two, or you may decide to delay buying a piece of equipment.

As a start we shall consider budgeting for profitability.

BUDGETING

It is usual to budget for a full year ahead. Some businesses add a rough budget for a further one, two or even four years, but this should not be necessary for a small business and is difficult in the present times of inflation. The budget is broken down

337

into months. It is common to use a year starting in April and finishing in March so that the year end does not come at the same time as Christmas. Taxes are often based on this same financial year.

There are three main classes of money to consider:
1. Income – mainly from sales of materials
2. Running Expenses – on wages, transport, rent etc.
3. Capital expenses – the buying of new machinery, vehicles, tools etc.

Sales budget

Income from sales is calculated by multiplying the amount expected to be sold by the price. It is prudent to make a cautious estimate of both. Leave a gap in sales during Christmas, Easter and any other holidays. Show any changes in amount or in price that you expect to occur. Even if you will not be paid cash on delivery of the materials, show the sale in the month when the invoice is presented. It is useful to draw up a budget of the weight of material you expect to deliver and convert that into a value of cash income.

If there is any other income, such as from the hire of transport to another collector or from the sale of objects salvaged from the wastes, it is best left out of the budget unless it is regular and dependable.

PLASTICS WASTE CASE STUDY 11

Penelope, Prida and Paulo budget their sales for their second year of business (Tables 17 and 18). Note the following:

    i) Sales to Bluetown Bucket Co. are at a steady amount but those to Bluetown Moulding Co. increase as the volume of collections of transparent scrap increase.

    ii) Prices for the recently negotiated sale to Bluetown Mouldings are constant but a reduction in prices from Bluetown Bucket Co. is expected as a result of the competition from the new Government plastics plant.

    iii) Although they collect large quantities of whole bags and sacks, these do not give any sales because they are used in the course of collections.

    iv) They have two weeks holiday in August, a week at

338

Table 17 Plastics waste case study 11—Sales plan in tonnes

Customer	Material: Grade	Material: Colour	Price in dollars a tonne	Number of Tonnes sold each month: Total	1981: April	May	June	July	Aug	Sept	Oct	Nov	Dec	1982: Jan	Feb	March
Bluetown Bucket Co	Normal	Transparent	250*	45	4	4	4	4	3	4	4	4	3	4	4	3
	"	Opaque white	150*	10½	1	1	1	1	½	1	1	1	½	1	1	½
	"	Pure colours	200*	21	2	2	2	2	1	2	2	2	1	2	2	1
	"	Mixed	50*	33	3	3	3	3	2	3	3	3	2	3	3	2
	Cleanest	Transparent	500*	10½	1	1	1	1	½	1	1	1	½	1	1	½
Total to Bucket Co				120	11	11	11	11	7	11	11	11	7	11	11	7
Bluetown Moulding Co	Normal	Transparent	250	61	5	5	5	5	4	5	6	6	4	6	6	4
	Cleanest	Transparent	550	29	2	2	2	3	1	3	3	3	2	3	3	2
Total to Moulding Co				90	7	7	7	8	5	8	9	9	6	9	9	6
Overall total				210	18	18	18	19	12	19	20	20	13	20	20	13

These prices are expected to reduce by 30% at the end of September.

339

Table 18 Plastics waste case study 11—Sales budget in dollars

Customer	Grade	Colour	Price in dollars per tonne	Total	1980									1981		
					April	May	June	July	Aug	Sept	Oct	Nov	Dec	Jan	Feb	Mar
Bluetown Bucket Co	Normal	Transparent	250*	9600	1000	1000	1000	1000	750	1000	700	700	525	700	700	525
		Opaque white	150*	1350	150	150	150	150	75	150	105	105	53	105	105	52
		Pure colours	200*	3600	400	400	400	400	200	400	280	280	140	280	280	140
		Mixed	50*	1385	150	150	150	150	75	150	105	105	70	105	105	70
	Cleanest	Transparent	500*	4500	500	500	500	500	250	500	350	350	175	350	350	175
Total to Bucket Co				20435	2200	2200	2200	2200	1350	2200	1540	1540	963	1540	1540	962
Bluetown Moulding Co	Normal	Transparent	250	15650	1250	1250	1250	1250	1000	1250	1500	1500	1200	1500	1500	1200
	Cleanest	Transparent	550	15950	1100	1100	1100	1650	500	1650	1650	1650	1100	1650	1650	1100
Total to Moulding Co				31600	2350	2350	2350	2900	1550	2900	3150	3150	2300	3150	3150	2300
Overall Total				52035	4550	4550	4550	5100	2900	5100	4690	4690	3263	4690	4690	3262

* These prices are budgetted to reduce by 30% from the end of September.

Christmas and a week at Easter, so the tonnes sold are reduced.

Expenditure budget

This needs more experience to estimate the costs that will be incurred but less arithmetic is involved. To do it the second time, based on experience in the first year, is very easy. The following costs may be included, but not all businesses will have them all.

i) *Rent* for land, buildings, any extra storage place. This may be a fixed sum per square metre or a total lump sum. It may be paid per year or half year or quarter, but in the budget it is shown spread evenly over each month.

ii) *Rates* are payments made to the municipality (for street lighting, cleaning, refuse disposal etc.). They may be yearly etc., but again are spread in the budget. There may be rates to a state or province, and even national ones. If these take the form of taxes, on the income or profit of the person or the business, they can only be budgeted for after this has been calculated.

iii) *Electricity* can be estimated if the power used by all lights, heaters and machines is added up and the cost per unit of electricity is known. It may be less trouble to make a guess the first year and check it after two or three months. In winter or a wet season more lighting and heating may be used. At holiday periods less is used, too. The bill may come monthly or every quarter.

iv) *Liquid or solid fuels* may be used for heating, for furnaces, and for processes such as drying, rendering or flame-cutting. They may be bought in bulk once or twice a year and, if they are a big item of cost, it may be better to spread the costs over each separate month; but remember the actual cash to pay for them goes out in lump sums after the bill is received.

v) *Insurance* is a regular payment (monthly or yearly) to an insurance company which will pay the costs if any disaster occurs: theft, fire, accidents etc. It is a wise arrangement but is often not used by small companies because they do not understand how it works, or because they do not want to pay the regular payments (called premiums). Poor people, who need protection against unexpected disasters more than anyone, never use it because they cannot afford it. Disaster usually leaves them ruined as a result.

A great benefit of insurance is that the small regular premium payments can be budgeted for by even a small business, whereas big costs of disasters: rebuilding a burnt-out factory, paying damages in a lawsuit, or compensation to the victim of an accident, can never be foreseen.

If your business is steady, even if it is small, contact an insurance company and ask them what it will cost you to insure against the most obvious dangers like fire and theft. Then include it in your budget; you will soon forget the small regular payments but, if disaster strikes, you will never forget the satisfaction when an insurance payment helps you get back on your feet.

Only two words of caution. *Do not* deal with small, cut-price insurance companies and *do* read all the small print in the insurance agreement (called a policy). It may be in difficult legal language so get someone to explain it to you.

vi) *Wages* of employees are easy to budget; do not forget to budget some pay for them during the holidays; their families do not stop eating! Some employers pay an extra bonus at festivals. If there is a state insurance scheme for employees or a state medical scheme, it is convenient to budget for this at the same time. Remember that months have different numbers of days.

Wages for yourself, the owner, are also important. You can either pay yourself a regular wage like any other employee, and treat profits quite separately (the simplest arrangement) or you can decide to take the profits each month as your reward. Provided you are clear about what you are doing it is easy to budget either way.

vii) *Transport and collection costs* will include not only petrol or diesel fuel for a vehicle or fodder for an animal, but also costs of new tyres, oil, maintenance and repairs (difficult to budget for unless you have costs from the previous year as a guide – but even then remember the vehicle is a year older and more worn so add 20%) for tax or licence costs, and insurance – often required by law.

342

It will also include two other charges that need to be explained carefully. They are called capital charges and because they are a little more complicated they will be dealt with at the end of this section.

viii) *Office costs.* Costs of paper and envelopes, invoices, any typing or photocopying, stamps, telephone bills, ink, pens, pencils and all the other little things you may need. Usually, a single monthly sum is put in to cover them all.

ix) *Selling costs.* Travelling to see customers, any small gifts to them, costs of sending samples, 'weighbridge' charges etc.

x) *Bank charges.* Normally, they are small, but if you borrow money from the bank they will include interest, and so will be much larger.

xi) *Maintenance costs.* Everything from repairs or spare parts for machinery to having the drains unblocked (a very common task in waste-paper depots – if they have drains!). Keep transport maintenance separate from other items so that you always know the full cost of transport.

xii) *Capital costs.* These are the costs of using capital (which means lump sums of money). Capital equipment is large pieces of equipment that need lump sums of money (i.e. someone's capital) to buy them. A baling press should be treated as capital equipment but a knife should not.
Interest and repayment of loans. If you borrow money to buy capital equipment, such as a vehicle or machine or building, you will have to pay interest as well as paying the loan back. Usually, the interest is a fixed percentage of the sum you have borrowed. As you pay the money back, the interest, at the same fixed percentage, becomes less. If you know the sum you have borrowed, the percentage of the interest rate and how quickly you are going to repay the loan, you can calculate the interest payments quite easily, and include them in the budget showing how they become less.

You also need to include the regular repayments in the budget. Keep them separate from the interest and show them continuously until the loan is repaid.
Interest on capital employed. If you borrowed money from the bank or (heaven forbid!) from the money-

343

lender, you will have paid interest; a fee for the benefit of using the money. If you use your wife's dowry, your grandfather's lorry or your own savings, should you not also charge your business either interest or a fee? Many businesses like to do so, to show the cost of using this capital. They usually include it in the budget as an expense equal to the money they would have received each month if the money (or lorry) had been lent or hired to someone else.

However, to do so is purely a calculation on a piece of paper. It reduces the amount of profit shown by the business. Some people prefer to leave such capital free so the final profit will be that much bigger. You may decide yourself which to do. If you have to pay tax on the profits from your business, one way may be better than the other; ask your bank manager. Otherwise, it must be stressed, there is no difference in actual money, only in how you show the figures.

PLASTICS WASTE CASE STUDY 12

Penelope, Prida and Paulo draw up their expenses budget for the coming financial year. Note the following about the budget in Table 19.

i) Rent, rates, insurance, and loan repayments, and office, selling and maintenance costs are shown to be constant month by month.

ii) Electricity varies with the amount of work done in the month.

iii) Lorry hire varies with the amount sold each month (from Table 17).

iv) Wages and costs of animal fodder vary with the number of days in each month.

If employees are paid a fixed sum per month, this can be avoided. Some people prefer to spread wages evenly, regardless.

v) Interest on loans decreases as the loans are repaid. The bank loan for the granulator was spread over three years and the interest rate was a reasonable 24% per annum (2% per month). The bank would not grant a loan for donkey carts because the bank manager thought they were old-fashioned so they had to go to the money-lender and pay a staggering 48% per annum. They therefore decided to pay this loan off quickly – in a year. The budget showed they could manage this. If they had not had such an assurance from the budget, they would not have dared to take a loan at such high interest, but the extra donkey carts were essential to collect more of the very profitable transparent, cleanest material for the new customer.

Paulo worked out the benefits of the second customer from the budget. Using only the figures for the total year, he saw that the extra sales were $31,600 and the extra costs were:

	$
Wages of the five extra employees	7820
One extra lorry trip a month	720
Capital costs of the new donkey carts: repayment and	4800
interest	1248
TOTAL:	14,588

Leaving an excellent profit of $17,000 despite the heavy interest rates.

Rule 26
By budgeting, you can spot the profitable activities and spend more money and time on them.

New and Replacement Capital Equipment
i) *Depreciation.* Finally, the budget must reflect one other fact about the use of capital equipment: that it is being worn out and, in time, cash will be needed to buy its replacement. This is true even if your loan has been fully repaid, even if you never needed a loan because your grandfather left you something when he died. In order to avoid ending up with no equipment, no money to buy any and in need of a new loan, use an idea in your budget called depreciation.

This is just a way of charging your business for wearing out its capital equipment. Instead of showing the full cost of the equipment in the month it was bought, the cost is spread over all the months during which it will be used until it will be worn out. The easiest way to do this

Table 19 Plastics waste case study 12—Expenses budget in dollars

Expense and how calculated	Total	Apr	May	Jun	Jul	Aug	Sep	Oct	Nov	Dec	Jan	Feb	Mar
Rent: workshop & land	7200	600	600	600	600	600	600	600	600	600	600	600	600
Rates and taxes	2400	200	200	200	200	200	200	200	200	200	200	200	200
Electricity: lights, granulator	1125	100	100	100	100	75	100	100	100	75	100	100	75
Insurance	1200	100	100	100	100	100	100	100	100	100	100	100	100
Wages: 3 owners @ $35pw each	5475	450	465	450	465	465	450	465	450	465	465	420	465
5 employees @ $30pw each	7820	643	664	643	664	664	643	664	643	664	664	600	664
Collection: 3 carts @ $20pw each	3000	240	260	240	260	260	240	260	240	260	260	220	260
Lorry hire: $60 per 7 tonne load	1980	180	180	180	180	120	180	180	180	120	180	180	120
Capital loan: repayments & interest													
Granr: repay $3600 over 3 yrs.	1200	100	100	100	100	100	100	100	100	100	100	100	100
interest on remainder @ 24%	732	72	70	68	66	64	62	60	58	56	54	52	50
Carts: repay $4800 in 1 yr.	4800	400	400	400	400	400	400	400	400	400	400	400	400
interest on remainder @ 48%	1248	192	176	160	144	128	112	96	80	64	48	32	16
Office and sales costs	600	50	50	50	50	50	50	50	50	50	50	50	50
Maintenance costs	600	50	50	50	50	50	50	50	50	50	50	50	50
Total	39380	3377	3415	3341	3379	3276	3287	3325	3251	3204	3271	3104	3150
10% extra for unexpected costs	3938	338	342	334	338	328	329	332	325	320	327	310	315
Total	43318	3715	3757	3675	3717	3604	3616	3657	3576	3524	3598	3414	3465

Abbreviations: $ = dollar, pw = per week, @ = at, yr. = year, & = and, % = percent.

is to guess how long it will last. A good rule is that a vehicle running on bad roads will last three years, one running on good roads will last five years, a piece of machinery will last eight or ten years and a building will last twenty or twenty five*. Next divide the cost of the equipment by this number of years and you have the yearly depreciation to put in your budget. For a monthly depreciation, divide this by twelve.

Depreciation is only an idea. It shows you, on your budget, what it is costing to use that equipment and wear it out. Later, when you work out your profit each month by subtracting the costs from the sales, your profit will have been realistically reduced by this amount. You may, as a result, decide to take less out of the business.

However, a different figure on a piece of paper does not mean there will be cash in the bank or under the floor as a result. You may not buy clothes for your family but you may spend the money on buying more materials from other collectors. But what will you do when the equipment finally wears out? How will you find the money to buy a replacement?

You have two choices: to do nothing and rely on getting a loan from somewhere; or to put enough money each month into a savings fund so that when the old equipment is worn out you have enough to buy the replacement. There is no fixed rule that says you must do one or the other; it is your choice depending on whether you are, or can afford to be, cautious and looking to the future, or whether you prefer, or are forced, to think only of the present.

ii) *Savings fund.* This is sometimes called a sinking fund and may be run in one of two ways. For either you need to open a separate bank account (keeping money under the floor of your home is risky and earns no interest).

You can transfer into the savings fund each month a

These periods are longer than are commonly used in industrialized countries but are typical for the Third World where equipment is normally allowed to become more worn before it is replaced. If you want to use industrialized country standards, use two, three, five and twenty years respectively.

sum of money equal to the depreciation of the original cost price of the equipment. If you use a bank deposit account, this fund will earn interest to help with the fact that, when you buy the replacement equipment, it will be at a much higher price than the old equipment cost. Even so, you will still probably need more cash than you will have in the savings fund.

Alternatively, you can calculate how much the price of this kind of equipment is going up each year, and make an allowance for this. You may need some help from your bank manager to do the calculation. It will mean using a rather higher sum each month in your budget than simply the old cost price of the equipment, depreciated over the number of years before it wears out.

Summary of capital charges

To summarize the rather difficult matter of capital charges, the following may be included in your expenses budget:

a) If you *borrowed money* to buy equipment you should include the regular repayments and the interest, which reduces as the loan is repaid.

b) If you used *your own* money or your wife's you may want to charge your business the interest that you could have earned if you had loaned the money out instead of using it yourself. Alternatively, you may prefer to leave that interest as part of your profits.

c) To show how your profit is being reduced, by the wearing out of your equipment in the process of running the business, include depreciation figures.

d) To make sure you will have cash to replace the equipment when it is worn out, start a savings fund and budget to pay into it (and in due course actually pay out) enough money to replace the equipment, possibly at a much higher price, in future. This is *instead* of depreciation in the budget.

Depreciation is only an accounting trick to make sure that, when calculating the profit made by a business, the use of capital is not ignored because it was spent in previous years. It is a way of spreading the capital costs, just as it is convenient to spread the electricity costs over all months when electricity is used, and not only the month when the bill was received.

Depreciation reduces the amount of profit that is calculated and discourages too much profit being taken out of the business, but it does no more than this. To ensure that this money is available to replace a vehicle or piece of machinery that has worn out, it is necessary to take the cash physically from the day-to-day finance of the business and put it in a savings fund to earn interest and be ready for the day when a new item must be bought. The amount that is put in the sinking fund *may* be the same as the amount shown for depreciation of the item but in times of high inflation it is necessary to put more away if the fund is going to be sufficient to buy a new item at much inflated prices.

Budgeting spending on new capital items

One of the most difficult things for a small business to obtain is the capital money needed to start a new activity. To borrow from a money-lender means a very high rate of interest. A bank will charge lower rates of interest but will want to be certain that a loan will be repaid (and repaid on time) and will ask for security or collateral. This usually means either that the borrower finds someone who will guarantee the debt (repay it themselves if the borrower cannot) or else that the borrower possesses some building or item of machinery that would become the bank's property if the loan were not repaid. As few small businesses can offer either of these, they have great difficulty in obtaining capital. However, there are certain agencies that may help poor people to obtain capital if they have genuine, well-considered plans to start a small business and these are discussed in the Appendices.

Once a business has started to trade, the problem of finding capital is a little less difficult. The best way to finance it is from the profits of the business if these are sufficient, and it is important to budget for these needs to avoid the money being spent as income by the owners of the business. Just as the replacement of capital equipment and vehicles is achieved by keeping a savings account, so the purchase of new capital equipment can be done in the same way.

PLASTICS WASTE CASE STUDY 13

Penelope, Prida and Paulo use the sales and expenses budgets to see what profits they are likely to make in the coming financial year, and to plan their capital spending. They have been hoping, for some time, to buy an extruder-pelletizer, for 9000 dollars. They do not want to borrow more money until the heavy interest debt on the donkey carts is paid off, but they believe the profit from the pelletizer will be high. The budget shows that:

if they actually make as much profit as budgeted and *if* they do not take these profits out of the business, they will nearly have enough saved for the pelletizer by the end of the next financial year.

Table 20 Plastics waste case study 13—Budget of profit and capital spending

	Budgeted value of sales (From Table 18)	Budgeted expenses (From Table 19)	Budgeted profit or loss
April	4550	3715	835
May	4550	3757	793
June	4550	3675	875
July	5100	3717	1383
Aug	2900	3604	(704)
Sep	5100	3616	1484
Oct	4690	3657	1033
Nov	4690	3576	1114
Dec	3263	3524	(261)
Jan	4690	3598	1092
Feb	4690	3414	1276
Mar	3262	3465	(203)
Total	52,035	43,318	8,717

Note: figures in brackets indicate a loss e.g. (704)

However, Penelope objects.

"First," she says, "we have been paying high interest rates on the loans for the donkey carts and the granulator. We should be depreciating these and putting money into a savings account to replace them when necessary. Secondly, we shall only receive a miserable 35 dollars a month from this business according to the budget. I have five children and my parents to support and my husband is dead; I want more money from the business to spend on

my family, not another machine for Paulo to play around
with!''

They are surprised by Penelope's outspokeness but
decide to look at the figures which show that the straight
depreciation of the donkey carts, assuming a life of five
years each, will be $4,800 over five years or $960 a year. If
prices go up 15% every year, replacement donkey carts
will cost about $9,650 so they would need to put $1,930 a
year for five years into a savings fund to replace them.

Depreciation of the granulator over eight years is only
3600 ÷ 8 or $487.5 a year, but a savings fund on the same
basis of 15% inflation, would need about $11,000 or
$1,376 a year.

They decide that:
  i) They will set up a savings fund for the donkey carts
     and charge the business $960 a year depreciation
     for this.
 ii) They had no difficulty getting a bank loan at
     reasonable interest for the granulator, so they will
     not try to provide for its replacement at present.
iii) That leaves a budgeted profit of $8,717 − $960 or
     $7,757 for the year. They will plan to use $6,000 of
     this for the pelletizer and to distribute the rest
     among themselves as profit; about $11 a week
     each. Any profit above or below this will be split
     50% : 50% between the pelletizer and themselves.

Rule 27
Budgets and cost actuals should take account of the depreciation of capital equipment, and cash may be set aside in a
savings fund so that equipment can be replaced when it is worn
out and new equipment bought.

CASH

One of the problems that faces any business, large or small is
the need to make sure that at all times they have enough cash to
meet their daily needs of paying rent, wages, bills etc. Short-
ages of cash may be caused by any of a number of things that
have nothing to do with whether or not the company is profitable. For example, a customer may be late in paying a large
bill, or money may be needed to pay for a big repair job, the
day after every cent has been scraped together to pay for a

new machine. One common cause of a shortage of cash among waste collectors is that a large supply of waste becomes available. They spend cash to collect or buy it and then find that, although their customers will buy it all in the long term, other collectors have also been delivering larger amounts and the customer's warehouse is full, so he will buy no more at present. The collector is left with a large stock of material but a shortage of cash for paying the wages or feeding his family.

There are a number of ways to act in this situation:

i) *Bring in any money that is owing* to the business.

ii) *Delay payment of bills* to other people as long as possible (but not so long that they refuse to do business in future!).

iii) *Delay all expenses.*

iv) *Arrange short term loan* from the bank or elsewhere, but this may cost heavy interest.

v) *Offer stocks at a discount* (a lower price) for a limited period to encourage customers to buy them sooner. However, this may result in a loss of profit.

vi) *Reserves* may be used such as the savings fund; it is most important that it be repaid as soon as the crisis is over.

vii) *Employees may be laid off* work without pay. This is a cruel action and should be avoided at all costs.

viii) *Equipment or buildings may be sold*. This is bad as it leaves the business unable to recover later and it is difficult to obtain fair prices if sales are made in a hurry.

The best solution is not to get into a cash crisis and this can be prevented as follows:

i) *Do not let customers run up large debts*. If they do, first remind them, then stop supplies.

ii) *Do not spend money* unless it is sure that (a) the business can afford it and benefit from it in the long term; and (b) there is cash for it without creating a dangerous cash shortage in the short term.

iii) *Keep some cash in the bank* as a reserve – but try to make sure it is earning interest.

iv) *Budget the cash movement* in and out of the business. This is done by a process almost the same as that for budgeting profit except that the sums of money are entered in the months when they will actually be paid. Thus, the entire electricity bill is paid in one month, not spread over all three months of the quarter. Sales are shown not in the month when the invoice is made out, but in the month when the cash is likely to be received. By budgeting and comparing actual performance with budget, the danger periods (e.g. holiday time when workers are paid but no cash is received from customers) can be spotted in advance and arrangements made to cope with them, such as help from the bank or post-ponement of a capital purchase.

v) *Bank managers.* Many people think of the bank manager as a kind of policeman whose job it is to dis-cipline anyone who draws more from the bank than he has in it. This is a pity because a bank manager can be a businessman's greatest ally if he is treated correctly. The bank manager will earn profits for his bank by helping his small customers to be successful and become big customers; his job is to lend the bank's money. How-ever, he has to make sure he does not lose money by doing so. The best way to reassure him is to be sure to tell him about your business and to seek his advice from time to time. He is probably one of the most experienced businessmen in your district, as well as being one of the only ones who will give advice free, so it is worthwhile to keep him well in the picture. Talk to him before you start a new venture, inform him when it is going well and discuss *in advance* what help he will be able to give in a cash crisis, and you will have little trouble getting reasonable help from him when things become a little difficult.

Rule 28
Avoid cash crises by budgeting cash movement, controlling debtors and getting support from your bank manager.

KEEPING THE ACCOUNTS
Like drawing up a budget, keeping a set of accounts is far simpler than most people think. It requires neatness, lined paper and no more arithmetic than that learnt in primary school. All you do is write down how much money you receive each time you make a sale, in one book, and how much you spend each time a payment is made in another. Each month (or quarter or year but monthly is better) you add them up and draw a line under the last figure. It is as easy as that!

There are really two kinds of accounts. *Book-keeping* is intended to make sure that the money is properly looked after; to check any theft or fraud; to show the bank manager to prove that your business is sound and that he need not be afraid to lend you money; to show the tax-man how little profit you made and how you cannot afford to pay any taxes and so on.

Cost accounting on the other hand is the analysis of your income and expenses in the same way used for budgeting. It also compares what you actually spend with what you planned (budgeted) to spend. Then you can see if anything is going wrong and take action to put it right. You can plan for the next year, too, or for a new venture, with more accuracy than last year.

Book-keeping

It is a good idea to have three separate accounts:
1. A current account at the bank.
2. A savings account for depreciation of equipment (the savings fund) at the bank.
3. A petty cash account. There is no bank involved.

All income, whether cash or cheque, is paid into the *current account*. Cash is paid in as quickly as possible so that it does not stay in the office for any length of time. The amount of money deposited in the bank must be the same as that shown on the invoice for the sale. All expenses are paid out of the current account either by cheque or through the petty cash account if they are by cash. At the end of each month, the receipts and payments should be compared with the bank statement, and a summary written out showing all the sales (split into those that have paid and those that still owe money) and all the expenses (split into those paid and those owing). Do not forget the depreciation charges. A total profit for the month can then be calculated.

The savings account receives the money that pays for the depreciation of capital equipment. At the end of each month, a cheque is written out to take money from the current account and transfer it to the savings account in accordance with the sum shown in the budget. If possible, the savings account should be a deposit account earning a reasonable rate of interest, but this is second in importance to it being totally safe. The savings must be transferred each month, even if this means no profit is left. If it is not and there is not enough money to replace equipment or vehicles when they are worn out, the business could collapse.

The petty cash account is kept in a tin or cash box. To start with, a current account cheque is cashed to provide a float of, say, $50. Whenever an item is bought from a shop it is paid for from the float in the box.

The receipt from the shop is added to the box. If no receipt is given the bookkeeper writes one out, signs it and puts it into the box. At the end of each day, the total of the receipts and the cash in the box are added up and should equal the value of the float. Any amount missing must be tracked down and replaced. When the cash is nearly used up, the value of all the receipts is added up and a current account cheque written for the total. This is cashed and the cash put in the box to bring the amount up to the original float. The receipts are kept together in an envelope with a note of the cheque number, the date and the total amount.

PLASTICS WASTE CASE STUDY 14

At the end of April 1981, Penelope, Prida and Paulo produced their monthly account of receipts and payments as follows:

	$
Income	
Income from Sales	4400
Debtors	Nil
Total sales in April	4400
Expenses	
Cheques drawn on current account	3500
Petty cash	85
Creditors	200
Total expenses in April	3785

	$
Depreciation (transferred to savings account)	140
Profit	475

While they are pleased to have a profit, they are

355

disturbed not to have made as much as they had planned in the budget and they do not understand why. They seek advice from their bank manager who suggests to them that they learn how to keep their accounts in such a way that they can easily find out what has gone amiss, using a system of cost accounting. He also shows them how to check or 'reconcile' their accounts with their bank statement, having first replenished the petty cash float with a cheque drawn on the current account for $85, see Table 21.

Rule 29
Only very simple book-keeping is needed for a small business with: A book to record payments and receipts, a petty cash box, a current account at the bank and a deposit account for the savings fund.

Year-end accounts are often demanded by the tax collector, the bank manager who has provided a loan, or by an agency that is giving financial assistance to a small business. If the business has kept good records of its receipts and payments, it can hand these to a qualified accountant to produce a balance sheet and a profit and loss account which are what will be required. It is not necessary for the business itself to do the rather more complicated system known as 'double entry book-keeping'.

COST ACCOUNTING
This has nothing to do with the bank or the tax-man or anyone else. It is a way of recording what has been spent or earned in such a way as to make it easy to compare with the original budget. By doing this it is possible to:
- Make sure the business is going as it was planned to do.
- Find out where and why if it is not.
- Take advantage of any improvements in the business.
- Budget better next time.

Costs are recorded under different headings and the headings used are exactly those that were used for the budget. At the end of the month, all expenses under a heading are added up. The total is called the cost actual because it is what was actually spent. It is then compared with what was budgeted.

356

Table 21 Plastics waste case study 14—Bank reconciliation

	$		$
Balance in current account at beginning of April	– 240	Balance in current account at end of April	915
Petty cash in tin	– 100	Petty cash in tin	100
Receipts from sales	– 4400	Cheques drawn on current account	3585
		Transferred to savings account	– 140
Total	4740		4740

Table 22 Plastics waste case study 15—Current account for June

Date	Description of payment	Cheque number	Total	Rates	Elec.	Ins.	Wages	Colln. costs	Lorry hire	Repay capital	Int. on cap.	Cap. deprec.	Office selling	Maintenance
3/6	12 sacks of wheat bran	342191	120					120						
4/6	Hire of lorry to Bluetown	342192	60						60					
5/6	To Petty cash account	342193	45				20	15					10	
5/6	Wages	342194	255				255							
6/6	Payment to electrician		25											25
8/6	Printed notepaper and envelopes	342195	(23										23	
8/6	Printed collection leaflets		(20					20						
8/6	Paint	342196	16											16
10/6	Quarterly electricity bill	342197	270		270									
12/6	Wages	342198	255				255							

Table 22—contd.

Date	Description of payment	Cheque number	Total	Rates	Elec.	Ins.	Wages	Colln. costs	Lorry hire	Repay capital	Int. on cap.	Cap. deprec.	Office selling	Main-tenance
12/6	Payment to electrician	342199	34											34
15/6	Hire of lorry to Bluetown	342200	60						60					
18/6	3 Sacks of Feed supplement	342201	45					45						
19/6	Wages	242202	255				255							
26/6	Wages	242203	255				255							
27/6	Rent	242204	600											
29/6	Rates	242205	200	200										
29/6	To bank	242206	168							100	68			
29/6	To money-lender	242207	560							400	160			
	TOTALS		3266	200	270	Nil	1040	200	120	500	228	Nil	33	75

For example, on a certain day the following payments are made:

	$
Three sacks of grain for the donkeys	39
A tin of paint for a cart	4
Payment to an electrician for repairing a light	15
A can of oil for oiling the granulator	5
A new lock for the front door	3

From this, $23 (electrician, oil can and lock) will be put down to maintenance and $43 (grain, paint) to collecting costs.

The same can be done with sales. Sometimes, with wastes, it is easier to study the number of tonnes that have been delivered to the customer instead of the value in money.

At the end of the second month, both the totals for the month and the combined totals for both months, are compared with the budget. At the end of the third month, the combined totals for all three months are compared with the budget and so on. These combined totals for every month since the budget began are called cumulative totals and they are more help than the totals for each month on their own, because they are not affected by small delays in payments which can alter one month's figures completely.

PLASTICS WASTE CASE STUDY 15

Acting on the bank manager's advice, Penelope, Prida and Paulo change the way in which they record the payments from their current account so that in June they produce an accounts record as shown in Table 22.

PLASTICS WASTE CASE STUDY 16

At the end of June 1981, after three months of the new financial year, Penelope, Prida and Paulo are studying the cost actuals for the month and comparing them with what they had budgeted to spend (Table 23).

They see that most headings show the same actual as the budget because they knew exactly what they would have to spend, for example on the rent. Electricity is badly overspent, however. They wonder if there is something wrong and whether they should call in an expensive electrician again. They know they are already overspent

Table 23 Monthly comparison of budgets and actual costs

	Month of June		
	Budget	Actual	Variance
Rent	600	600	0
Rates	200	200	0
Electricity	100	270	+ 170
Insurance	100	0	− 100
Wages	1093	1040	− 53
Collection costs	240	200	− 40
Lorry hire	180	120	− 60
Capital costs	728	728	0
Office and selling costs	50	33	− 17
Maintenance	50	75	+ 25
Contingency	334	0	− 334
Total	3675	3266	− 409

on maintenance and are trying hard to economize on this. Lorry hire is underspent and they are pleased about this until Prida points out that it is because the last load of the month was delayed (because one of Penelope's sorters was sick), which means that, although they saved on lorry hire, they also are under budget on their tonnage of sales. Penelope promises that they will work extra hours this coming month to catch up the lost output.

Table 24 Cumulative comparison of budget and actual costs

	June – Cumulative	
	Budget	Actual
Rent	1800	1800
Rates	600	600
Electricity	300	270
Insurance	300	300
Wages	2400	2400
Collection costs	740	650
Lorry hire	540	480
Capital costs	2238	2238
Office and selling costs	150	91
Maintenance	150	292
Total	9218	9121

They then go on to look at the cumulative actuals for the three months (Table 24).

This shows them that the electricity is not faulty; the high bill in June was the bill for all the three months together! So they do not need to call in an electrician, but even so the increase in their maintenance costs is rather worrying. They decide to get out all the bills for maintenance and study them together. When they do so they notice that:

i) They have bought five different lots of paint. They have all been brightening up their own parts of the business with the result that they have overspent on this heading and they now have five half-full cans of paint in different places! They agree that in future Paulo will do all the buying and he will prevent this kind of mistake happening again.

ii) They have called the electrician in five times in three months. They decide that nothing can be done, as it is unsafe for anyone else to do electrical work, but they decide that Prida will try and agree a lower price per hour with the electrician in exchange for a promise that they will give him first chance to do any work for them.

Table 25 Comparison of budget and actual tonnages—Plastic waste case study 16

| | | | June – Cumulative | |
			Budget	Actual
Bucket Co.	Normal	Transparent	12	14
		Opaque white	3	4
		Pure colours	6	4
		Mixed	9	9
	Cleanest	Transparent	3	4
		Total	33	35
Moulding Co.	Normal	Transparent	15	12
	Cleanest	Transparent	6	4
		Total	21	16
		Overall total	54	51

They finally look at the cumulative tonnages of material that have been delivered to the customer (Table 25).

They see that they have been delivering a little over the budgeted quantities to Bucket Co. and a little under to Moulding Co. As Moulding Co. pays a better price, and they have doubts about the future market with Bucket Co., they decide to alter this and make sure that Moulding Co. gets the larger share of transparent material and that any shortfall of transparent material to Bucket Co. can probably be made up with coloured or white material.

They are pleased to see that, if a small correction is made for the lost load at the end of June, they are ahead of budgeted production and this, combined with being a little below budgeted costs, means that their profit is likely to be better than budget if they can continue the same way for the rest of the year. Paulo decides he will write to one or two companies for details of their pelletizers. Penelope decides on the sort of clothes she will buy her children.

Rule 30
Sales and cost actuals can be compared with the budget to find out what is going wrong, how to put it right, improve the business and budget better in future.

Costing different materials
Every collector or processor of wastes has to make the initial choice of which material to collect. Is it more profitable to collect a large quantity of good material from a distance than scattered arisings of poor quality material from just around the corner? The methods of budgeting and book-keeping that have been described will provide an answer, provided that records and accounts are kept up to date.

The price per tonne for which he sells such material is known to him. However, some may cost more than others. The invoices tell how many tonnes were delivered. He needs to know the total cost of collection, processing and delivery of all those tonnes.

363

Allocating costs

If a cost is due entirely to one batch of material this is easy. However, if a cost is incurred on an operation that produced a mixed quantity of materials then it is more difficult; the cost has to be allocated (or separated) between the different materials in a sensible way: by weight, by sales value, by time spent on each etc. There are no true answers, no right and wrong method; the right way is the way that seems to you to be right.

For example, a collection that obtained 200 kilos of bad material from calling at houses for six hours and then obtained 400 kilos of good material by two one-hour calls on factories could have its costs allocated either by weight or time. In the former case, the good material would carry two-thirds (400 kg out of 600 kg) of the costs, in the latter the good material would carry only one-quarter (two out of eight hours) of the cost. By taking more time for a collection you have to pay the collector higher wages; by collecting more weight you give the donkey a heavier load to pull home. Obviously, time has more effect than weight on the cost and in this example it would be better to allocate by time.

Those processes and costs that cannot be allocated are split up in any way that seems intelligent. The rent and rates may be allocated in proportion to the amount of space taken up by each material: if they are similar this is probably the same as splitting them by weight. The office and selling costs might be split up according to the sales value. If one material, such as paper, is inflammable and another, like iron, is not, then perhaps the paper should stand all or most of the insurance costs.

All the costs during a given month can be totalled up to be split between the different materials, and these costs subtracted from the value of the sales of each. It will then be clear which material makes the greatest contribution to the overall profit and which makes the least. Some material may be seen actually to reduce profit and, after the calculation has been carefully checked to make sure there is no error, it may be decided to stop collecting it.

However, if no alternative can be collected in its place it may be that this material helps to cover the fixed costs: rent or vehicle tax that cannot be reduced just by stopping that collection, only by selling the building or vehicle which would ruin the rest of the business. Decisions to stop a material must only be taken on the basis of the real savings they make.

PLASTICS WASTE CASE STUDY 16

Because they get a much better price for the clean material, Penelope, Prida and Paulo decide to study how much profit they make on clean material and how much on dirty. They decide to make the calculation on the budgeted figures for sales tonnage and value and for expenditure. They know that it would also be possible to do the calculation on the 'actuals'. However, they only have actuals for three months of the year so feel the budget will be better.

They decide to allocate the costs as follows:

Collection costs will include the wages of Prida and three collectors, fodder and maintenance of the carts and the capital costs of the carts. These will be allocated according to the number of days each week that are devoted to collecting each kind of material. In practice, clean material requires one day for each of the three carts; dirty material takes the other four days, twelve in all, but they decide to reduce this to eleven as there is often some reason why one cart does not turn out.

Cleaning costs only apply to dirty material. This includes wages for Penelope and Peter and about one-quarter of the rent (because a quarter of the depot space is devoted to washing), and half the rates (because washing uses water which is a major part of the total rates bill).

All other costs apply to all materials and they agree to allocate these by weight of sales. They draw up Table 26, using the annual cost totals from the budget (Table 19) and allocate 39½/210 to cleanest material and 170½/210 to normal material (from Table 17 Annual totals of weight). They simplify this to one-fifth for cleanest and four-fifths for normal.

From Table 26 it is evident that:

1. Their profit is, in fact, coming from cleanest material (20,450 – 7,610 dollars, line 11 – line 10) and there is an overall loss on normal material (31, 585 – 35,708 dollars, line 11 – line 10).

Table 26 Plastics waste case study—16 Cost per tonne of materials

Line	Source	Cost	Total for the year	Clean	Normal
	Table 19	*Collection costs* allocated in the ratio		3/14	11/14
1.	"	Wages of collectors + Prida @ 125 dollars a week	6500	1393	5107
2.	"	Fodder and maintenance of carts	3000	643	2357
3.	"	Capital costs of carts	6048	1296	4752
4.	Lines: 1 + 2 + 3	Total collection costs	15548	3332	12216
	Table 19	*Cleaning costs* all allocated to normal		0	100%
5.	"	Wages of cleaners Penelope and Peter @ 65 dollars a week	3380	–	3380
6.	"	One quarter of the rent	1800	–	1800
7.	"	One half the rates	1200	–	1200
8.	5 + 6 + 7	Total cleaning costs	6380	–	6380
	Table 19	*All other costs* allocated in the ratio		1/5	4/5
9.			21390	4278	17112
10.	4 + 8 + 9	*Total costs*	43318	7610	35708

Table 26—contd.

Line	Source		Cost	Total for the year	Clean	Normal
10.	4 + 8 + 9	*Total costs*		43318	7610	35708
11.	Table 18	Total sales value		52035	20450	31585
12.	Table 17	Total tonnage sold		210	$39\frac{1}{2}$	$170\frac{1}{2}$
13.	10 + 12	**Cost per tonne**		**206.27**	**192.65**	**209.43**
14.	Table 18	Price per tonne	Transparent		500 & 500	250
15.	"		Opaque white		–	150
16.	"		Pure colours		–	200
17.	"		Mixed		–	50
18.	14 – 13	Profit per tonne	Transparent		307 & 357	41
19.	15 – 13		Opaque white		–	– 59
20.	16 – 13		Pure colours		–	– 9
21.	17 – 13		Mixed		–	– 159

2. However, transparent normal material makes a profit of 41 dollars a tonne. (line 18)
3. Opaque white and pure colours normal material make a small loss. (lines 19 and 20)
4. Mixed normal makes a heavy loss (line 21).

They decide that:
1. They will speak to their customer and explain that they are making a loss on normal material, especially mixed, and ask him for a price rise.
2. If they cannot raise the price they will stop collections from sources of normal material that do not yield a high proportion of transparent material as well.
3. They will explain the costings to their collectors so that they search out the most profitable material.
4. They will reconsider the calculation in a month's time and study the possible effect of stopping collections of normal material altogether.
5. They will consider whether they can increase the volume of normal material by enough to spread the fixed costs (rent, insurance, office costs, etc.) over more material without greatly increasing the variable costs (those that increase with volume of material such as hire of lorry, wages of collectors etc).

Rule 31
The profit per tonne of each kind of material can be calculated to show which collections should be increased and which should be stopped.

INCREASING PROFIT
Case study 16 gave an example of the possible ways in which profit can be increased:
- Increase selling price.
- Cut costs.
- Increase total volume of sales without increasing costs in proportion, i.e. on materials whose variable costs are low compared with fixed costs.
- Increase volume of sales of profitable materials.
- Reduce or discontinue collections of less profitable or unprofitable materials.

It also showed how the different, simple costing methods described help make these possible. Even the increase in sales

368

price might depend on being able to convince a customer that you are serious in your threat to stop supplies of one material because it is not profitable; without your impressive figures he may think you are just a good salesman with a cheeky bluff!

There are many, many other methods of accounting that will help a small businessman to do other things for his business. Some of them are just as simple as those described here; others are more complicated. Readers who have felt happy in their understanding of this chapter (or who felt it was so impossible to understand they would like a more competent explanation!) may consult the books in the further reading section.

Rule 32
By learning how to improve your budgeting, accounting and costing you will improve your control of your business and your profits.

Summary of Rules for Creating Work from Waste

1) Find out which wastes occur in the district that are not being used.

2) Find out the quantity if possible.

3) Find out the uses of markets that exist before starting to collect waste material.

4) Find out the quantity and quality required, where the markets are and the price that might be obtained.

5) Decide on the type of technology needed to change the material from the form in which it occurs into the form in which it can be sold and whether further technology is desirable.

6) Remember that with simple, home-made technology you can often process material cheaply to increase its sales value and reduce transport costs.

7) Leave complicated technology until you are familiar with the product and the market and can find the money needed without endangering your business.

8) Transport is one of the highest costs in a waste business. It may decide which sources of supply or markets are economic.

9) Transport costs can be reduced by:
- making door-to-door visits on foot with a back-up vehicle;
- using carts drawn by people or animals instead of motor vehicles;
- hiring vehicles for part-time work; and
- compressing materials and organizing material handling to reduce the time the vehicle is required.

10) Plan your workplace to minimize rent, transport costs, handling effort and outside interference. Decide which services and space you need now and which can be added later.

11) Although waste may be dirty, heavy, infested or of low value, the people who handle it should be treated as valuable assistants and provided with reasonable pay, food and drink and washing places and treated with courtesy.

12) Management is the most important activity but is done best by people closely-involved in the running of the business. If all share in the management of a small business there will be a greater sense of

partnership but some do certain jobs better than others: only one person should be responsible for each activity and a procedure for taking big decisions is needed.

13) House-to-house collections should be planned to keep the distance covered low, the handling of materials easy and to get co-operation from householders by taking careful account of their social preferences.

14) Compact materials during collection, using waste containers or other simple means.

15) Plan your depot so that:
– materials travel in one direction, a minimum distance;
– there is sufficient storage space;
– employees can work comfortably and safely; and
– costs are kept low;

16) By grading materials, their value is increased, often by much more than the cost of the job and additional employment can be created.

17) Keep material clean and separate from dirty material to obtain the highest prices.

18) When going for an interview, always wash thoroughly, be tidy and dress as smartly as you can manage. Wear a tie (which means a shirt as well!) Behave with quiet confidence and good manners.

19) Find out as much as possible about the markets into which you are selling, using sources of written information such as libraries and talk to people, especially the managers of factories that use your products.

20) Use the information you obtain to plan your marketing so you do not depend on a single outlet. Sell to final users, not middle men.

21) As with rule number sixteen, be professional in your salesman-ship — in telephone calls, letters and especially visits. Plan ahead, be neat, clean and courteous.

22) Never negotiate a price without first finding out what price you ought to get; what otners get, your own costs and how much your customer needs your material. Work out the lowest price you can accept and start by asking for more.

23) Transport is one of the highest costs in waste handling but can be reduced in many ways. Use of your own lorry is one of the most expensive forms of transport.

24) All deliveries of material to a customer should be accompanied by suitable paperwork.

25) The safety of your business and its people can be ensured by learning and acting on a few simple rules — and in the long run these will increase your profits too.

26) By budgeting, you can spot the profitable activities and spend more money and time on them.

27) Budgets and cost actuals should take account of the depreciation of capital equipment and cash may be set aside in a savings fund so that equipment can be replaced when it is worn out.

28) Only very simple book-keeping is needed for a small business with a book to record payments and receipts, a petty cash box, a current account at the bank and a deposit account for the savings fund.

29) Sales and cost actuals can be compared with the budget to find out what is going wrong, how to put it right, improve the business and budget better in future.

30) Avoid cash crises by budgeting cash movement, controlling debtors and getting support from your bank manager.

31) The profit per tonne of each kind of material can be calculated to show which collections should be increased and which should be stopped.

32) By learning how to improve your budgeting, accounting and costing you will improve your control of your business and your profits.

APPENDICES

Conversion Table

Quantity	Imperial units to Metric units		Metric units to Imperial units	
Power	1 h.p.	= 0.746 kW	1 kW	= 1.34 h.p.
Energy	1 B.T.U.	= 252 calories	1 calorie	= 0.00397 B.T.U.
Weight	1 lb	= 0.454 kg	1 kg	= 2.205 lb
Volume	1 gal	= 3.785 litre	1 litre	= 0.265 gal
	1 cu. ft	= 28.33 lit.	1 cu. m	= 35.316 cu. ft
Length	1 inch	= 25.4 mm	1 mm	= 0.039 inches
	1 ft	= 30.48 cm	1 cm	= 0.393 inches
Area	1 sq. ft	= 0.092 sq. m	1 sq. m	= 10.764 sq. ft
	1 sq. yd	= 0.836 sq. m	1 sq. m	= 1.195 sq. yd
	1 acre	= 0.404 ha	1 ha	= 2.47 acres

Temperature °Centigrade = °Fahrenheit × 9/5 (then add 32)
°Fahrenheit = °Centigrade × 5/9 (after subtracting 32)

Where to obtain more information and aid

Where to get general information

The Telephone Directory often shows the kind of business run by each listed company.

The Classified Telephone Directory (sometimes called Yellow Pages) can only be found in some cities and countries. It is an invaluable help to anyone starting a business. If it exists, buy your own copy; it can save you hours!

Other directories (e.g. Kompass) list companies, their products etc. They are usually found in libraries and information centres. Perhaps a local factory manager will let you look at his copy.

Libraries may also contain:
- Technical books
- Technical and trade journals (magazines)
- Encyclopaedias, especially the huge Encyclopaedia Britannica which has much information on wastes and on materials and processes generally.

Library staff are trained (and paid) to help you find information; ask them for help.

Materials Reclamation Directory is published every year by the Trade Journal 'Materials Reclamation'. This contains a great deal of up-to-date technical information about recycling. Similar publications may be obtained from the U.S.A. and certain other countries by applying to the information offices attached to their embassies.

Intermediate Technology Publications Ltd. publish many books on different kinds of simple or "appropriate" technology and industry. Write to 9 King Street, London WC2E 8HN, U.K. for their latest publications list, free of charge.

Where to get technical help

University and Technical College lecturers and technicians will often give help direct or suggest where it may be found.

Customers usually know more about their own business than anyone else. Remember that their answers may be designed to persuade you to do what will benefit them, not you!

Trade, Technical and Research Associations often run an advice and information service. Sometimes this is only available to their members but usually will be made available for genuine enquiries from small businesses. The names of such associations can be obtained from a library or from the Ministry of Trade or Industry.

United Nations Special Agencies such as UNDP (United Nations Development Programme) and the ILO (International Labour Office) often employ technical staff to assist the development of new industry. Many cities have excellent United Nations libraries. Some of the larger industrialized countries also offer such help. Ask at their embassies.

The British Council which has offices in many capital cities (and libraries in some) can give you the names and addresses of the Trade associations which cover the activities of most parts of the reclamation industry in Britain and who *may* be willing to give advice to enquirers from overseas.

The Intermediate Technology Development Group of 9 King Street, London WC2E 8HN, U.K. runs an advisory service for enquiries from developing countries and employs specialists in many different branches of technology other than waste. Enquiries about waste and its uses can be addressed to the author at this address.

Appropriate Technology Institutions such as:

VITA – Volunteers in Technical Assistance, 3706 Rhode Island Avenue, Mt. Rainier, Maryland 20822, U.S.A.

NDRC – National Research Development Corporation of India, 20 Ring Road, Lajpar Nagar III, New Delhi 110024, India.

ATDA – Appropriate Technology Development Association, P.B. 311, Gandhi Bhawan, Lucknow 226001, U.P., India.

TCC – Technology Consultancy Centre, University of Science and Technology, University Post Office, Kumasi, Ghana.

Where to get business advice

Your Bank Manager is one of the most experienced businessmen in your town or district and will know many of the other businessmen who are his customers. It is in his interest to help your business prosper, so usually his advice will be to your benefit.

Small Business Associations (which are often a section of an Industry, Trade or Commercial Association) exist in many cities and some smaller towns. It is a good idea to become a member if you can. You will meet people who can help you in your own business and you may have opportunities to attend lectures or meetings that will be helpful. Usually these associations try to raise the social standing of their members and small waste collectors may find they do not get a warm welcome! The answer to this is to wear a suit, collar and tie, to wash and polish your shoes before you go and to say little but listen well.

Governments (usually the Ministry of Industry) often run an Industrial Promotion Service to help small firms get started and, once started, to stay healthy. They are often difficult to deal with due to red tape (official forms, regulations etc.) but may genuinely try to be helpful and flexible towards less experienced or less educated enquirers. They often have access to large sums of money from which to grant technical and financial help but, all too often, demand more security for loans than should be expected from a new business.

United Nations Agencies as well as the governments of some of the industrialized countries, may run business advice services. Ask at individual embassies.

Where to get financial help

Yourself if possible. The very best source of finance (money) to start a small business is your own earnings or those of your close friends and family.

Your bank makes its living not only by keeping money safely for people like you, but also by lending its (and other peoples') money to people like you, to invest in businesses that will help the money grow. Never be afraid to ask your bank for money. Dress properly and be prepared to answer searching questions about the business and your plans for it. If possible take along papers to show that you have done some careful planning.

Government Small Business Promotion Centres often have funds to help small companies get started.

United Nations Agencies and agencies set up by foreign governments may be able to help with money but usually there is too much red tape for it to be effective.

Development Agencies that are not run by or connected with Governments are much more flexible and easy to deal with. There are many and they differ in different countries but some of the best and most helpful are:

Agencies of the World Council of Churches The name and address of the person in your country or district or town who works with them can be found by asking your local priest or minister. It may even be him. The Roman Catholic Churches often work separately but will also help.

Oxfam, the agency for which the author worked for five years, has staff and offices in many countries of the world. Oxfam is dedicated to helping the poorest people and those who are unable to obtain help from elsewhere but they would rather support a genuine attempt by a group or a community of people to start a business that will create employment than to help a business that will only benefit one man or one family.

Other Development Agencies in the British Commonwealth, their names, addresses and the kind of work they do or support, can be found from directories published by The Commonwealth Foundation, Marlborough House, London SW1Y 5HX, England and they will send them free of charge.

REMEMBER   If you write to an address to ask for assistance or information, do give a clear address to which the reply can be sent. Write in **BLOCK CAPITALS** and include:

Your name

The number of your house or the house of a friend who will take letters for you. If you have no house ask at the Post Office for a Box Number for a short period.

The name of the street

377

The district

The town or city

The country in which you live

You do not need to send a stamp for the reply when writing to any of the bodies listed in this Chapter, but *do* put the right value stamp on the letter you write or it may never arrive.

Further reading

Accounting

Accounting in Business No. 1 by Frank Wood. Longman Group Ltd., Longman House, Burnt Mill, Harlow, Essex CM20 2JE, U.K.

Accounting in Business by R.J. Bull. Sweet and Maxwell Ltd., 11 New Fetter Lane, EC4P 4EE, U.K.

Introduction to Book-keeping by C.W. Smith. East African Publishing House Ltd., P.O. Box 30571, Nairobi, Kenya.

Bigger Profits for the Smaller Firms (2nd Edition) by E.G. Wood. Business Books, 24 Highbury Crescent, London N.5., U.K.

Biogas

A Bibliography of Methane Generation. Intermediate Technology Publications Ltd., 9 King Street, London WC2E 8HN, U.K.

A Chinese Biogas Manual, edited by Ariane van Buren. Intermediate Technology Publications Ltd.

Composting / Use of Nightsoil and Sewage

Biological Reclamation of Solid Wastes by C.G. Golueke. Rodale Press, Organic Park, Emmaus, Pennsylvania 18049, U.S.A.

Compost, Fertilizer and Biogas Production from Human and Farm Wastes in the People's Republic of China by M.G. McGarry and J. Stainforth (Eds). International Development Research Centre, P.O. Box 8500, Ottawa, K1G 3H9, Canada.

379

Management of Solid Wastes in Developing Countries by F. Flintoff. World Health Organization, New Delhi, India.

The Forge and the Foundry

Foundry Work by Stimpson and Gray. American Technical Society, Chicago, U.S.A.
The Iron Foundry – an Industrial Profile. Intermediate Technology Publications Ltd.
Forging by Hand by Alexander G. Weygers. Van Nostrand Reinhold Co., 450 West 33rd Street, New York 10001, U.S.A.
Metal Forging and Wrought Iron Work by John A. Gross. Mills and Boon Ltd., 17–19 Foley Street, London W1A 1DR, U.K.
Oil Drum Forges. Intermediate Technology Publications Ltd.
Small Scale Foundries by John Harper. Intermediate Technology Publications Ltd.
Guidelines for Establishing a Demonstration Foundry in a Developing Country. UNIDO, Felderhaus, P.O. Box 707, Rathausplatz 2, A-1010, Vienna, Austria.

Glass

Handbook of Glass Manufacture by Fay V. Tooley. University of Illinois, 55 West 42nd Street, New York 36, U.S.A.
Making Glass. Glass Manufacturers' Federation, 19 Portland Place, London W1N 4BH, U.K.
Modern Glass Practice by Samuel R. Scholes. Cahners Publishing Co., 89 Franklin Street, Boston, Mass. 02110, U.S.A.

Metals

Metals in the Service of Man by Alexander and Street. Penguin Books Ltd., Bath Road, Harmondsworth, Middlesex, UB7 0DA, U.K.

Minerals

Blastfurnace and Steel Slag by A.R. Lee. Edward Arnold Publishers Ltd., 41 Bedford Square, London WC1B 3DP, U.K.

A Survey of the Locations, Disposal and Prospective Uses of the Major Industrial By-products and Waste Materials. Building Research Establishment, Garston, Herts. WD2 7JK, U.K.

Paper

The Paper Chain by Christine Thomas. Earth Resources Research Ltd., 40 James Street, London W1, U.K.
Small Scale Papermaking by A.W. Western. Intermediate Technology Industrial Services, Myson House, Railway Terrace, Rugby, CV21 3HT, U.K.

Use of Sewage/Nightsoil

Sanitation in Developing Countries by Arnold Pacey (Ed.) John Wiley and Sons Ltd., Baffins Lane, Chichester, Sussex, PO19 1UD, U.K.
The Disposal of Sewage Sludge to Land. H.M.S.O., Atlantic House, Holborn Viaduct, London EC1, U.K.

Recycling and Reclamation – general

Formation and Use of Industrial By-products: A Guide by A.W. Neal. Business Books Ltd., 24 Highbury Crescent, London, N5 1RX, U.K.
Industrial Waste by A.W. Neal. Business Books Ltd.
Materials Reclamation Directory. Materials Reclamation, P.O. Box 109, Davis House, 69 High Street, Croydon CR9 1QH, U.K.
The Recycling and Disposal of Solid Waste by Henstock (Ed.) Pergamon Press, Headington Hill Hall, Oxford, OX3 0BW, U.K.
Recycling Waste by Paul Slee Smith. Scientific Publications (G.B.)
Recycling, Resources, Refuse by Andrew Porteous. Longman Group Ltd.
Recycling, Use and Repair of Tools by Alexander G. Weygers. Van Nostrand Reinhold Co.

Material Gains by Christine Thomas. Earth Resources Research Ltd.
Repairs, Re-use, Recycling – First Steps Towards a Sustainable Society by Denis Hayes. Worldwatch Paper 23, Worldwatch Institute, 1776 Massachusetts Avenue NW, Washington D.C. 20036, U.S.A.

and Small Industry Research Institute, P.B. No. 2106, 4/43 Roop Nagar, Delhi 110007, India.
which is a source of several relevant reports.

Glossary

Abrasion	Wearing by rubbing
ABS	A polymer
Activated sludge	Process for sewage treatment
Activator	Substance that starts off a process
Additive	Chemical added to oil to improve its function
Adhesion	Ability to stick to a surface
Aerobic	Kind of bacteria that need air
Aggregate	Filler used in concrete
Alloy	Mixture of metals
Amortize	Gradually write off initial costs of
Anaerobic	Bacteria that can or must live without free oxygen from the air.
Analyze	Break down to examine
Anneal	Heat and cool slowly to prevent cracking of metal or glass
Anode	Positively charged metal or carbon plate for passing electricity through liquid
Atom	The smallest quantity of an element that can exist
Ballast	Stones under a railway line
Ballotini	Tiny balls of glass used in reflective paints
Batch	Single quantity of raw material, not continuous
Bead	Extra thickness at a rim
Berlins	Knitted wool rags
Binder	Material that holds fibres or particles together
Biogas	Methane, a gas that can be safely burned in the home
Bituminous	Black, sticky and tar-like
Bloom	Slab of metal for rolling or forming

Blown film	Thin plastic sheet, used for sacks and bags
Bolt croppers	Tools for cutting steel bars or bolts
Brass	Alloy of copper and zinc
Briquette	Compact block of a loose substance
Burr	Rough edge remaining on cut or punched metal or paper
Bus-bar	Copper bar for conducting electricity
Buyer	Person in a company who buys materials and goods
Cadmium	A soft metal
Carborundum	Hard, rough mineral used for grinding
Cardboard	Board made from paper fibre
Casein	Organic substance present in milk
Cellophane	Transparent wrapping material made of viscose
Charge	Appropriate quantity of material to put into a receptacle
C.I.F.	Cost, insurance and freight. Commercial term for the price of goods or materials
Clinker	Lumps of mineral left after a solid fuel has been burned
Cold worked	Bent, twisted, hammered etc. without being heated
Combustion chamber	Part of a furnace in which the burning takes place
Comforters	Knitted woollen rags
Compound	Substance made by combining other substances
Compound interest	Interest added to the original sum, year by year
Confidential	Secret
Contaminated	Dirty
Contingency	Unexpected event
Contrary	Impurity in waste, not acceptable to the process in which the waste is used
Crates	Boxes that hold bottles during transport
Crumb	Small, solid shapeless particle
Cupola	A kind of furnace for melting cast iron
Cure	Process to preserve or harden a material
Cutting oil	Oil used to assist cutting of metal etc.

384

Cutting rooms	Workshop where cloth is cut to pattern to make clothing
Daylight	Gap between the moulds in a rubber press
d.c.	Direct current – electric current that flows one way only
Deposit account	Bank account in which the money earns interest
Detinning	Removing the tin layer from tin plated steel sheet
Develop	Convert the light affected grains on a photographic film to silver
Devulcanize	Process rubber to remove its elasticity, make it mouldable
Diaper	Baby's napkin
Die casting	Casting using a die (metal mould)
Digest	Break down under the action of bacteria
Digester	Tank in which fermentation takes place
Direct reduction	Reduction (of metal ores) without melting
Disinfectant	Substance for preventing infection by killing bacteria, commonly used on wounds
Doghouse	Compartment of a glass furnace into which raw material is loaded
Double entry	System of book-keeping in which each item is recorded twice
Dross	Dirt and impurities that float to the top of molten metal
Electrolytic deposition	Plating of a metal on to an electrode, by action of an electric current
Extruder	Machine for shaping material
Feed-rollers	Rollers that pull or push material through a machine
Feedstock	Raw material input to a process
Ferment	Activity of bacteria on organic material, giving off heat and gases
Fettle	Trim rough edge of metal casting
Filler	Fine material that fills in gaps between larger particles
Fireclay	Natural clay, containing alumina, that can withstand high temperatures

Flash	Thin layer of waste material on a casting or moulding at the mould joint
Flash dehydrator	A device for removing water from a fluid
Float	Sum of cash to start a petty cash fund
Float	To move, free from rigid support
Flow path	Path through which goods move without obstruction
Flue	Passage through which smoke leaves a furnace
Fluting	Corrugated centre of cardboard
Flux	Non-metal that covers a molten metal to prevent oxidation
F.O.B.	Free on board: commercial term for the price of export goods not including insurance or freight
Formulation	List of substances to be mixed to make rubber goods
Foundry	Workshop where metal is cast
Friable	Easily crumbled
Friction	Rubbing against a rough surface
Gate	Channel in a mould along which molten metal can pass
Gob	Round mass of molten glass ready for moulding or blowing
Grade	Level of material quality
Grain	A small particle
Granulate	Chop into small pieces
Granulator	Machine for granulating plastic, metals etc.
Gravity die casting	Casting non-ferrous metal or plastic by pouring into a die
Grog	Mixture of crushed, burnt fireclay in water
Gross weight	Weight of vehicle plus load
Half shaft	Half the rear axle of a lorry or car
Hand shear	A huge scissor with a lever arm
Heat	A series of melting operations without the furnace cooling in between
Heat treatment	Heat process used to change properties of a metal
Hollander	Type of beater for pulping waste paper

386

Hot shortness	Cracking of steel during hot rolling due to impurities such as tin
Homogeneous	Of the same kind all through
Hydra-pulper	Cylinder with rotating arms for pulping waste paper
Hydraulic	Using liquid flowing through pipes
Inflammable	Easily catches fire
Injection moulding	Process for moulding plastics by forcing them into a mould
In series	Way of connecting electrical components end to end so that the same current flows through them all
Integrated mill	Mill that both makes and uses a material like steel, textile etc.
Jerrican	Can for carrying petrol or water
Knits	Knitted rags
Kraft	Strong brown chemical wood pulp
Ladle	Container for carrying hot liquid or molten metal
Ladle skulls	Solidified metal remaining after a ladle is emptied
Latex	Juice of the rubber tree from which rubber is made
Leach	Wash out or through with liquid
Letterhead	Notepaper bearing a Company's name and address
Lifting eyes	A steel loop into which a hook can be inserted to lift a heavy object
Liners	Replaceable wear surfaces
Loading dock	A hard surface beside and higher than a road to assist in loading vehicles
Marl	Mixture of clay and limestone
Master batch	Colouring added to plastic raw materials before moulding
Mesh size	Sizes of mesh or net through which a material will and will not pass
Micron	One thousandth part of a millimetre
Mild steel	Most common form of steel, low in alloys
Mill	Factory that makes raw materials
Mini-mill	Small steel mill that rolls but does not make steel

387

Misprint	Item that is scrapped due to incorrect printing
Molecule	The smallest quantity of a substance that can exist alone
Mould	Surface to give shape to a solidifying liquid
Muck out	Remove excreta-soiled bedding from animal pen
Mulching	Mixture of wet straw, leaves, etc., spread to protect roots of young plants
Multilayer board	Cardboard made from several layers
Needle felt	Felt made by compressing textile waste and piercing with barbed needles
Nett monthly cash	Payment at the end of the month following delivery
Nett weight	Weight of the load without the vehicle
Nightsoil	Human excreta, collected from homes without their own means of disposal
Noils	Short fibres left from combing wool
Nutrient	Part of a feed or fertilizer that has food value
Offal	Non-edible parts of animal carcass
Opaque	Unable to be seen through
Outlet	Customer, selling agent or retailer
Oxide	Compound of a substance with oxygen
Pan	Wash gold-bearing gravel in pan
Parasites	Animal or plant living in or on and drawing nutriments from another
Parison	A bubble of glass, the first stage in blowing a glass container
Pelletizer	Machine used in the processing of waste plastics
pH	Number that measures the acidity or alkalinity of a material
Picker	Person who collects material from a refuse dump
Pile	Fibre that rises above the surface of a textile
Platten	Strong horizontal plate of a press (to which the upper part of a die may be fixed) that is forced down when the press operates

Plough back	Use profit from a business to finance new plant or activities of the business
Poling	Dipping green timber in molten metal to refine the metal
Polymer	Plastic
Porosity	Ability to soak up liquids or gases
Precipitate	Solid that grows in a liquid due to chemical action
Precipitation iron	Iron used to recover copper from its ore.
Pressure die casting	Method of casting non-ferrous metals in which the molten metal is forced into the mould under pressure
Primary air	Air needed for the first stage of burning
Primary wood pulp	Pulp made direct from wood, containing no recycled material
Projections	Objects that stick out from a surface
Promote	Encourage the sale of a material
Proprietary	Material known by the makers special name e.g. Pepsi Cola
Protein	Organic material containing nitrogen, a necessary part of the food of all living animals
Pull	Separate knitted or woven textile fibres for re-use
Pulp	Mass of fibres in water from which paper is made
Pulping	Process of freeing fibres from what it is that binds them together
Quicklime	Calcium hydroxide which is produced by burning calcium carbonate in air and becomes slaked lime when added to water
Quotation	Statement in advance stating the price to be charged for work done
Reclamation	Recovery of waste material for further use
Reconcile	Make two things agree
Recycle	Use a second time
Red tape	Official rules and paperwork
Reduce	Convert into a simpler form
Refuse	Rubbish

Reverberatory furnace	A furnace in which heat is reflected off the roof on to the charge
Revulcanize	Vulcanize a second time
Rip-top	Type of drink can that is opened by tearing the top.
Riser	Passage in a mould that holds molten metal to top-up shrinkage, also known as a "feeder"
Roughage	Fibrous part of food or crop
Ruminant	Animal, such as a cow, with two stomachs that can digest fibrous material
Scarecrow	Rough human figure to frighten birds away from crops
Scavengers	People who live by collecting material from rubbish dumps
Scrap	Waste material
Screen	Vibrating sieve for size-sorting material
Seals	Rubber strips that prevent passage of fluid
Secondary air	Air for the second stage of burning
Secondary pulp	Paper pulp made from waste paper
Seediness	Small bubbles in glass
Septic	Poisoned
Sewage	Human waste material carried away by pipes
Shore A scale	A commonly used measure of hardness
Short circuit	Incorrect passage of electric current
Shred	Tear into small pieces
Skeleton	Framework of a solid object
Skip	A large container for waste
Slab	Rectangular lump
Slag	Non-metallic material that floats on molten metal to prevent oxidation
Slip casting	A method of making pots
Sludge	Wet, solid material that settles from sewage or other solution
Spinning	Process of twisting fibres to produce yarn
Sponge tin	Sponge-like mass of impure tin
Sprue	Hole or passage through which material is poured into a mould. Also used for the solidified material left by the pas-

	sage when the casting is withdrawn.
Step	Square corner
Sub-contracted	Pass work on to someone else to do
Substrate	Material on which bacteria or other organisms can be grown
Suspension	Even mixture of undissolved solid in a fluid
Tamp	Press down with repeated blows of a stick
Tap	Open a solid object or container to allow liquid to flow out
Tare weight	Weight of a vehicle without load
Thermoset	Plastic that cannot be reshaped
Tinsnips	Small shears for cutting sheet metal
Ultra-violet	Wavelength beyond violet end of visible spectrum contained in the sun's rays
Vibration	Rapid movement to and fro
Viscous	Sticky.
Volatile	Evaporating rapidly.
Vulcanize	Make rubber elastic by combining with sulphur
Weighbridge	Machine on to which vehicles can be driven to be weighed
Wet strength	Paper that keeps its strength when wet
Woody	Containing wood that has not been fully pulped
Work	To shape by hammering, bending etc.

Note

For reasons of space, the definitions of chemical names have been omitted. Reference should be made to a chemistry textbook.

Index